Baker & Botts in the Development of Modern Houston

Baker & Botts in the Development of Modern Houston

*by Kenneth Lipartito
and Joseph Pratt*

University of Texas Press, Austin

First Edition, 1991

Requests for permission to reproduce material
from this work should be sent to Permissions,
University of Texas Press, Box 7819, Austin, Texas 78713-7819.

Library of Congress Cataloging-in-Publication Data

Lipartito, Kenneth, 1957–
    Baker & Botts in the development of modern Houston / by Kenneth
Lipartito and Joseph Pratt. — 1st ed.
        p.   cm.
    Includes bibliographical references and index.
    ISBN 0-292-70782-7 (alk. paper)
    1. Baker & Botts—History.   2. Law firms—Texas—Houston—History.
3. Houston (Tex.)—History.   I. Pratt, Joseph A.   II. Title.   III. Title:
Baker and Botts in the development of modern Houston.
KF355.H68L56   1991
340'.06'07641411—dc20   90-48256
                                                                                CIP

Frontispiece: One Shell Plaza

Contents

Illustrations

Preface

T HIS IS THE HISTORY of a major Houston law firm—and
more. Baker & Botts was founded as a two-member partnership
in the early nineteenth century. It has since grown into an organization of more than 370 lawyers with offices in Houston, Washington, D.C., Dallas, and Austin. In the 1980s the firm was in the
public eye as counsel for Pennzoil's successful effort to recover
billions of dollars in damages from Texaco over the acquisition
of the Getty Oil Company. But for most of its history, Baker &
Botts has remained outside the spotlight, quietly handling legal
affairs for such blue-chip clients as the Southern Pacific Railroad
(SP), Houston Lighting & Power Company (HL&P), and Tenneco,
Inc. As Houston's oldest corporate law practice, Baker & Botts
has long occupied a prominent place in the city's legal, economic, and civic life. We have tried to capture a sense of the
complex interrelationships between Houston's emergence as a
modern city and Baker & Botts's growth into a national law firm.

The law firm and the city literally grew up together. Baker &
Botts was founded in 1840, when Peter Gray first entered the
practice of law with his father, William Fairfax Gray. At that time,
Houston was a small dot on the map of the Republic of Texas. As
the city steadily expanded and Texas entered the Union, Gray
did path-breaking work on the early legal codes of the new state.
After the Civil War, he returned to the practice of law in partnership with Walter Browne Botts. Gray & Botts took on a new name
partner in 1872 with the addition of Judge James A. Baker. As
Baker & Botts evolved to meet the legal needs of an industrializing city, other prominent lawyers earned places as name partners (table 1). Finally, in 1971 the practice of adding new name
partners was ended, and the firm took as its permanent designation Baker & Botts. To avoid confusing the reader, we have chosen

viii

Baker & Botts
in the
Development
of Modern
Houston

to use this name throughout the book. Although table 1 shows the evolution of the firm's "official" name, for most of its history the firm has been known as Baker & Botts or Baker, Botts.

Given the firm's long history and its parallel development with Houston, it is not surprising that the initial impulse for writing this history came from Baker & Botts. As the firm approached its 150th anniversary, the partners quite naturally felt an impulse to pause and look back over the terrain their organization has traveled. Yet the decision to commission a professional history was by no means an exercise in either nostalgia or self-congratulation. In recent decades, Baker & Botts and the legal profession as a whole have been challenged by far-reaching changes in the practice of law. In the midst of such change, history is more than comforting; it can be instructive. The broad contours of the firm's past provide a useful context for contemplating the pace and direction of change in the future. A historical understanding of the organizational structure of the firm helps to identify traditional strengths. A study of its diverse roles in the development of the Gulf region adds a much-needed long-term perspective to any discussion of the ongoing relationship between Baker & Botts and its home base of Houston.

Once the firm decided to commission the writing of a professional history, it did not have to look far for a historian. Joseph Pratt was in the Baker & Botts archives completing research on a history of Texas Commerce Banks, a major Houston-based bank holding company, which was a long-standing client of the firm. Preliminary discussions led to a practical plan: an oral history project, which would be accompanied by a survey of archival sources to determine the feasibility of writing a full-scale firm history. As the interviews moved forward, the potential for a book became clearer. Pratt, a business historian whose previous work had focused on the history of the oil industry and the development of Houston, was soon joined by Kenneth Lipartito, a historian of the American economy, who had just completed a study of the telephone industry in the South. Together, these coauthors planned the history project.

The contract between the coauthors and the firm granted the authors full editorial control and final disposition of the manuscript. It also assured them full access to firm records and personnel, as conditioned by the constraints necessarily imposed by

TABLE 1
DEVELOPMENT OF FIRM NAME

Name	Years Used
Gray & Botts	1865–1872
Gray, Botts & Baker	1872–1875
Baker & Botts	1875–1887
Baker, Botts & Baker	1887–1893
Baker, Botts, Baker & Lovett	1893–1904
Baker, Botts, Parker & Garwood	1904–1931
Baker, Botts, Andrews & Wharton	1931–1946
Baker, Botts, Andrews & Walne	1946–1947
Baker, Botts, Andrews & Parish	1948–1953
Baker, Botts, Andrews & Shepherd	1954–1962
Baker, Botts, Shepherd & Coates	1962–1970
Baker & Botts	1971–

the confidentiality of client records. Under the contract, Baker & Botts provided funds for Pratt to take time off from his teaching position at the University of Houston, for Lipartito to devote two years to the project (during which time he was an employee of Baker & Botts), and for a part-time research assistant. The coauthors agreed to produce a "university press–quality" history of the firm. Appended to the contract was a chapter outline for the project developed by the coauthors and reviewed by the firm. By anticipating areas of possible conflict before research began in earnest, the contract laid the foundation for a smooth working relationship between the authors and Baker & Botts.

As work began, the authors soon recognized that Baker & Botts was an excellent vehicle for studying the process of economic and business development in Houston. The members of the firm were active in the legal affairs of many of the major corporations that shaped the early growth of Houston; thus, much of the city's economic life flowed through the offices—and through the records—of this firm. These lawyers were in a crucial position to encourage the "absorption" of their region into the modern American economy.

So vital was their influence, indeed, that some thoughtful readers may wonder if the authors claim too much, if their emphasis has been skewed by their access to the heretofore untouched historical records from one group of lawyers. After all, lawyers have seldom played such a central role in the published histories of America's economic and urban development. Yet the authors invite the reader to entertain these thoughts: the sources needed to describe the roles of lawyers have not been available to researchers; historians have thus concentrated instead on the activities of politicians, whose records are in the public domain, or flamboyant big business executives, whose activities could be followed through court and regulatory archives. With so few thorough studies of the histories of major law firms, it is not surprising that the impact of lawyers on history is so little understood and so often neglected. Time and again the historical sources suggest that the power of lawyers has always been acknowledged and often feared by their contemporaries. We trust that this study of one major corporate law firm in one developing city can help place the influence of these partnerships in proper historical perspective.

The assistance of a number of people made this book possible. Chris Castañeda served as our research assistant and archivist. His work in organizing records proved invaluable in preparing our history and in preparing the Baker & Botts Historical Collection for deposit at the Woodson Research Center at Rice University. Other research assistance came from Elisabeth O'Kane, Patience Evans, and Ann Hardikar. In the initial oral history phase of the project, Robert Calvert and Karl Conrad conducted interviews.

The manuscript benefited greatly from a vicious editing job by Louis Galambos. He helped turn a long manuscript into a shorter, more clearly focused one by cutting out all of the good parts. Our thanks for his efforts on the project, as well as on the more demanding, longer-running project of training both of us to be professional historians. Others who commented on all or lengthy parts of the manuscript include John Boles, Robert Gordon, Thomas Green, David McComb, Mark Steiner, and an anonymous reviewer for the University of Texas Press.

We enjoyed an excellent working relationship with Baker & Botts. Our primary sponsor within the firm was managing partner E. W. Barnett, whose strong commitment to a professional history written by outsiders never wavered. J. H. Freeman, who originally came to work at Baker & Botts before World War II, helped us in all phases of the project. He was a guide to the firm's personnel and records, a link to its history, and a constant source of encouragement and goodwill. James Doty, the partner in charge of the history project, read early drafts with the sharp eye of a lawyer-historian. He was replaced late in the project by Charles Szalkowski, who helped push various aspects of the project through to completion. Judge Joe R. Greenhill and Edwin Bell helped track down information on Captain Baker. In both formal and informal interviews, many other retired and current members of the firm provided valuable perspective on issues raised in our history.

Our research was facilitated by numerous records specialists and archivists, notably Millie Carey, Jennie Mendoza, Bob Downie, Trisha Fabugais, Nancy Boothe, Louis Marchiafava, Maury Klein, and James Aldridge. Cindy Moore Landry helped get the project organized. Our thanks also to Lauson Stone and Walter Isaacson. The preparation of the manuscript was efficiently handled by Mary Jauer, Hazel Rowden, and Lillian Stern, who wore out several word processors in the process of typing and revising.

One final note. Our research and writing were facilitated by the excellent environment in which we worked. The tone at Baker & Botts felt familiar to us as academics; there was a deeply shared commitment to both history and ideas. Our academic home, the University of Houston, also provided a stimulating intellectual environment and various other assistance.

Baker & Botts in the Development of Modern Houston

Introduction

LAW FIRMS have exerted a powerful and continuing influence on modern American economic history. As advisers to business, firm partners assist in the organization and financing of modern corporations. As intermediaries between big business and the larger society, they help corporate managers adapt to changing regulatory demands. As business executives, they direct some of the nation's largest enterprises. As politicians, they help write many of the laws that govern business behavior. For this work, they have been well compensated by clients and often soundly abused by critics.[1]

Both the criticism and the compensation reached formidable proportions around the beginning of the twentieth century, when the modern corporation and large law firms such as Baker & Botts were experiencing profound changes. Over the past hundred years, these law firms have evolved from small, often temporary, two- or three-person partnerships operating in a single region to much larger institutions whose work often spans the national and at times the international economy. Resembling modern businesses in scope and organization, corporate law firms have performed critically important functions that have shaped the evolution of the modern American business system. Responding to their clients' need for continuous service and expert advice, these organizations have had the opportunity and the motivation to burrow deeply into common law doctrine, to monitor and lobby legislatures, and to search for means to extend the reach of business, even in the face of resistance by critics of the corporate sector. Lucrative retainers from clients have allowed these partnerships to assemble excellent legal talent to perform these services.[2]

Given the importance of corporate law firms in the history of big business, it is somewhat surprising to find how few of these legal institutions have been studied by historians. The existing literature on the subject consists primarily of retired partners' accounts of life in the firm, sociological treatises on the firm as an organization, or potboiler exposés of greed and corruption. The first group supplies useful information, but the works are generally anecdotal and laudatory and consist largely of detailed sketches of partners and their most important cases.[3] The second group, though grounded solidly in theory and committed to analysis, generally lacks the intimate inside knowledge of how a firm actually operates and what larger social functions it fulfills.[4] The last group, predictable in tone and content, is a variant of the muckraking studies that have always found an audience in a society prepared to believe the worst about its large institutions.[5] Although at times entertaining, the exposés focus on the chaff while largely ignoring the wheat; they blend real with imagined abuses and provide little insight into the workings of a large law firm or its impact on society.

We hope to help fill the void on the history of modern corporate law practices with this study of the Houston firm of Baker & Botts. Since its beginning in 1840, Baker & Botts has run the full gamut of changes characteristic of modern legal organizations. Today it is one of the leading corporate firms in Houston and resembles in size, structure, and client base other major law firms in other large cities. Baker & Botts's history helps us understand the transitions that firms of its type have experienced over the past century. Because the firm early on established a practice among the major corporations active in Texas, its history also reveals how corporate law firms paved the way for the expansion of big business in a nation eager for economic development yet skeptical of the power of large corporations.

Baker & Botts's history is of course in some respects unique. Located in Houston, the firm's progress has followed the trajectory of the city's economy. Houston was far from a metropolis when Baker & Botts was founded. But this frontier town of a few thousand hardy souls steadily grew into an important regional center of economic activity for the upper Texas Gulf Coast and then into a city of national significance. With Houston grew Baker & Botts.

Perhaps the clearest way of understanding the history of the firm and its city is through the Baker family itself. Judge James Addison Baker moved to Houston in 1872 and joined the partnership of Peter Gray and W. B. Botts. Baker's expertise was in railroad law, an important area of practice when the railroad was the foremost corporate enterprise on the Gulf Coast. Judge Baker's son, Captain James A. Baker, grew up with the firm and the city and was from young manhood a confident member of provincial Houston's small but active elite. His familial connections and outgoing manner enabled him to move easily among the many business activities in early-twentieth-century Houston—banks, real estate, oil, lumber, utilities. By the 1950s Houston had grown much larger, and Captain Baker's son, James A. Baker, Jr., followed in his father's footsteps, ascending quickly to the partnership, taking a seat on the boards of various local institutions. But in Baker Jr.'s day Houston had already become too diverse for one man to participate in the whole of its economic life, as Captain Baker had. Competing circles of elites vied for power as the city emerged as a metropolis of national significance. At the same time, Baker & Botts's law practice began to serve clients who operated in the national and international economy.

James A. Baker III illustrates well this break in Houston's and Baker & Botts's past. In the late 1930s the firm recognized the need to make its organization more professional and passed an antinepotism rule, which excluded Baker's participation in the firm that bore his family name. Joining longtime rival Andrews & Kurth, Baker enjoyed the advantages of his family's history in Houston, but he moved beyond the city to the national stage, as the Southwest began to produce a new generation of economic and political leaders. James A. Baker III does not, as did his grandfather, operate in a tight local elite; rather, as secretary of state, he symbolizes the new national and international significance of Houston and its leaders.

The history of the firm from the first Baker to the most recent one comprises three stages of development: (1) from 1866 to 1914, Baker & Botts can best be characterized as an elite firm in a colonial economy; (2) from the First World War through the 1920s, it was a leading regional firm in a maturing region; and (3) from the Great Depression to the present day, it has grown to become a national firm in a major city. We have organized our chapters around these three eras, bringing our study to the recent past, despite the perils of analyzing contemporary events.

"Colonial" aptly describes the Houston-area economy in the years before World War I. As a part of a region that was undeveloped relative to the industrial Northeast, Houston was a small city with big aspirations. In the late nineteenth century much of its nascent industrial sector was composed of national corporations headquartered outside the state. In transportation, oil and gas production, insurance, electric power, steel and other industries, northeastern companies exerted a profound influence over Houston and the region's economy.

These "foreign" corporations chartered largely in other states held the key to rapid economic growth in the Gulf Coast. As they reached out to exploit the region's resources—first cotton, then timber, then oil—they required legal experts in Texas, a populist state with highly restrictive laws governing the activities of big corporations. Baker & Botts filled this role after it was chosen to be general counsel in Texas for one of the major railroad systems in the state, the Southern Pacific. In this capacity, Baker & Botts became the leading corporate law firm in Texas. Its essential task was to help the Southern Pacific, and later other corporate clients, learn to operate within the confines of Texas's unfamiliar and often hostile legal environment while working to adapt the laws of the state to the needs of modern business. Slowly, in many cases almost imperceptibly, the firm's efforts opened the state to new business development.

This work brought far-reaching changes to Baker & Botts, which grew much larger than most of its local competitors and came to resemble in size and tone the leading Wall Street law firms of the day. Through this colonial era, Baker & Botts's members were a critical part of the economic and civic elite of Houston, and they helped build the infrastructure needed to foster local development and to absorb the resources and people coming into town. Thus while representing large corporations often based outside the state, Baker & Botts helped to prepare the region for participating more fully in the growth of the national economy.

The opening in 1914 of the Houston ship channel to the Gulf of Mexico symbolized the beginning of a new era for the region and the firm. In the two decades after 1914, Houston became more tightly integrated into the nexus of national economic activity. The region's recently discovered oil deposits fueled the expansion of an already healthy economy, giving Houston a new and important identity within the nation's business system. Baker & Botts emerged as a major regional law firm, the label applied to prominent legal organizations in outlying cities such as Houston. In the early twentieth century the leading Wall

Street practices took care of most of the work arising from the organizing and financing of the nation's largest businesses; the leading regional firms handled the essential but somewhat less glamorous work generated as these corporations moved beyond the northeastern states.

In the 1920s and early 1930s several changes in the firm's practice enhanced its standing as an important regional firm. The consolidation of nearby utilities into sprawling national systems held together primarily through common ownership by holding companies involved the firm in the intricacies of corporate reorganizations and finance. Meanwhile, the expansion of the southwestern oil industry presented Baker & Botts with opportunities to become a national leader in areas of the law affecting this vital industry. The firm remained primarily a specialist in the laws of Texas, but it prospered and matured as an institution in a booming, oil-led economy.

The Great Depression slowed the regional boom while undermining the value of the firm's traditional focus on the laws of Texas. The federal government's response to the depression included a wave of new regulations affecting various sectors of business. Although this rush of legislation encompassed many often-contradictory impulses, one significant impact was the "federalization" of corporate law, as new federal statutes created unprecedented powers for the national government in areas as diverse as securities trading, oil and gas production and transmission, the organization of public utility holding companies, and labor-management relations. Regional firms such as Baker & Botts faced a critical choice. They could remain specialists in state laws and watch their influence decline, or they could begin to master the new federal laws and attempt to compete more effectively with the traditional leaders on Wall Street in an increasingly national market for legal services.

As it pursued the second path into a new era, Baker & Botts was most fortunate to be based in Houston. A postwar boom in the city, led by the dynamic oil, natural gas, and petrochemical industries, provided a range of growing Houston-based clients of national significance. Along with several of its aggressive competitors in the city, Baker & Botts prospered in the 1950s and 1960s. By the early 1970s it had developed into a major corporate law firm on the national scene. In the eighties, Baker & Botts joined the other leading law practices throughout the nation in adapting to the demands that accompanied larger size, geographical expansion through branch offices, and growing competition for both clients and lawyers.

During each of these three eras, Baker & Botts partners have been closely involved in the complex economic, political, and cultural changes taking place on the Texas Gulf Coast. They have participated in Houston's development not only as legal experts and general business advisers, but as entrepreneurs, civic leaders, and policymakers. Through their firm and their personal and professional contacts, they have been part of a tight "circle of influence" that has cut deep marks in their city's history. Viewed in this light, the firm and its members have been among the most important city-building forces in twentieth-century Houston.

As a major force for change in its region, Baker & Botts inevitably became enmeshed in the conflicts that surrounded modern economic development. At the turn of the century, when rural values still predominated in Texas, many farmers saw lawyers in three-piece suits—an early trademark of Baker & Botts, even in the long, hot summers of Houston before air conditioning—as symbols of all that was wrong with their world. In their minds, lawyers who served corporations had helped to bring on the abuses of monopoly, alien capital, and the evil city ways that accompanied industrial growth. Since these farmers and others with similar attitudes often made up the juries that decided the cases involving Baker & Botts's clients, members of the firm had to walk a fine line. In turn-of-the-century Texas, it was no easy feat to remain a respected part of the local society while representing large corporations based outside of the state. Lawyers at Baker & Botts maintained the balance by combining active involvement in civic affairs with an intense commitment to professional excellence. This theme runs throughout the firm's history. The members of Baker & Botts have sought to meet the demands of leadership both in their local community and in the professional community of corporate lawyers. As we shall see, the two did not always mix harmoniously.

Criticism from other Texans was especially troublesome to the early practitioners of corporate law at Baker & Botts. Many of the firm's members had grown up in small-town Texas and shared their society's feelings against bigness, the North, and cities. Such personal biases could and did change with exposure to the world beyond the Texas countryside. In their professional lives, moreover, these lawyers committed their intellect and discipline to the legal issues raised by the coming of industrialism.

Their professional energies and the needs of their clients made
them agents of cultural change whether or not they fully em-
braced the values of twentieth-century urban and organizational
culture. As decades passed and the social tensions generated by
the initial impact of industrialization subsided, the members of
Baker & Botts and most of their fellow Texans appear to have
accepted the values and accompanying economic growth characteristic of an urban industrial society.

Yet tensions of another sort followed Baker & Botts as it proceeded into the twentieth century. Texans continued to debate
important questions of power: Who should control the process of
change, and how would the costs and benefits of industrialization be divided? These choices were vitally important, for they
defined what "modern" was to mean in the state. As advocates
for big business, Baker & Botts's partners remained in the middle
of these policy debates. Members of the firm helped to set legal
precedents and public policy on a wide variety of issues, including railroad regulation, antitrust law, the leasing of oil- and gas-
producing lands, labor unions, municipal control of utilities, pol-
lution regulation, and state tax policy. They generally turned
their talents to widening the discretion enjoyed by their corporate clients. Trial lawyers challenged and thus helped to define
business regulations; lobbyists sponsored laws that sidestepped
Texas's constitutional prohibitions on business consolidation; experts in corporate and financial law engaged in detailed negotiations with public officials and private interests to permit the
erection of the financial and managerial structures common to
modern enterprise.

For this work, some critics angrily denounced Baker & Botts.
When they did, the firm pointed to the right of all citizens, including corporate entities, to legal representation. In an adversarial legal system, they noted, lawyers' responsibility was to
represent their clients' interests as thoroughly and as aggressively as possible. While such appeals to the imperatives of professional ethics seldom quieted the critics' complaints about the
broad social impact of large corporate law firms, Baker & Botts's
lawyers could also respond that they had helped foster the economic progress that had accompanied the problems that drew
the critics' fire.

However one judges these matters, it is clear that Baker &
Botts exerted a strong voice in deciding what shape Houston

and, indeed, modern Texas would take. What follows, then, is a history of legal and economic change in the state as seen through the life of one important institution. It is a case study of elite leadership, not of broad social movements, popular action, or everyday life, though it will touch on such things. Full coverage of the important transformation of Texas between the nineteenth and the twentieth centuries would certainly demand a view from the bottom as well as the top of society. Our focus, however, is on one key institution whose often anonymous individual members have over 150 years helped to shape both the law and the economy of the state. The firm as an ongoing institution brought the talents of many specialists to bear on the complex legal issues raised by the expansion of the American business system.

PART I
AN ELITE FIRM IN A COLONIAL ECONOMY, 1840–1914

Breaking with Tradition

IN 1865 Peter Gray and Walter Browne Botts returned home to Houston after service in the Confederate Army. What they found was not, by today's standards, very impressive. The city was then a small island of commerce in a sea of cotton farms. It was not a particularly promising location for ambitious new ventures; indeed, it was little more than a cluster of wooden buildings tied together by unimproved roads and possessing almost none of the amenities already common in larger, more-developed cities in the East. A local newspaper noted several of the distinguishing characteristics of Houston in this period: "oceans of mud, and submerged suburbs, the home of the frog and the cradle of the musquito [*sic*], the birthplace of fever."[1] Amid the dislocations brought by the Civil War and Reconstruction, Houston remained in its infancy, a trading center on the flat, humid coastal plain of Texas. It was far removed from the seats of political and economic power in the nation. With a population of fewer than ten thousand, it was roughly one-twentieth the size of New Orleans, the reigning urban center on the Gulf Coast. Houston did not even dominate its immediate surroundings. Forty miles to the southeast stood the substantially larger port city of Galveston, which enjoyed a long head start over its inland rival in the competition for Gulf Coast trade. Yet with an optimism that seemed blind to reality, boosters of Houston predicted future expansion.

From its founding in 1836 by the original boosters, the Allen brothers, Houston had generated such enthusiasm. When pressed for details, boosters pointed to the city's excellent location squarely in the path of the potential inland transportation connections between New Orleans and California and between the Gulf of Mexico and the centers of midwestern trade, Saint

Louis and Kansas City. Houston might someday become a major port, they observed; all that needed to be done was to dredge a deepwater channel to the Gulf via Buffalo Bayou and Galveston Bay. There were ample natural resources nearby. Huge timber stands lay just to the east, and cotton and other farm products could be grown in abundance in the hinterland connected to Houston by navigable rivers.

Skeptics might have noted that similar prophecies were ringing forth from boosters throughout the United States. But America's nineteenth-century economic dynamism was making many such prophecies come true. The industrializing Northeast was reaching out to markets and for raw materials throughout the nation, and the energies so evident in industrial centers before the Civil War were to surge across much of the remainder of the country in the decades that followed 1865. Those well situated with talent, ambition, a sense of timing, and a touch of luck would have many opportunities to prosper.

Peter W. Gray and Walter Browne Botts had all of these qualities and some other advantages as well when they returned to Houston to rebuild their lives and their careers after the war. The cousins from prominent Fredericksburg, Virginia, families had migrated to Houston before the war in search of new opportunities. The primary skill they brought with them was legal training, in each case acquired by reading law under the guidance of family members. Gray also came equipped with a formidable reputation and a network of contacts in Houston and the state, the legacy of his well-known father.

Peter Gray had moved to Houston with his father, William Fairfax Gray, when the "city" was a rough commercial outpost on the banks of Buffalo Bayou populated by a few thousand recent migrants. Texas was then not even a part of the United States. Visions of Houston's future were of necessity tempered by the realities of survival in a hostile, rugged environment. The elder Gray quickly rose to prominence as a lawyer, an official in the government of the Republic of Texas, and the district attorney of a broad region in Southeast Texas. While helping to create a legal system for the new republic, he also laid claim to more lasting historical fame as a diarist whose vivid description of the region remains among the best portraits of life in early Houston.

William Fairfax Gray died in 1841, but Peter Gray continued in his father's footsteps. He was admitted to the bar in 1840, and briefly practiced law with his father. When Texas became a state in 1845, Gray served in both houses of the legislature, where he wrote the first procedural code, the Practice Act of 1846, which defined the laws of pleading before Texas courts. He also served as a judge on the 11th District Court. Following the outbreak of the Civil War fifteen years later, Gray was elected as Houston's representative to the Confederate Congress. Amid the chaos of Reconstruction, Gray would remain a builder and would quickly become a recognized leader of the bar in his region.

Walter Browne Botts first made the trek from Fredericksburg to Houston in 1857. He also brought to the city a strong family background in the profession and training acquired by reading law in the offices of his father. He returned to Virginia to fight for the Confederacy, but once back in Houston "Colonel" Botts formed with Peter Gray a legal partnership, the firm of Gray & Botts.

The new practice resembled other law firms in post–Civil War Houston. Such partnerships generally had two or three members who carried on their individual work while sharing overhead expenses in a common office. These firms at times made use of "clerks"—apprentices who were studying the law under the guidance of one of the partners—to perform routine tasks. Those who "read law" in such an office were being trained to be admitted to the bar, not to be admitted to membership in the firm. Traditional practices generally focused on legal issues involving property, with land law, business contracts, and personal finances, including trusts, as prominent concerns. Individual lawyers often built their reputations through theatrical performances in courtrooms. Firms were as well known as their most visible partners, and the leading ones often included lawyers who had gained fame outside as well as inside a courtroom, with prominent politicians leading the way. Few firms were permanent institutions, for traditional partnerships in law—as in the small businesses of the day—tended to dissolve when one of the partners died or withdrew in search of better opportunities.[2]

In the 1860s the legal profession in Texas was as yet only loosely organized. Though Peter Gray had made a lasting contribution to the codification of the state's legal system with the Practice Act of 1846, there were still no well-established law schools in the state. Nor was there an ongoing association of the bar at the local level before 1870, or at the state level before 1882. The legal libraries in Houston belonged to individual lawyers and their partners. The system for reporting precedents from the various courts was unsystematic and difficult for practicing attorneys to use. The common law of contracts and commercial law—vital concerns in subsequent decades to business lawyers—"remained almost static" during the nineteenth century. There was no need for banking law, to give the extreme example, because the Texas Constitution of 1845 had outlawed the incorporation of banks. In short, the legal environment of the newly established firm of Gray & Botts reflected the needs of a sparsely settled, little-developed region populated mainly by small farmers.[5]

This world began to change with the coming of the railroads to Houston. No industry in the nineteenth century had such a pervasive impact on the Texas economy or on its legal system. As rail lines bridged the vast gulfs of land that separated the state's scattered towns and nascent cities, commerce bloomed. So too in many ways did the practice of law. Railroads needed more capital and higher levels of coordination than did traditional Texas businesses, which raised a host of new legal issues in the areas of finance and corporate organization. As interstate businesses, railroads also generated new regulatory questions. Law firms that responded to railroads' legal needs, as Gray & Botts did, moved away from the traditional, nineteenth-century practice of law and edged toward the emerging corporate practice that would become characteristic of large firms in the twentieth century. In this sense, the railroads transformed the practice of Gray & Botts as they transformed the economy of Houston.

The partners had an early opportunity to become involved in railroad law when a group of ambitious Houstonians founded the state's first railroad, the Buffalo Bayou, Brazos and Colorado. Their venture symbolized the hope that rail transportation represented. The new line was to extend across the three bodies of water—Buffalo Bayou and the Brazos and Colorado rivers—most important to Houston and bring hinterland trade to the interior port. In doing so, the line would help the city compete with its larger rival to the south, Galveston. Other towns had similar plans, of course, and competition for trade stimulated a railroad boom in Texas, just as it had a generation earlier in the East.[4] As railroads penetrated the state, Gray & Botts gradually built up a substantial railroad practice, culminating in the firm's appointment as general Texas counsel for the giant Southern Pacific system in 1893.

At first, the attorneys served these railroads much as they had

their other clients. Railroading was just one more local business, easily added to the partners' ongoing work with wills and estates, investigation of trust deeds, and small commercial suits. Representing lines such as the Fort Worth and New Orleans Railroad and the Waxahachie Tap Railroad, Gray & Botts continued to do business in the traditional manner.[5]

But the railroads did not long remain like other businesses.[6] As the lines grew longer, much larger, and more interconnected, they transformed both the economy of Texas and the practice of the law firm. The direction of change had already been apparent in the East before the Civil War. Great systems—the Pennsylvania, the New York Central, the Baltimore and Ohio—took shape and transformed transportation into an interstate business. After 1869, and a decade of wartime building, financiers and speculators unleashed a flurry of competitive construction and consolidation, which reshaped the nation's railroad map. The construction of transcontinental lines and the consolidation of local roads into regional and national systems quickly made railroading into a new type of industry run by professional managers and dominated by a few leading investors.

The efforts by powerful eastern and midwestern railroad barons to forge self-contained systems for their roads brought financiers to Texas in search of local lines to buy. After 1873, when a general financial panic swept the country, many of the small, undercapitalized lines running throughout eastern Texas fell into receivership. Local investors, seeing their personal fortunes and their dreams for the future threatened, had little alternative but to solicit funds from the capital-rich East and North. Texas railroads began to pass out of local hands.[7]

As Texas roads fell into the hands of eastern financiers, they came to symbolize the power outsiders had over the local economy.[8] A prominent supporter of the Farmers' Alliance voiced the fears of many Texas farmers: "Wall Street owns the country. It is no longer a government of the people, by the people and for the people, but a government of Wall Street, by Wall Street and for Wall Street. The great common people of this country are slaves, and monopoly is the master. The West and South are bound and prostrate before the manufacturing East."[9] An almost obsessive fear of "foreign" control gripped many Texans as their state began to industrialize. The interstate railroads became the focus of these fears.

"Slavery," "monopoly," and "exploitation" were the terms farmers and merchants used to condemn their loss of control over transportation. Decisions about where to place a line or how much to charge to ship a particular product were now in the hands of faraway traffic managers who seemed insensitive to local needs. Farmers and merchants complained when a rail line bypassed their town and sent trade to some urban rival. Even when they succeeded in landing a link to the expanding rail network, they found that the new national transportation system could be a two-edged sword. The same lines that allowed them to market their crops brought the bad news of worldwide price declines. Those who had eagerly sought the railroads because they could promote prosperity now viewed them with anxiety because of their potential to inflict damage on their communities. As the president of the Texas Farmers' Alliance warned, "Railroad corporations are penetrating almost every locality with their iron rails, they are binding the people in chains and strangling to death the industries of our state" (*Southern Mercury,* 21 August 1888). When Texas farmers decried the control of their lives by "foreign railroads," they voiced a fear of large-scale, northeastern-based corporations that would reverberate throughout the state for decades.[10]

The struggles of those hurt by the railroads prompted a political response. One result was a new Texas constitution in 1876. Supported by Democrats and a strong Granger party, the new constitution was designed to bring the railroads to heel. Outside control of vital transportation lines was prohibited, as was acquisition of one road by another. The constitution also restricted the issuance of rail construction bonds by municipalities and limited the amount of state land that could be given to the railroads as a subsidy. It was hoped that railroads would thus be deprived of their leverage against communities, that is, the threat of bypassing a town used to extract subsidies and concessions. The constitution also made rates subject to regulation by the legislature, though it provided no effective means for enforcing this provision.[11]

The combination of a new constitutional setting and a powerful set of hostile economic interests increased railroad demands for local legal services. It fell to lawyers to resolve many of the complex issues stemming from the broadly worded new law. This sort of work, combined with the new areas of corporate finance and organization, made railroads leading clients for ambitious lawyers. One of the most prominent members of the Texas bar, Galveston attorney William Pitt Ballinger, captured the sentiment of many specialists in business law when he admonished himself in his diary: "I must make myself thorough in Railroad law."[12]

Gray & Botts also recognized the trend and added James A. Baker from Huntsville to their partnership. Baker had arrived in Texas from Alabama in 1852. "Judge" Baker built a thriving practice as a prominent citizen of Huntsville, in part through legal work involving local railroads. Yet at the age of fifty, he chose to migrate seventy miles south to Houston and embark on a new phase of his career.[13] The death of three small children over a twelve-year period no doubt prepared the Baker family to leave Huntsville; the lure of practicing law in the emerging railroad center of Houston helped draw Judge Baker to his new home.

On Baker's arrival at Gray & Botts in 1872, the firm became Gray, Botts & Baker. In 1875, after Peter Gray left to join the Texas Supreme Court, it became Baker & Botts.[14] With his political activities and professional prominence, Gray had given the fledgling firm high standing within the city and state. While still with the firm, he had served in 1870 as the first president of the Houston Bar Association. His appointment to the Texas Supreme Court further enhanced his reputation, as well as that of his firm. Gray died only months after his appointment, however, at the age of fifty-four, and the firm that he had founded faced the challenge of building new strengths.

When Judge Baker joined the firm in the early 1870s, its railroad work was confined primarily to the smaller roads within Texas. It acted as general attorneys for the Missouri, Kansas and Texas (Katy), an important line in the northeastern part of the state, and the Houston and Texas Central (H&TC), a railroad linking Galveston and Houston to Austin and Dallas.[15] These roads' legal problems included the touchy matter of disposing of land grants, which the state legislature demanded be sold quickly.[16] There were as well more routine matters—suits by shippers against the lines for failure to deliver freight on time and other questions of common carrier law.[17] Soon, however, the partners became involved in the machinations of the railroad giants. Working for Texas lines such as the Katy and the H&TC put Baker & Botts in contact with the most famous railroad magnate of the 1880s, Jay Gould.[18]

Gould had already made a name for himself in the East by

gaining control of lines through clever legal and financial manipulations and then running them into the ground and reaping windfall profits by speculating in their stocks. But the infamous financier also had ambitions as a builder. In Texas he set out to integrate some of the state's most important railroads into the national system he was building. After winning a fierce, controversial struggle with the experienced railroad leader Tom Scott, Gould gained control of the Texas and Pacific Railroad, which he hoped would provide him with a link from his growing transportation empire in the middle of the nation to the Pacific.[19]

Next to face off against Gould was Collis P. Huntington from San Francisco, one of the builders of the transcontinental Central Pacific Railroad. Huntington and Gould battled for years in the courts as well as in the marketplace for control of the southern transcontinental route, and not until the early 1890s was peace declared, with Huntington the victor.

Baker & Botts had gradually been drawn into this extended legal and economic combat. When Gould acquired control of the Katy through a leasing agreement, the law firm was in effect working for him. Later, the partners became general Texas counsel for Gould's Missouri Pacific. Much of the legal work arising out of Gould's disputes was handled by his New York attorneys, the firm of Shearman & Sterling. But Baker & Botts assisted in the many suits and countersuits in Texas that grew out of the wrestling of the giants. At one point, Judge Baker was one of the two main Texas counselors whom Gould used to argue his position. By the early 1890s, as Gould's strength faded and a new era in Texas railroading began, Baker & Botts was well situated to play a major role in the industry's legal affairs.

The history of railroads in Texas changed in 1893. Two years earlier, Gov. James Hogg and the Texas legislature had created the Texas Railroad Commission, and now that body began to regulate the roads in earnest. At the same time, Collis Huntington, victorious over Jay Gould, had begun to consolidate his many holdings in Texas, placing them all under a new Southern Pacific (SP) holding company chartered in Kentucky. It was this corporation that was denounced by western farmers as a grasping "octopus." In 1893 this controversial railroad combine named Baker & Botts as its general counsel in Texas. The appointment made the firm quite important to the SP, since Texas contained a significant portion of the properties of the company.

By this time, the firm was an acknowledged regional leader in railroad law.[20]

The impact of Baker & Botts's new scale of railroad practice was most evident in its hiring of new lawyers. Between 1893 and 1915 the firm added eight new partners, five of whom had extensive experience with railroad-related work before joining the firm. As was common around the turn of the century, Baker & Botts generally sought new members from among the ranks of experienced lawyers, not from the small numbers of graduates from law schools each year. Thus when the firm's work load increased, it invited into the practice lawyers with proven ability in court in the sort of railroad work that was the backbone of Baker & Botts's early practice.

The most prominent new partner was Robert Scott Lovett (1860–1932), who attested to the members that their firm had "arrived" on the national legal scene. This son of an East Texas farmer had postponed high school and begun his railroad career literally at the bottom, digging stumps for one of the Gould lines. After reading law in the offices of a Houston attorney, he began to practice in Coldspring, a small town some sixty miles north of Houston. One local client was a railroad that was part of Gould's Texas & Pacific line, and Lovett's excellent work quickly propelled him up the ranks of the lawyers employed by that system. The Texas & Pacific named him its general attorney in 1891; two years later, Baker & Botts made him a partner.

Lovett's upward march continued, and Baker & Botts proved to be a stepping-stone in an improbable journey from a dirt farm in East Texas to the chair of one of the nation's largest railroads. While working for the Southern Pacific in Texas, Lovett caught the eye of Edward H. Harriman, who had taken control of the road. Harriman brought the Texas lawyer to New York in 1903 as the general counsel in charge of the Legal Department of his mammoth Union Pacific–Southern Pacific system. Lovett succeeded Harriman following the latter's death and, after the separation of the SP and the Union Pacific, he headed the Union Pacific until 1932. Even after leaving Houston in 1903, Lovett retained close personal and professional ties to members of Baker & Botts, thus linking the firm to the eastern establishment.[21]

Even before Lovett's departure, the firm added several other new lawyers. These included two who would later exert a profound influence on the organization: Edwin B. Parker, a legal workhorse who coordinated the increasingly complex railroad work and set up the first firm management plan, came into the business in 1894; and Jesse Andrews, who developed a branch office in Kansas City, joined in 1899. The immense potential for litigation in railroad work also encouraged the partners to add superior litigators, such as Clarence Wharton, a well-known trial lawyer in Richmond, in Fort Bend County southwest of Houston. Wharton's skills in the courtroom made him a partner in 1906, and the firm relied on him to try many of its most important cases in these years. In 1904 Baker & Botts brought in Hiram Garwood as a partner through a special arrangement to represent the Southern Pacific in Austin. As a member of the Texas legislature in 1886 and 1890, Garwood had helped write the Texas Railroad Commission Law. He had also served briefly as a judge, and he provided the sort of political connections the railroad desired in Texas. Judge Garwood was much more than a good lobbyist; his reputation as a trial lawyer equaled that of Clarence Wharton, and he handled a wide variety of cases for the firm.

By the early 1900s Baker & Botts had clearly broken away from the traditional pattern of Texas law firms. It was much larger than others in the state; it also specialized in railroad work to a remarkable degree. As the partners noted in 1897, the demands of railroad law had forced them to subordinate general practice. Most of the office space, clerical help, and lawyers' hours had to be given over to their most important client simply because of the size and complexity of the work.[22]

The addition of Clarence Carter in 1907 and Jules Tallichet in 1909 confirmed the trend to specialization. Carter had roots in East Texas, where his family was prominent in the lumber business. Before coming to Baker & Botts, he spent four years as a division attorney in Houston for the SP. Tallichet was the Austin-born son of a French Canadian professor of romance languages at the University of Texas. He had worked for nine years as an SP attorney in his hometown and then in West Texas. Baker & Botts brought him to Houston to make use of his highly refined talents in this work. He balanced Wharton's and Garwood's litigation skills by burrowing deeply into the intricacies of office law.[23] So closely attached was Tallichet to the railroad that, though a partner in the firm, he was also paid a salary directly by the Southern Pacific.[24]

In this era as much as half of Baker & Botts's total revenue was generated by its railroad practice.[25] In 1893 the firm received retainers from the various SP lines in Texas; $6,000 per year for representing the Houston and Texas Central, $4,040 for the Houston East and West Texas. In 1894 an additional $1,875 came in from the Galveston, Harrisburg and San Antonio (GH&SA) and the Texas and New Orleans (T&NO) lines.[26] In addition, the Katy still paid the firm $2,500 for handling litigation in Harris County, and the parent Southern Pacific Corporation provided a steady $5,000 biennially to lobby in Austin.[27]

At the turn of the century, the firm's financial position improved even more. Its compensation from the H&TC increased to ten thousand dollars, while payments from the GH&SA and the T&NO increased more than fivefold, also to ten thousand dollars. By 1912 the firm's total retainer from the Southern Pacific alone was more than twenty-five thousand dollars, at a time when the annual wage for an average industrial worker was about five hundred dollars.

Work for the Southern Pacific was also significant in another way: it was the cornerstone around which Baker & Botts built the leading business law practice in Texas. From the 1890s through the 1920s, railroad work fostered the steady expansion of the firm. Baker & Botts gradually took on the distinctive organizational form and attitudes characteristic of the small fraternity of large law firms that had arisen in New York and other large cities to meet the changing legal needs of big business. As a nationally recognized specialist on the laws of Texas, Baker & Botts developed strong correspondent ties with influential corporate law practices in New York and other commercial centers. Through these contacts, the firm monitored closely the transformation of the practice of law in this particular segment of the legal profession. Client referrals also flowed through these ties.

Like leading law practices throughout the nation, Baker & Botts became a different sort of organization in these years. The firm began to develop an associate system for recruiting and promoting to full partnerships young lawyers who had demonstrated ambition and intellectual promise in a leading law school. It also took a more systematic approach to management under the direction of a managing partner, who was responsible for the smooth workings of the growing organization. Although the firm continued to excel in trial work, it took on a growing amount of office work performed by specialists who seldom ventured into a courtroom. Large enterprises in transportation, in manufacturing, and in finance were creating a high-volume legal business that could no longer be handled by the old style of law firm, whether in New York or Houston. If attorneys wanted this business, they had to change the nature of their practices and their organizations. The partners at Baker & Botts were determined to stay abreast of this forceful tide.

In size and organization, Baker & Botts was quite similar to the major New York law firms from the earliest years of modern corporate practice.[28] All of these large firms became ongoing institutions with numerous lawyers instead of temporary alliances of a few partners. Baker & Botts joined such rising Wall Street firms as Shearman & Sterling, Sullivan & Cromwell, and Cravath, Swaine & Moore in the vanguard of the movement toward new methods of organizing the practice of corporate law. These firms and others entering this relatively new area of specialization focused their practices on the rescue of ailing corporations, particularly railroads, the creation of new companies and the consolidation of existing ones, and the arrangement of financing for corporations. To manage such work effectively, Baker & Botts and other emerging corporate firms in this era required larger size and greater specialization.

Yet, the Houston firm also had unique aspects. There were distinct differences between the practice of the leading corporate law firm in a relatively poor, though dynamic, southwestern state and that of the emerging giants on Wall Street. Much of the difference reflected the fact that Houston at the turn of the century was still a small town compared to New York City, the center of the nation's financial and economic systems. It is not surprising that high finance and corporate mergers and reorganizations were not as important on the Gulf Coast as they were in New York. Indeed, the total bank deposits in Houston in 1905 were less than 10 percent of the deposits then held by one major New York bank.[29] Even that figure probably exaggerates the real power of Houston's banks, which considered themselves fortunate to handle the local payroll account of a regional railroad. Houston was not yet home to major industrial corporations, whose legal work went primarily to firms located near the sources of financing in the East. The highly restrictive state incorporation statutes in Texas were in sharp contrast to the permissive holding company laws of Delaware and New Jersey. As a result, even the large oil corporations that started their operations in Texas after 1901 would ultimately make their legal homes outside the state.

Baker & Botts represented the major regional utilities, but they, too, were small relative to the much larger utility systems serving northeastern cities. Although Baker & Botts remained roughly the same size as the largest Wall Street firms, its practice differed in content from that of its counterparts in New York.

Still, Baker & Botts clearly no longer resembled most other law firms in Texas. Turn-of-the-century Houston still had numerous practices similar in stature and style to the traditional partnership of Gray & Botts of the 1870s. Several prominent lawyers headed these sorts of firms. They included Mayor Ben S. Campbell, the senior partner in the Houston firm of Campbell, Sewell & Myer, and Jonathan Lane, member of the firm of Lane, Wolters & Story and "one of the most prominent citizens and well known attorneys of Houston and Texas." But these and other law firms did not at this time develop a strong, ongoing relationship with a major railroad system. They were not influenced, as Baker & Botts was, by the transformation of the practice of corporate law. This meant that within its region and its state, Baker & Botts early on differed in size, tone, and organization from other firms. It was no longer tied to the attitudes, procedures, and client bases of traditional local practices.

The new style of law practiced at Baker & Botts exposed the firm to often-biting criticism as the prime local example of a haven for the dreaded "corporation lawyer." An editorial in the *Houston Chronicle* on 1 November 1907 captured the tone of such criticism: "Nevertheless close observers of our times note the evil example of two extreme types, the corporation lawyer, who tends to become as soulless as the corporation he serves, and the 'shyster lawyer,' who is a troublemaker and everything which a good lawyer ought not to be." The editorial asserted that "of the two the corrupt corporation lawyer is the worst," as the "capitalist's caddie does a greater amount of harm." The key complaint against corporation lawyers was their willingness to conspire with big business and against the broader society: "Every captain of industry has a lawyer lieutenant who shows him how to do his tricks without getting caught."[30] By casting its lot with the industrial forces that were beginning to transform a state with strong rural traditions, Baker & Botts became an obvious symbol in Houston of a corporate world that made many citizens distinctly uncomfortable.

The firm also became an agent of change in the legal profession of Texas. First, in serving as a model for the organization of a large-scale corporate legal practice, it indirectly influenced the practice of law by other Texas firms. More important, in carrying out its work for the Southern Pacific, Baker & Botts also exerted a much more direct influence on the state's legal system. Part of the firm's responsibility for its client included hiring lawyers capable of handling the railroads' legal work throughout the state. While identifying and retaining good counsel for the SP, Baker & Botts also sought to inculcate values and procedures compatible with its own within this growing network of Texas railroad lawyers. The firm encouraged the spread of a "Wall Street" approach to the practice of law while directly shaping the evolution of a number of major law firms in other Texas cities. Baker & Botts was thus an outpost of the attitudes and techniques of "modern corporate law" in a state in which the legal profession was still dominated by traditional partnerships.

Within the extensive system of local counsel used by the SP, Baker & Botts served in a managerial capacity. The firm replaced traditional correspondent ties between law firms with what might best be termed corporate relationships. Heretofore, informal working arrangements between firms had emerged through experience working on cases together, references from mutual acquaintances, and personal ties developed during the study of law or through political and social contacts. Such correspondent relationships were then used to refer clients or to seek advice or assistance in trying cases outside of a firm's immediate region or outside its primary areas of expertise. The corporate ties within the SP's legal network, however, were more formal and more systematic, that is, more bureaucratic. These ties resembled more those that bound employees to employers in a business organization. Such corporate relationships were foreign to turn-of-the-century Texas lawyers, and they at first generated considerable tension. The lawyers and their firms gradually adjusted to the new constraints, soothed, no doubt, by the financial and professional benefits of representing one of the largest corporations active in their state.

The SP legal network constituted a four-tiered pyramid. At the top of this pyramid were the lawyers and traffic managers in the railroad's corporate offices in San Francisco and New York. These men set legal policy for the company as a whole under the direction of the corporation's chief counsel, a position filled for a while by one-time Baker & Botts partner Robert S. Lovett. In the second tier was Baker & Botts, which enjoyed considerable tactical autonomy in carrying out the corporate legal strategy within Texas. A major part of this work involved organizing and managing the activities taking place on the two lower tiers, the division and the local attorneys throughout the state.

The primary contacts of Baker & Botts were the division attorneys in major Texas cities served by the SP, including El Paso, San Antonio, Waco, and Victoria. Division attorneys tended to be partners in well-established firms having strong reputations for railroad work within their area. Counsel was needed throughout the state to file documents, register mortgages, and oversee the road's vast landholdings. Division attorneys performed this routine work while also handling suits that arose over such matters as charter violations, large personal injury cases, and the payment of taxes. Under them, local attorneys in the smaller towns took care of the innumerable claims and damage suits that arose in the normal course of railroad operations. These local attorneys generally were just starting their legal careers, and they usually worked on a contingency fee basis.

In this setting, the practice of law went forward under a chain of command similar to that used in a modern, decentralized corporation. Although lawyers at all levels retained the autonomy to try cases as they saw fit, policies established by those above the trial lawyers in the hierarchy dictated the types of cases that should be tried, the range of permissible settlements, and the compensation of the attorneys. The SP's legal network was no doubt more flexible than most of the management systems used in industry, if only because it employed a relatively small number of lawyers who had a strong professional tradition of independence. Nevertheless, individual lawyers in this network faced constraints unfamiliar to traditional practitioners and they often voiced concerns about their loss of autonomy. Baker & Botts had to manage the trade-offs between independence and central control in a way that would keep the network operating effectively.

Typical of the problems that arose were those discussed in an exchange of letters in 1904 between Baker & Botts and the firm of Proctor, Vandenberge & Crain in Victoria, Texas, about 125 miles southwest of Houston. Proctor was a prominent Texas lawyer and politician who headed a well-established firm that had represented several local railroads before they were acquired by the Southern Pacific. As the general attorney for these local roads, the firm had enjoyed direct access to top managers and considerable discretion in meeting the legal needs of its clients. When Baker & Botts sought to integrate the Victoria firm into the SP's legal network, a heated dispute quickly arose.

The immediate issue was the authority of the Victoria firm to request complimentary passes from SP management for those it judged important to the smooth functioning of the railroad in its area. Baker & Botts resented the attempt by the division attorney to bypass it in the chain of command. After Baker & Botts asserted its authority, the Proctor firm sent an indignant letter of protest to the president of the railroads in question (along with a copy to Baker & Botts). As asserted in the letter: "Ever since the Southern Pacific Company has had control over our lines, and even prior thereto as respects the G. W. T. & P., we had the entire control, management and responsibility of every particle of litigation against these companies." Further, "We cannot see the necessity that we should make requests for passes through them [Baker & Botts], or that our requests upon you should be referred to them." This well-established firm had represented lines affiliated with the SP even longer than had Baker & Botts. It did not relish the idea of "reporting" to its neighbor in Houston. To emphasize its point, the firm signed its correspondence "General Attorneys," the designation it had held for the local lines before their absorption by the SP.[31]

The response of Baker & Botts left no doubt as to which firm would use the title "General Attorney" in the future. Baker & Botts explained that it had not intervened previously because "we found this litigation was having most intelligent and efficient attention and no good purpose could, in our opinion, have been subserved by our giving detailed attention to it." But now the Houston firm was ready to assert its authority: "This firm has been for years, however, and still is, held responsible for the general conduct of the legal affairs of the two roads mentioned, and it is contemplated that we shall in a general way look after all matters affecting their organization and shape the general policy to be pursued insofar as their legal affairs are concerned, to the end that the general policies . . . may be uniform." By achieving "a very clear understanding as to the authority and responsibility of our respective firms," Baker & Botts concluded, they would prevent "annoying misunderstandings in the future."[32]

Determined to have the last word and to forestall any future conflicts, Baker & Botts played its trump card: its close relationship with former partner Robert S. Lovett. Where the Victoria firm had submitted its grievance to the president of the local roads, Baker & Botts sent the entire series of letters to Lovett, SP's chief counsel. Its report of this episode to the Victoria firm left no room for continued controversy: "For the purpose of confirming our own understanding of the respective status of your firm and ours . . . we have submitted to Judge Lovett—who is here today—your letter to Mr. Van Vleck of the 30th ultimo, who confirms the correctness of our previous understanding."

The question had been decided. By explicitly leaving to the Proctor firm the "absolute control" of litigation affecting lines within its area (so long as it stayed within "the general lines of policy"), Baker & Botts kept this particular division attorney in the network. Once satisfied on this crucial point, the Proctor firm settled into a smooth, effective division attorney relationship under the general direction of Baker & Botts. The new hierarchy worked.

At times Baker & Botts and the division attorneys had to implement SP-established policies that ran counter to the professional judgment of the network's attorneys. By the early twentieth century, for example, routine commercial and personal liability suits had become a major source of concern to the railroad. Farmers took the SP to court for damage to their livestock; passengers sued for injuries sustained in the course of travel. According to Edwin B. Parker (Baker & Botts), such cases had become a highly lucrative business for members of the "damage suit fraternity."[33] In West Texas in particular, local resentment against the railroad found expression in such suits. Juries composed of resentful cattle ranchers, many of whom had outstanding claims against the railroad, had awarded large judgments in several cases.[34]

In response, the SP developed a new policy. To quell antagonism toward the railroads, the division attorneys were to help "promote good feelings between the Company and the people."[35] "Every effort was to be made," wrote Parker, "to mold public opinion and create a sentiment favorable to RR companies."[36] To accomplish this herculean task, attorneys were instructed to litigate claims only as a last resort, relying on negotiated settlements to avoid the tensions raised by jury trials. Now instructions from above, not the judgment of the individual lawyer, dictated the strategy to be taken in the courthouse.

To help implement this policy, Baker & Botts was able to supply legal advice to division attorneys and to assist them in preparing briefs when matters went to court. The Houston firm also provided retainers from the SP rather than case-by-case fees, eliminating any economic incentive the lawyers might have had to bring cases to trial. At the same time, the firm charged local attorneys with new responsibilities: they were to work under division attorneys and perform services such as monitoring juries and keeping track of citizens who were known to be antagonistic to the railroad.[37] Selecting lawyers well acquainted with the areas in which they operated, Baker & Botts directed that they get to know every person on the jury panels and "bring every legitimate influence to bear to overcome any local prejudice which may exist against the railroad."[38]

This new set of policies involved a fundamental reshaping of the legal structure of the SP in Texas. Division attorneys in even remote counties became more specialized in railroad work. Local attorneys acquainted themselves with all aspects of the railroad business and its effect on their locality. The railroad spared little expense in assisting them. In response to ongoing antagonism in the key city of El Paso, it sent a claims agent with instructions to watch juries and investigate witnesses to "learn of any attempts to improperly influence or corrupt jurors, [or] color the testimony of witnesses."[39] When cases came to trial, the railroad provided money for the expenses of jury investigation and the payment of witnesses, evidently believing that if it could begin a case with parties at least unprejudiced toward railroads, it stood a fair chance of winning.

Such efforts were obviously aimed at a broader goal than winning the SP more favorable results in cases immediately brought to trial. The railroad now had a long-term perspective on its problems in Texas. In one case, for example, the road paid eight thousand dollars to a plaintiff in an injury suit. In the bargain, however, it gained a valuable ally in the plaintiff's lawyer. As part of the settlement, he agreed to keep the terms of the award confidential, to refuse to take any more antirailroad cases, and to provide information on certain cases still pending. His firm later became local attorneys themselves for the SP in Hondo, a relationship that continued until 1967.[40]

The new SP legal policy clearly limited the traditional independence of the lawyers who served the railroad. Edwin Parker put the matter simply: all railroad lawyers should follow company policy even if it conflicted with their own opinion or advice for their client. The object, according to Parker, was to make "every attorney who represents the Sunset Central [SP] lines to feel a *personal* interest in *all* that affects these lines."[41]

While some corporate policies of the SP were implemented easily, others generated recurrent problems for Baker & Botts. The tensions inherent in corporate relationships were most clearly evident in disputes over compensation. Traditional firms set fees according to the experience and sense of fairness of individual attorneys, but fees for SP lawyers were set by corporate officials and enforced by Baker & Botts within Texas. The Southern Pacific carefully compared the charges paid to attorneys performing similar services. Changes in existing charges had to be approved by corporate officials. Using a rudimentary variant of the cost-accounting calculations originally developed to manage other aspects of the railroad's operations, the SP's Legal Department set standards for the compensation of lawyers based on the number and the types of cases they handled.

Baker & Botts, which had only limited discretion to depart from these standards, had to field numerous complaints from the network's attorneys over these fees and retainers. Seldom could the Houston partners grant requests for increased payments. The firm often responded to complaints by developing statistical evidence to persuade the SP's Legal Department of the need for adjustments. But the SP did not make changes in existing fee schedules lightly. In this unpleasant aspect of its dealings with other attorneys in the state, Baker & Botts could normally do little more than explain that its hands were tied by corporate policies. Those network attorneys who were satisfied with the steady income, prestige, and client referrals that flowed from railroad work stayed with the SP.

Such referrals at times made it possible for firms to specialize in corporate law even in Texas towns seemingly too small to support such a practice. The promise of referrals from a major Houston law firm that represented clients active throughout Texas could be a strong incentive for a small-town practitioner surrender a measure of autonomy and become a part of the SP's network. But this new business came with strings attached. One ready source of income for attorneys in towns near railroads was the representation of suits against the roads for damages caused by their operations. Obviously, employment with the SP foreclosed the acceptance of such cases. In fact, the corporate policies of the SP—and other major lines—went a step further and forbade attorneys representing the SP from taking plaintiff suits against any other railroad.

More than money was at issue for many local attorneys who sought to balance the costs and benefits of working for the SP. In rural Texas at the turn of the century, the label "railroad lawyer" may have been a badge of professionalism to some, but to others it carried a social stigma. A lawyer so marked risked losing acceptance within the community. The local attorney for the SP in Wharton, a small town southwest of Houston, explained to his "supervisors" at Baker & Botts in 1915:

> There is an element involved in this matter of being an attorney for a railway company, in the country, which you gentlemen in the city may not appreciate. The railroads come into contact with the people in so many ways that there exists, always, more or less friction, although much of it does not develop into litigation, and an attorney who is known as a representative of a railroad company is looked upon by many people with more or less disfavor, and often looses [*sic*] business that would have come to him otherwise.[42]

In a state with a strong populist tradition, those who chose to represent the railroads could not escape the skepticism of segments of the community. In recruiting and retaining good local attorneys, Baker & Botts had to convince able young lawyers that their futures lay in the practice of twentieth-century railroad and corporate law, not in the traditional type of small-town practice common in the nineteenth century.

This argument was somewhat easier to make in the case of division attorneys. The Southern Pacific needed experienced, aggressive attorneys in the larger cities along its lines. A firm with good standing in its community, a proven record before juries, and the political and social connections to represent the railroad effectively seldom needed coaxing to see the long-term advantages of working for the Southern Pacific. Neither was it likely to accept easily intervention in its affairs by Baker & Botts. In the abstract, the interests of Baker & Botts were identical with those of the division attorneys; however, in the real world of day-to-day work on cases of immediate importance to the SP and thus to Baker & Botts, the Houston firm inevitably intervened aggressively in what had traditionally been considered the internal affairs of other firms. Even on the most fundamental of all decisions made by a law firm—the choice of partners—the leverage provided by the Southern Pacific's work allowed Baker & Botts to intervene decisively on occasion in the internal affairs of a major law firm.[45]

In these and other ways as well, Baker & Botts used its position as the general manager of the SP legal network in Texas to shape the practice of corporate law in the state. The firm's influence seems to have been particularly strong in the years before World War I, when Texas still lacked fully developed bar associations or regional law schools. From the firm's filing system to its close attention to detail, it held up procedures and attitudes for other lawyers in the SP's legal network to emulate. Those who chose to affiliate themselves with the railroad were asked to meet the firm's standards of professionalism. Many of the first generation of corporate lawyers received a part of their initial exposure to modern corporate law in this way.

As Baker & Botts rode the railroad to professional prominence, it invariably became enmeshed in controversy and conflict. Many farmers and small-town business leaders regarded corporate lawyers not as the bearers of new high standards of professionalism, but as mouthpieces for vested interests running rampant in the state. Yet increasingly, the firm would of necessity ally itself with these interests. The remuneration offered by corporate giants such as the SP was simply too enticing for entrepreneurially minded attorneys to pass up. As Baker & Botts made itself into a corporate law firm, it was called on by its clients to open up (or find ways around) laws and regulations in Texas that blocked the growth of big business. The lawyers had their first exposure to such work through their representation of the railroad.

Advocate for the Octopus

Representing railroads placed Baker & Botts on the frontier of law in Texas. When the firm began this type of practice the state had few statutes concerning modern corporate entities, little common law precedent for dealing with large-scale private enterprise, and few members of either the bench or the bar acquainted with the problems of these new business organizations. With its legislature dominated by rural citizens suspicious of corporations, there was little prospect that statutes would evolve quickly to meet new needs. Indeed, to many of the Texans who sat on the benches of state courts or served on their juries the law was seen largely as a bulwark to protect the people from large alien forces such as the railroad. Such conditions were not conducive to rapid legal or political change in favor of corporations. Nonetheless, through the efforts of lawyers such as the partners of Baker & Botts, the laws of Texas gradually changed, tentatively embracing the railroads and other forms of big business.

As a large, modern, well-established legal organization, Baker & Botts was well prepared to take on a variety of jobs for its most important client. The firm's representation of the Southern Pacific Railroad involved it in numerous activities, from trying cases, to lobbying in the state legislature, to representing the SP before the Texas Railroad Commission. In particular, the firm steadily gained experience in two vital areas of modern corporate law: the consolidation and reorganization of corporations; and government regulation, particularly as it applied to the rate-making process.

In handling these legal issues, Baker & Botts provided services not readily available from either the railroad's chief corporate counsel or other Texas firms. Regulatory work, for example, required a thorough knowledge of both Texas law and popular attitudes toward the railroads. Certainly, fear of public controversy had played no small part in Collis P. Huntington's decision to add Baker & Botts to the SP's Legal Department in 1894. Texas had a strong tradition of antirailroad sentiment. The creation of the Texas Railroad Commission represented the political mobilization of this vague, unfocused, but deeply felt desire to maintain local control of railroad rates and service. The state's stringent statute prohibiting "foreign" control by corporations chartered outside of Texas also prevented the SP from formally consolidating its Texas lines, while the passage in 1892 of a stock and bond law regulated the practice of stock watering (issuing securities in excess of capital needs or property values).

Though the vagueness of these laws and the limited staff of the Texas attorney general's office meant that the statutes were often ignored, they still impinged on the operation of the SP, generating substantial work for Baker & Botts. The railroad, which was chartered in Kentucky, owned the stock and bonds of most of its major Texas lines and leased other, less important, ones.[1] But under Texas law, it could not formally consolidate these holdings into a unified, centrally managed system. For that reason it had to maintain a Houston office to coordinate its Sunset Central lines—the name it gave to its Texas railroads to distance them from the Southern Pacific. Because of the danger of political attacks and competitive incursions from other carriers, as well as its loose organizational structure, the SP needed "strong local management," which meant both competent local executives and strong support from local lawyers.[2]

In an era when management techniques and business communications were still in their infancy, legal advisers played a critical role in running a large, distended enterprise like the SP. Disputes and conflicts that are now internalized by businesses or settled through bargaining and arbitration often found their resolution through litigation. In such a situation, the expert opinions of Baker & Botts served to educate SP executives about the options available to them in charting strategy in Texas and in negotiating with public officials. In the absence of strong federal law, decentralized legal procedures were the rule. Matters that later would be handled in-house or over the telephone required local representatives on the spot who knew the law and the society in which their client operated.

Baker & Botts attended to a variety of commonplace tasks for its largest client—calling annual meetings, seeing that directors were properly elected—but it also repeatedly performed important managerial functions. Attorneys Parker, Tallichet, and Garwood served at various times as directors of the GH&SA, one of the SP's main Texas lines. Reporting to Houston-based SP executives, who were formally under the corporation's New York headquarters, they exercised considerable initiative in Texas. In 1911 Parker recommended expanding the role of the road's general manager, allowing him greater autonomy from the president in matters of capital expenditure, while Garwood suggested restructuring the company to allow greater functional division of work by creating directors of maintenance and operations and traffic.[3]

As the SP sought to improve coordination within its expanding Texas system, Baker & Botts also worked to bring about a major transition in the Texas law on formal mergers. Since the Texas constitution still prohibited mergers of competing lines, the law firm had to lobby for a special legislative act to enable the railroad to consolidate some of its properties. Baker & Botts engaged Hiram Garwood, a former state representative and well-known trial lawyer, who used his contacts in Austin to good effect in presenting the case for consolidation. In 1905 Garwood helped obtain legislative authorization for the SP to take control of the New York, Texas and Mexican Railroad, the Gulf, West Texas and Pacific Railroad, the Galveston, Houston and Northern Railroad, the San Antonio and Gulf Railroad, and the Gonzales branch line.[4] The Southern Pacific was permitted to collapse all of these roads into its main Texas subsidiary, the GH&SA.

Getting the needed legislation was only half the battle. Baker & Botts also had to negotiate agreements with the numerous private parties who opposed consolidation. Even when the railroad already had a controlling interest in the lines involved, it often had a difficult time with bondholders and minority interests.[5] Shippers who enjoyed low rates because of competition also could be a source of opposition. Farmers whose livelihood turned largely on the prices they had to pay for moving their crops to market feared the impact of a consolidated rail combine.

The Texas legislature's Consolidation Act explicitly recognized some of these interests. It made the SP liable for all outstanding debts and prevented the sale of any line until it was approved by three-quarters of the stockholders.[6] Some creditors and stockholders resisted consolidation.[7] Though the potential benefits of being acquired by the SP were great, some hesitated to surrender control of their properties or capital to a distant corporate giant. The common law offered a remedy to those who felt they were being deprived of their property without due process; and it was in the subtleties of interpreting this law that Baker & Botts contributed to the process of consolidation. The Houston attorneys worked closely with Robert Lovett's Corporate Law Department, providing the expertise in state law and the experience before Texas judges and juries the SP needed.[8]

After lengthy negotiations with old owners and debt holders, Baker & Botts was able to stamp out a number of legal brushfires. The firm supplied legal opinions on the interpretation of debt contracts and it sought a consistent definition of net earnings of the line, which would serve as a basis from which dividends would be paid. Such work was tedious but fruitful.[9] Typical of the problems the partners faced were those created by the New York, Texas and Mexican Railroad, which lacked the resources to declare a dividend. Worse, ownership of one-quarter of its stock was considerably muddled because of the unusual origins of the road. It had been originally financed by New York millionaire J. W. MacKay, who placed much of the early capital with European investors through Count Joseph Telferner, an Italian nobleman.[10] Despite its grand name, the NY,T&M consisted of a scant seventy-nine miles of track, and its investors were either long gone or unknown.

While the law provided general means to cut through these problems, Baker & Botts's skillful and original interpretations of the measure were essential in the untangling of this situation and others like it. Drawing heavily on their contacts in the national legal profession, they adapted familiar principles of corporate, contract, and property law from the East to frontier Texas, easing the way toward consolidation.[11]

The route to centralization was tortuous, and the law firm could not always be satisfied with the results it achieved. Some of its difficulties stemmed from the efforts the legislature had made to protect local capital, a matter of great concern in turn-of-the-century Texas. Other troublesome provisions of the act included those aimed at preventing overcapitalization and stock watering.[12] There was as well a nagging conflict that arose out of a suit brought by Thomas T. Hubbard. In 1890 Hubbard (a former GH&SA executive and a substantial bondholder of the line) and other GH&SA bondholders had agreed to receive the interest on their bonds out of net earnings.[15] Apparently, this was done because year after year the road had defaulted on its interest payments, endangering the bondholders' investment and the credit of the road.[14] Though the SP contended that Hubbard and the others had expressly agreed to convert their mortgage bonds to income bonds permanently, Hubbard's suit maintained that with the consolidation, the crisis had passed and the bonds should again be treated as mortgages.[15]

To SP executives, Hubbard's claims amounted to nothing more than a form of blackmail, a "strike suit" by a minority of bondholders to force a lucrative settlement before they would agree to go along with reorganization. Hubbard, on the other hand, charged the SP with "milking" subsidiary roads like the GH&SA out of their profits and juggling its accounts to make it appear as though no money existed to pay the debts.[16] Appealing to the public's sympathy for "local" interests, he sought to block the road from issuing more debt until the earlier obligations were fulfilled.[17] Playing on the fears of "foreign capital," he threatened to undermine the SP's effort at consolidation. The railroad won the first trial, but the appeals court overturned the decision and ruled that the bondholders had not given up their lien on the GH&SA property.[18] It was incumbent on the SP as owner of the GH&SA to make a good faith effort to pay the mortgages.

Before the suit was finished in court, the SP and Hubbard came to terms, settling his claim for fifty cents on the dollar.[19] In addition to achieving a lucrative settlement, Hubbard had made an important point. Unable to consolidate all of its Texas railroads into one organization, the SP had for years depended on less-formal methods to manage its sprawling empire. It had leased Texas lines to a holding company, sent all of the profits to New York, and paid a rental to the Texas roads. In this way, the combine had been able to manage all of its properties in accord with a unified corporate strategy. Yet the legal basis for this structure was quite shaky, as Hubbard revealed. His suit voided the lease and forced the SP to pay the Texas line's debt obligations in accord with the original terms of the mortgage. In response to the court decision, the SP created a sinking fund for those GH&SA mortgages that did not have one and applied surplus funds to back payments, thereby quelling fears that the SP was milking its Texas roads.[20] But this was an expensive way to solve a problem that the SP and its law firm had hoped to finesse.

As the problems associated with the GH&SA consolidation demonstrated, there was far more slack in the application of the law than was apparent in theory. In an age before standardized accounting practices or regulation of securities markets, concepts such as net income, profit, mortgage, and the like were open to widely varying interpretations. The traditional legal system centered around real property was giving way to one based on new definitions of property associated with corporate securities. In such a transition, lawyers helped frame new definitions in the course of settling disputed financial issues.

In seeking such resolutions, Baker & Botts also sought the best interests of its client. The lawyers successfully avoided legal restrictions on corporate finance to send funds to what were deemed more valuable purposes.[21] They helped move properties and cash from the GH&SA to the account of the Southern Pacific, where they would be free for general use.[22] In another instance, when the GH&SA could not pay for needed equipment out of its earnings, they drew up the documents that allowed the road to lease what it needed from the SP, thereby complying, in fact if not spirit, with Texas statutory limitations on railroad capital.[23] Ambivalence toward corporate entities had left gaps in Texas law, and Baker & Botts lawyers worked to fill in those gaps.

Even when the law seemed clear, specific actions raised difficult questions. What was the value of intangible property? How much new debt could be issued for needed improvements without violating the law? How much "flexibility" was there in a debt contract entered into years earlier under far different conditions?[24] Contending interests often viewed efforts to answer these questions as attempts to avoid legal obligations, but a successful resolution was necessary if new capital was to be raised. The state participated in this process of legal change, pretending that the SP lines were Texas entities, when in fact they were run in accord with the parent railroad's corporate strategy. This fiction allowed the SP to consolidate its Texas operations without seeking change in existing laws that would have reopened political debates on a controversial issue. Compromise allowed all parties to "slide" around regulations that, if strictly enforced, would have blocked the growth of modern corporate structures.

The Texas Railroad Commission was an important actor in this drama. Dealing with this potentially powerful regulatory body was Baker & Botts's second major area of railroad practice. From the commission's inception in 1892, the firm was involved in cases to test and define its powers. In 1892 then-partner Robert Lovett and John Dillon, a former federal judge who had turned his talents to the defense of some of the largest railroad corporations in the nation, had prepared the first challenge to the law.[25] After a series of adverse lower court decisions, they took the case to the United States Supreme Court. The high court decided in favor of regulation but stipulated that rates had to be set so as to provide a fair return for the lines.[26] To do otherwise, the court ruled, would be to confiscate property without due process. Thus, while the court upheld the authority of the state commission to set rates, it sought to safeguard the railroads against regulations that threatened their economic well-being.

Pursuing this point of law, Lovett challenged the commission once more in 1898.[27] With all of the major Texas lines participating, he and his colleagues argued in federal court that the rates set by the commission were too low to earn a fair return for the Texas lines. The case went in favor of the roads, as Judge A. P. McCormick held that the commission's valuation omitted important assets and property.[28] In the future, the commission would have to show that its rates were fair and equitable. They could not be too low to prevent the earning of a fair return, nor could they discriminate against specific carriers. In this decision, McCormick followed the same reasoning that the United States Supreme Court would use that year in *Smyth* v. *Ames,* which set the precedent for use of rate-of-return rate making. But McCormick carried the concept of a fair return on property fairly valued one step further by adducing specific criteria for determining fair value. He decreed that the state had to consider growth, improvement, and betterment in roads over time, including additions for intangible assets such as goodwill and franchise, and even the investors' expectations of profits. As he wrote, "Promoters and proprietors of roads have looked to the future, as they had a right to do." The commission could not simply calculate the replacement cost of a line plus interest.[29]

This decision paved the way for a compromise in public policy toward the railroads in Texas. Lovett and the other lawyers had not sought to destroy the commission's powers, but rather to define them. Taken to its logical conclusion, McCormick's ruling might have virtually eliminated administrative rate making or financial control. Absent was the notion of a "fair" rate of return, which would balance the economic needs of individual railroads against the interests of other members of society. Not seeking to return to unfettered competition, the railroads used their bargaining power to strike a compromise with the regulators. A committee representing the major lines, including Robert Lovett for the SP, came back to the commission and offered a compromise rate schedule. Over the objection of at least one commissioner, but with the support of Gov. Joseph Sayers, the parties reached an accord.[30]

Compromise between the emerging regulatory power of the state and the existing power of the corporation became the essence of Baker & Botts's extended experience in the rate-making process. The firm effected a compromise between the commission and its client, for instance, in the definition of value. Despite many court rulings, this concept was still vague in Texas, as it was in the rest of the country. In this era, most major railroads and urban utilities were seeking to come to grips with a new regulatory rate-making system, and their lawyers joined Baker & Botts in hammering out mutually acceptable accommodations between the regulated and the regulators in important—if often tedious—case-by-case bargaining.

Particularly important for Baker & Botts was its work in the massive valuation case arising out of the 1905 GH&SA consolidation.[31] As the SP moved forward with new financing for the consolidated lines between 1909 and 1911, critical questions arose regarding the value of these lines for the purposes of extending new capital and establishing a new rate base. At the urging of former partner Robert Lovett, Baker & Botts's lawyers spent months poring over old railroad records, looking up mortgages, checking receivers' financial statements for records of money spent on betterments and improvements. These efforts paid off for the railroad; following arguments presented by the lawyers, the commission raised its original valuation figure.

Typical of the ad hoc, bargaining manner in which their accommodation was achieved was the commission's decision to add 6 percent for the road's "franchise." This open-ended category, which included intangibles such as goodwill, was essentially a political device to bring the two sides together.[32] The use of such an adjustment did not completely satisfy everyone, for it revealed the rather arbitrary nature of decision making in this formative era of railroad regulation. Baker & Botts attorney Edwin Parker applauded the commission for having "corrected" its earlier figures, but he lamented that there was no sound objective basis for determining value.[33]

Not so Robert Lovett, who quickly approved the revised figures, which raised the consolidated GH&SA's value from $7.6 million to $9.7 million.[34] Lovett recognized that any method of arriving at the value of railroad lines was bound to be somewhat arbitrary. The Texas roads had been refinanced so many times and had passed through so many hands that any notion of a "true" value of the property was ephemeral, particularly in light of the 1898 court decision. Given this precedent, and the state's work force limitations, arbitration between railroad lawyers and regulators offered the most effective available method for determining capital values.

In that process, Baker & Botts gave the SP a crucial advantage over the regulatory body—superior technical and legal talent. Though mandated with the responsibility for overseeing railroads, the commission was in a weak position to monitor the inner workings of these giant interstate corporations. It could not readily combat the determined, sustained efforts of the railroad's Texas attorneys.

As a former railroad employee who had spent almost fifteen years as an apprentice lawyer specializing in railroad work, Edwin Parker was especially effective in this work. He generally succeeded in winning interpretations of the law that allowed the railroad a higher valuation and more financial freedom than it otherwise would have received. Parker was already developing a reputation as a tenacious advocate for his clients against what he regarded as "arbitrary and capricious" state action. Hardly a closed-minded, provincial conservative, he accepted the legitimate basis for some government involvement in private affairs. Later in life he would make a reputation for himself in service to the War Industries Board during World War I, and after the war by serving on the international reparations and claims commissions, earning the appellation "judge" for his high-minded, even-handed resolutions of these frequently tangled and charged issues. But as a firm believer in progress, science, and, above all else, hard work, Judge Parker had little tolerance for the easy-going compromises of political life.[35] There was little doubt in his mind that his efforts on behalf of the SP were improving an imperfect system of regulation.

As Parker's jousts with the regulators revealed, a basic weakness of the commission was its dependence on the entities it regulated for information and expertise. Baker & Botts lawyers and the commissioners became more like partners in a joint en-

terprise than antagonists in a courtroom drama. Thus, in deciding the difficult question of how property such as contracts and
leased rolling stock should be valued, the commission merely
stated that it should be set at an amount equal to the reasonable
cost of carrying on the business of the lines.[36] Such resolutions
left attorney Parker satisfied that the commission had been fair,
and for the next ten years, the firm and the regulators enjoyed
amiable relations.[37]

By the 1910s business regulation in Texas was losing some of
its obsessive fear of corporate size. The overall trend in court decisions and administrative actions was to increase the freedom
of large-scale railroad systems in Texas. Baker & Botts hastened
this trend. In its dealings with both public officials and private
interests, the law firm performed a type of legal entrepreneur-
ship. The lawyers and the courts gradually adjusted the social,
political, and legal environment of Texas, allowing the SP greater
scope for its interstate system, despite the attempts of Texas to
maintain local control of its railroads.[38]

Although primarily concerned with statutory and common
law issues, Baker & Botts also served the SP as a lobbyist, an activity that the firm at times found quite troublesome.[39] Early on,
both Lovett and Parker regularly spent blocks of time in Austin.
The firm received additional compensation for this work, as well
as expense money for the hiring of professional lobbyists for specific bills. When the legislature was in session, Hiram Garwood
worked virtually full time in Austin, assisted by John Garrison,
who had excellent political connections. During the legislative
session, Garwood and Garrison placed car and chauffeur at the
service of lawmakers.[40] Baker & Botts also sent a representative
to every important hearing held by the Railroad Commission.[41]
Such work stretched the notion of service to a client further than
many in the firm wished to go.[42] Yet lobbying was at times critical
to the SP, and Baker & Botts remained an important ally of the
railroad in Austin.

Lobbying of a different sort also went forward at the grass-
roots level throughout the sections of Texas served by the Southern Pacific. With its network of division and local attorneys
scattered along its right-of-way, the railroad had well-placed
representatives capable of bringing influence to bear on public
officials. Baker & Botts oversaw this network, providing through
the railroad one form of political "currency"—passes for transportation. The passes served a variety of purposes, including

supplementing the relatively low legal fees paid by the railroads by enabling lawyers, their partners, and their families to travel free. But of course it was the other uses that sparked political controversy, in particular, their use to create a favorable political climate and to restrict legal challenges by buying off potential opposition.

Railroads freely distributed passes to achieve both of these goals. Local and division attorneys requested them for important clients, local magistrates, and active competing attorneys to keep them favorably disposed toward the corporation. Distribution could be extensive. Indeed, when Baker & Botts refused its request for more passes, the Victoria firm of Proctor, Vandenberge & Crain responded in astonishment that they asked for "practically no passes, except for the district judge, the district attorney, for bondsmen, two local attorneys, and sheriffs."

The use of such passes to limit the number of lawyers taking cases against the railroads raised serious questions. As mentioned earlier, all of the state's major roads agreed that any attorney representing any one of them would not be permitted to take cases against other railroads. Such accords were enforced in part by the withdrawal of railroad passes from attorneys who refused to cooperate.

This alienated many independent-minded lawyers in the state. One division attorney stated that the secret agreements caused him no end of trouble with other clients, who did not understand why he would not represent them in their claims against the railroads. Another firm complained that it was denied the chance to earn a six thousand to ten thousand dollar retainer from local property owners to represent them against the Texas and Pacific. Others denied that the agreements did much good. "We incline to the opinion," wrote El Paso lawyers Beall and Kemp, "that the same number of damage suits will be brought and our work will be about the same as before."[43]

As the SP's general Texas counsel, Baker & Botts oversaw the enforcement of these agreements. The firm arranged for passes from other railroads to mollify attorneys. At times, this included obtaining SP passes for the general attorneys of competing lines who might otherwise have been tempted to handle suits against the SP. This was not a case of avoiding conflict of interest, at least as that phrase generally applied to the traditional clients of lawyers; rather, it was a corporate decision aimed at limiting the number and the quality of plaintiff's lawyers available to sue the railroads. As such, it limited the traditional discretion of individual lawyers to choose which clients to represent.

To critics of railroads, passes used in this fashion were simply bribes. As one wrote, the railroads exercised such power over the state that "[the] legislature has taken no action on the subject of railroads except to pass resolutions thanking the railroads for the passes furnished its members."[44] Not surprisingly, they became a source of great controversy and a target for regulation. The first effective effort to regulate them came in 1908, when Texas enacted an antipass law designed to limit their use. But loopholes reduced the law's effectiveness. Not until the federal government curbed the practice in 1916 was the free pass issue put to rest. Even then, local and division attorneys in Texas continued to view the passes as entitlements. Baker & Botts had to plead with attorneys to reduce their requests. "We are anxious to be as liberal as the law and rules will permit us to be," Edwin Parker wrote in June 1916, "but in view of the approaching vacation period, again call attention to the restrictions imposed upon us."[45]

Federal intervention, which resolved the controversial pass issue, gradually settled more significant matters of railroad law in Texas. Most important, it finally set to rest the debates surrounding railroad consolidation. Beginning around World War I, a series of decisions in the federal courts addressed matters previously dealt with on the state level. The most important of these cases was the Supreme Court's precedent-setting *Shreveport* decision of 1914, which held that when federal and state regulations were in conflict, federal law was supreme.[46]

The *Shreveport* case was a long time coming and it held national significance.[47] In 1886 the Supreme Court ruled in the *Wabash* case that a state could regulate only those lines wholly contained within its borders; since then there had existed the grave danger of conflict between state and federal railroad policy. This conflict finally became manifest in the *Shreveport* case. The problem lay in a much-debated and little-understood issue known as short haul/long haul discrimination. Railroads frequently charged more for short trips than for long ones. There were several reasons for this. It often cost nearly as much to send freight a short distance as a long one, since the fixed costs of loading and unloading were often the same in each case. But long-distance shipments, because they included freight added from stops along the way, were frequently cheaper per unit than short ones. Competition also drove down the price of long hauls, while monopolies over the short routes kept their prices up. Whatever the reason, however, the practice was much resented by shippers, who could not understand why it cost more to send a ton of grain or cotton from Houston to Austin than it did to New York or Chicago.

States like Texas were determined to do something about this practice to protect citizens' interests. But because of the *Wabash* decision, they could not touch the long-haul rates, which involved interstate commerce. Their response was to lower the price of short-haul intrastate commerce, which they could regulate. This was exactly what the Texas Railroad Commission had been doing since 1899, when it found that merchants within Texas, who were paying high intrastate shipping prices, were not able to compete with merchants from nearby Shreveport, who enjoyed low through rates on interstate shipments. In 1910 the Shreveport shippers finally struck back, applying to the Interstate Commerce Commission (ICC) for help.[48]

By ordering intrastate rates below interstate ones, the Railroad Commission was not only hurting Shreveport interests, it was challenging the existing national rail pricing system. Railroads depended on the profits from short-haul shipments to keep down rates in competitive long-haul markets. If the commission's orders stood, some railroads would eventually face bankruptcy. Rivalries would turn the rail system into a hodge-podge of conflicting rates as each state tried to favor its own commerce over that of neighbors. On this basis the ICC ordered the railroads to equalize charges on interstate and intrastate routes of the same distance so as to eliminate the discrimination under which Shreveport interests were laboring. Immediately the Texas Railroad Commission and the state's railroads filed a protest. Eventually, however, the Supreme Court upheld the ICC decision, recognizing that purely intrastate regulatory decisions could have an indirect impact on interstate traffic. Where this conflict existed, the court ruled, federal policy was supreme.

Baker & Botts lawyers had been involved in the case when the decision of the Texas Railroad Commission was first challenged by Shreveport interests. Curiously enough, however, their client, the Southern Pacific, at first opposed federal intervention into state matters and was willing to live with the low rates mandated by the commission. Apparently, the SP feared that it would have to contend with two regulatory agencies and that rates would be equalized not by raising intrastate charges, but by lowering interstate ones. Once it became apparent that state regulation was being eclipsed by federal authority, however, the railroad changed its tune. It authorized Baker & Botts to apply to the Texas Railroad Commission for a 15 percent increase on intrastate routes.[49] When this request was refused, the lawyers simply went to the ICC to get the increase.

Following *Shreveport*, the federal government began to take a stronger hand in railroad regulation. This change allowed Baker & Botts to help the Southern Pacific unify its operations in Texas, eliminate the locally based structures of earlier years, and integrate Texas's transportation network into the national system. While over the years the firm had enabled the SP to burrow out a fairly free field of operations (a field protected from the public by the umbrella of government sanction), neither the railroad nor the law firm found it expensive or onerous to adjust to a strengthened federal agency. Now, in similar cases, the railroad could deal with one authority, a national one less concerned with local matters.[50]

The resulting shift in regulatory power greatly reshaped the practice of Baker & Botts, bringing the firm directly into the national regulatory arena in cases before the Supreme Court and the ICC. Over the next several years the firm's lawyers worked out the adjustments in rates and railroad policy needed to comply with the new ICC oversight. After the end of World War I, during which the government took charge of the roads, Robert Lovett took the lead as railroad voice for a new national policy. As Lovett explained: "No railroad executive or banker or investor with whom I am acquainted considers the abolition of government regulation among the possibilities, or even favors it."[51] What Lovett now wanted to eliminate were the often-conflicting state regulatory policies that at times still hampered the railroads. As he wrote to a friend in Dallas: "Like you, I am a 'States Right' Democrat; but that relates to purely local questions, and the national railroad system is not a local question."[52] Lovett and other railroad leaders were satisfied with the Transportation Act of 1920, which in several regards replaced state with federal regulation.[53] Under the provisions of the new law, Baker & Botts filed an application with the ICC for a certificate of public convenience and necessity to lease all of the SP's Texas lines to one subsidiary, the T&NO.[54] In this way, the SP moved one big step on its long journey toward consolidation of its Texas operations.

From its first regulatory case through its application of the federal Transportation Act, Baker & Botts helped to shape the development of railroad law in Texas. Bringing to bear legal and political pressure on restrictive statutes and regulations, the firm was one of the primary agents for opening the door for the integration of the state enterprises into national rail systems. Such work was controversial, identifying the firm with the emerging corporate economy that was being angrily denounced by many farmers and small businesses then in Texas. The law firm became embroiled in disputes such as those surrounding the use of railroad passes. Baker & Botts's legal work allowed its clients to reorganize critical sectors of the political economy of Texas, and the new order that emerged hardly satisfied everyone. But the state was far better equipped to work with the nation's large business organizations than it had been in the preceding populist and Granger regimes.

From the firm's point of view, Texas's best path out of colonialism was by way of absorption, not containment, of the energies of large corporations. By opening legal space for their operations, Baker & Botts helped introduce into the region a strong impetus toward economic development. But the firm's efforts did not stop there. As individuals concerned with the growth of their city, Baker & Botts partners also worked to bind the fate of such corporations to that of Houston and to build a city capable of making good use of the resources and people flowing into the region. On the foundations laid by the transportation revolution, a new, more diverse industrial economy was emerging in Houston. The lawyers at Baker & Botts, with the head start gained from representing the state's major railroad system, were well positioned to become leaders in this growing metropolis.

Civic Leadership in a Growing City

I N 1900 Houston was still small and provincial by national standards. But it had grown steadily in the late nineteenth century. By the turn of the century the city had more than forty thousand residents, finally surpassing its rival, Galveston. Much of the city's success was due to its civic leaders. Overlapping circles of influence, composed of business leaders, bankers, land developers, politicians, professionals, clergy, and their numerous family and friends, had seized the advantages brought by inland rail connections. No matter the populist rhetoric against railroad monopolies, they had made Houston a comfortable home for Texas's railroads. Open and inclusive, these circles continued to absorb the creative energies of talented, ambitious, and wealthy individuals from inside and outside of the region. Though loosely bound, the city's elite kept itself fixed on the ob jective of further growth. It shaped modern Houston and accounted for much that was both good and bad about the course of the city's growth.

Baker & Botts formed an important segment of this civic leadership. As attorney Clarence Wharton, the unofficial firm historian, explained in the 1920s, the firm had contributed to Houston's rise in numerous ways:

> One of the most interesting features of our professional life is the constant contact we have had with the growth of the community. There is scarcely a great enterprise in Houston or the surrounding country in which we have not figured in some way. As you look out on the large buildings that have been constructed in the last 25 years, you will find that we had something to do with the preparation of the contract, or that we represented the builder, or if we had no professional interest in the matter otherwise, we represented the insurance company that carried the risk on the building.[1]

Wharton's point was well taken, for it emphasized the special resources the lawyers brought to city building—numerous contacts within and outside of Houston gained from corporate representation.

In putting these resources to work in city building, Baker & Botts's efforts were typical of those of other law firms. In the twentieth century the firms that became Vinson & Elkins, Andrews & Kurth, and Fulbright & Jaworski also became focal points of influence. The pattern in each case was the same: each partnership forged ties to a local bank. Clients of the firm often became customers of the affiliated bank; major borrowers from the bank often turned to the affiliated law firm for legal services. Both law and finance required intimate knowledge of a client's personal affairs and character. Circles of influence naturally spread out in these client networks; within such circles flowed knowledge of opportunities for investment, offers of seats on boards of directors, money for projects, and membership in elite social clubs.

More than simple civic pride and a belief in "progress" motivated lawyers to take an active role in city building; most correctly understood that their careers and fortunes were tied directly to the fate of the city's economy and that of the surrounding region. In pursuit of personal as well as civic self-interest, Baker & Botts as an institution and its members as individuals employed their contacts to help lay the foundations of Houston's economic infrastructure and to build several of the city's key civic and cultural institutions.

No one recognized more clearly than Baker & Botts's first managing partner, Edwin Parker, the need to cultivate economic, social, and cultural ties to the city. Because of his keen interest in the firm's organization and his faith in scientific management, Parker actually strove to "systematize" these otherwise casual personal contacts. "*All* members of our organization," he admonished his partners, "should make it a part of their daily duties never to overlook an opportunity to keep in touch with friends made in college, in clubs, in the army, in social and business associations." Noting that many firm members belonged to the Houston Country Club but that no one was attending its meetings, he proposed that at least one partner go and represent the firm. "Through systematic and cooperative effort, we can constantly extend our activities in influencing Houston."[2]

Few members of the firm shared Parker's zeal for institutionalizing what they no doubt regarded as a highly personal part of their lives. Still, the ambitious managing partner had hit on a key theme in Baker & Botts's culture and self-identity. Articulating what many already knew, Parker reminded his colleagues: "The firm *is primarily* a Houston institution, however important and diverse its contacts outside of the city."[3] It was only good business, therefore, to cultivate these connections and take responsibility in community affairs. But to Parker, there was another purpose in such activity. As a Houston institution, Baker & Botts could be a "MORAL FORCE exerting very real and tangible influence for the good in the community of which we form an integral part."[4] With this bold statement, Parker expressed his and many of his partners' deeply felt belief that their firm was more than a vehicle for making money; it was as well an institution of power and responsibility that could shape the destiny of a community.

While Parker expressed most forcefully the importance of local leadership, Capt. James A. Baker most clearly exemplified leadership in action. Baker's numerous connections to local business, banks, real estate endeavors, and civic organizations made him one of the best known and most respected men in the city. Through his law firm, he also enjoyed direct access to eastern business, whose capital was so vital to local development. Spending considerable time in New York serving his firm's corporate clients, he had his feet planted firmly in two worlds. This position helped make him one of Houston's preeminent leaders. From the 1880s until his death in 1941 he and other members of his family remained at the center of one of the city's most influential clusters of business and civic leaders.

In dress and manner Captain Baker epitomized the southern gentleman of the nineteenth century. His large oval face, thin mustache, and level, at time piercing, gaze suggested a confident, alert mind. Outgoing and by nature a joiner and a booster, Baker was able to relate to a variety of personalities. He frequently exhibited the ability to soothe the egos of the often-temperamental lawyers of his firm and of others in the many public and private institutions of which he was a member. Yet those who mistook the white summer suit and light touch for the marks of softness were sometimes surprised. Nearly six feet tall and solidly built, Baker could turn quickly from the affable uncle to the stern patriarch. Much as his countenance and upbringing suggested the courtly ways of the nineteenth century, Captain Baker was also a man rooted firmly in the modern era, ready to adjust his firm and himself as the times required.

Captain Baker joined his father's practice as a clerk after graduating from the Texas Military Institute in Austin. He was admitted to the bar in 1881 and became a partner in the firm six years later. But lawyering was only one of his many activities. During his legal apprenticeship, he devoted much of his time to establishing the contacts with local business and civic organizations that would make him one of the most powerful men in Houston.

Joining the Houston Light Guards soon after finishing school, Baker rose to the rank of captain (from which he gained his life-long title) and position of commander. The Light Guards was a voluntary organization whose function was vaguely military; it was eventually absorbed into the Texas National Guard, and its members served as a unit in the regular army during the Spanish-American and the two world wars. But in Captain Baker's day, its purpose was mostly social, as members devoted their time to national competitions among military drill teams.[5] At a cost of eighty-eight dollars for the custom-made uniform, plus dues of three dollars per month, the leading young men of Houston society could join this fraternal organization. Leadership in the Light Guards helped Baker establish a web of friendships— many of which would last for a lifetime—with other prominent Houstonians.

During the 1890s Baker's ties to the regional economy gradually became more complex and rewarding. In 1890 he was appointed vice-president of the Texas Rolling Mills; in 1894, president of both the Houston Abstract Company and the Citizens' Electric & Power Company. He also served for a time as president of the Houston Industrial Club. In subsequent years Baker served as vice-president of the Merchants and Planters Oil Company, the Texas Trust Company, and the Bankers' Trust Company. He moved from vice-president to president of the Houston Gas and Fuel Company. In 1896 he was elected to the board of directors of the Commercial National Bank, and after its merger with South Texas National Bank in 1912, he became president of the combined institution. He also remained active in a second financial institution, the Guardian Trust Company. He was as well a partner in several real estate development ventures, and he established close ties with others in the city who had money to invest in real estate.[6] Widely respected and trusted, he was appointed receiver for the Houston and Texas Central and the International and Great Northern railroads.

Baker's blend of local influence and contacts can be seen most clearly in his work in banking and finance. Banks in early-twentieth-century Houston were small by national standards. They did not have close connections to major national industries, which depended on the much-larger New York banks for their financing. But as one of the prime vehicles for the circulation of capital in their own community, Houston banks touched a wide variety of local enterprises. Baker and several of his law partners played leading roles in the organization and management of several of the major turn-of-the century Houston banks, most especially the Commercial National Bank, which was founded in 1886. Baker, Lovett, and Parker all served on Commercial's board of directors, and their firm represented the bank in its legal affairs. Other members of the bank's board included the president of the Southern Pacific Railroad in Texas and Louisiana, and the head of the Houston Street Railway—both prominent Baker & Botts clients—as well as the president of the Illinois Central Railroad, several prominent cotton brokers, and numerous local business leaders.[7]

As was the case with most of the local banks, in its early years Commercial National focused on the financial needs of the cotton trade and of local concerns such as hardware and dry goods stores. In 1912 Commercial merged with South Texas National Bank, creating the South Texas Commercial National Bank, which remained one of the two largest banks in Houston until the 1930s. This new institution retained Baker & Botts as counsel and kept several of its partners on the board: Captain Baker served as either president or chairman of the combined enterprise from 1914 until his death in 1941.

Baker's participation in two other financial institutions—Second National Bank and the Guardian Trust—gave him and his colleagues a vehicle with which to direct investment funds into two dynamic sectors of the local economy: oil and gas, and real estate.[8] The Guardian Trust specialized in financing real estate.[9] In addition, Baker's partner Judge Garwood handled the organization of the Second National Corporation, an offshoot of the Second National Bank formed to "handle real estate loans, possibly engage in some real estate activity, and perform certain other functions which are not proper for a national bank." Drawing on their understanding of the law as it had been applied in more commercially developed states, the lawyers adopted a style of organization that had "been used by several of the large financial institutions of the country in similar circumstances." The officers of the Second National Bank declared a dividend of twenty-five thousand dollars and paid it over to the officers of the Second National Corporation, who, acting as trustees for this money, used it to organize the new corporation. Under the terms of this arrangement, the trustees would always be officers of the Second National Bank. Without formal ownership of the stock of the Second National Corporation, the Second National Bank was thus able to control its subsidiary organization.[10]

In these endeavors, as with his position of responsibility at South Texas Commercial National, Baker was in close touch with some of the most prominent entrepreneurs of the region. As Baker and his peers managed the affairs of their banks, including the crucial work of monitoring the loan and discount committees, they came to share an understanding of the local economy and to build strong personal relationships that would endure for many decades. At Guardian Trust, for example, Baker sat on the board with Hugh Hamilton. A self-made man, Hamilton had emigrated from Scotland and founded the Houston Ice & Brewing Association and then built up a diversified set of local interests. His investments in land brought him into the hotel business, where he underwrote the construction of several prominent ventures, including the original Rice Hotel of Houston and the Galvez Hotel of Galveston. Baker worked with Hamilton in the founding and development of the Guardian Trust Company, and Baker & Botts served as executor of his estate.[11]

These banks, like the law firm, also gave the partners of Baker & Botts a window on the world beyond Houston. Although relatively small and often unable to meet the financial needs of their largest clients directly, Houston's regional banks maintained correspondent relationships with larger institutions in Chicago, New York, and Saint Louis. Through its correspondent accounts, South Texas Commercial kept money on deposit in these larger banks, ensuring its access to money-center funds when needed. The metropolitan banks served South Texas Commercial by clearing notes and securing additional lines of credit for valued customers, particularly those involved in financing the cotton trade from the Texas interior through Houston and Galveston. Such ties were another way of integrating the local business system more tightly into the national economy. Within the region, Houston itself became the center of finance and commerce. Its largest banks performed functions for the smaller banks in the surrounding countryside similar to those provided by New York banks for Houston. Their services bound the region more closely and reinforced Houston's preeminence in the economy of the Texas Gulf Coast and the related timber and cotton regions in the interior.

The major industrial concerns of the Houston region rounded out this banking–law firm network. The SP placed local officials on the South Texas Commercial board and used the bank as a depository for money needed to pay for its regional operations. Since the SP was one of the largest employers in the area in the early twentieth century, its payroll funds alone were substantial. These deposits helped the bank fund its local lending activities. A similar pattern emerged in the relationship of South Texas Commercial to the large oil companies after 1901. Both Humble Oil and Refining (a major regional firm ultimately acquired by Exxon) and the Texas Company (Texaco), which was founded in Texas but quickly became active throughout the world, had high-ranking officials on the board of South Texas Commercial and kept deposits in the bank. Connection to such major corporations gave the bank and its lawyer-managers additional funds, investment opportunities, and a broader view of economic trends affecting the nation and the region.

As corporate lawyers, the members of Baker & Botts provided essential advice to business leaders; as lawyer-bankers, they helped to provide another essential commodity, credit. This interaction of law and finance with the modernization of Houston is most clearly illustrated by Captain Baker's involvement in Rice Institute. As trustee for the school's ample endowment, Baker helped to fund a variety of local projects.

Rice Institute received its endowment from the estate of William Marsh Rice, one of the most important business leaders in the region in the late nineteenth century. Rice had made his fortune in Houston after migrating from Massachusetts in 1839. He operated a highly successful dry goods business and diversified into cotton merchandising, land, cattle, timber, mortgage notes, and railroads, growing rich as the Houston economy expanded. He established strong ties to Baker & Botts, beginning in the 1840s, when Peter Gray first served as his attorney. Rice continued to use the firm throughout his life. The merchant's connections with Baker & Botts grew stronger when he became a major investor in the Houston and Texas Central Railroad, which was represented at the time by Judge Baker. Business ties were cemented by the friendship of Judge Baker's son and two of Rice's nephews, who were contemporaries of Captain Baker at the Texas Military Institute.[12]

By the 1890s Rice was ready to retire, and he decided to establish an institution of higher education in Houston. The following year Baker & Botts drew up the charter for the "William M. Rice Institute for the Advancement of Literature, Science and Art." Rice named himself treasurer and appointed to oversee the trust a seven-person board of trustees consisting of himself; his brother Frederick Rice, who was a banker and treasurer of the Houston & Texas Central Railroad; Alfred S. Richardson, a director of the same railroad; James McAshan from the South Texas National Bank; Cesar Lombardi, the president of the Houston School Board; Emanuel Raphael, president of Houston Electric Light and Power Company; and, as head, Captain Baker.[15] Although the board subsequently added Rice's two nephews, who were prominent in local business, it otherwise stayed remarkably stable for several decades. Baker remained head for fifty years.

The trust was one of the largest accumulations of capital in the region, but before this money could be put to use, Rice's estate was plunged into legal and criminal intrigue. When his wife died in 1896, the merchant discovered to his chagrin that her will left bequests not to his cherished educational enterprise, but to her own charities, friends, and relatives. Since Texas was a community property state, the situation posed a serious challenge to Rice's plans for an institute. Captain Baker took charge of the defense of Rice's property, and hence the future Rice Institute, against the claimants to Mrs. Rice's will. Arguing that the Rices were actually residents of New York, which had no community property law, he moved to have the will declared invalid. Rice had earned most of his money in Texas. But after the death in 1863 of his first wife, Margaret Bremond Rice, he married Julia Elizabeth Baldwin Brown in 1867, after which he and his wife had lived most of the time in New York. On this basis Baker had a solid case.

Before the will controversy could be settled, however, criminal charges pushed these legal issues backstage. Rice died suddenly in New York, and in what became one of the most spectacular cases of the day, a New York attorney, Albert T. Patrick, and Rice's valet, Charles Jones, were shown to have murdered the aging merchant and prepared a false will. Patrick had been hired by Oran T. Holt, the Texas lawyer representing the beneficiaries of Mrs. Rice, to take depositions in New York. Apparently, Patrick concocted a scheme to defraud and murder Rice after forging a will appointing him trustee of the Rice estate. The Patrick will, like that of Mrs. Rice, left a considerable fortune to certain Texas charities and relatives and a lucrative fee to Captain Baker, seeking to appease those who might raise objections. But the false document made no mention of an endowment to start a school in Houston. If this will were declared valid, the educational institute was doomed.

From the very beginning Rice's death aroused suspicion. From New York his bankers wired Captain Baker that the circumstances of Rice's demise required investigation. Baker quickly moved to prevent disposal of the body, which Patrick and Jones were arranging to have cremated. Arriving in New York, Baker met with Patrick to discuss the legal arrangements for the Rice estate. By this time the police, too, had begun to suspect something was amiss, and Baker soon found himself party to their criminal investigation. They quickly uncovered Patrick's crime. The role Baker actually played in discovering the murder is unclear, but when the story hit the newspapers, his name received prominent display. For days the tale of Rice's murder and the false will played in the *New York Times* (25, 28 September, 8 October 1900) and other dailies. Such unsolicited publicity placed the name of Baker & Botts prominently before readers of northeastern newspapers, enhancing the firm's reputation in that region.

For the Rice Institute, still only in the planning stages, Baker's work in the Patrick case was invaluable, but there was still the hurdle of Mrs. Rice's disputed will to be cleared. Not Holt, who stood to gain handsomely as trustee (a position entitling him to a 10 percent fee on all estate transactions), or the numerous distant Rice relatives who suddenly appeared, or the many Houston churches and charitable organizations named as beneficiaries were about to drop their claims.[14] The will controversy had grown into an ugly and expensive battle, involving attorneys from New York and Houston who represented dozens of claimants. While the time-consuming legal work paid Baker & Botts well, it drained needed funds from the institute's endowment. Baker, as head of the board of trustees, was responsible for that fund. Rather than let the case drag on, possibly for years, he moved in 1904 to settle. By paying out almost one million dollars to various relatives and organizations and their lawyers, he was able to quell the controversy. Though costly, the settlement allowed Rice to open with its large endowment unencumbered.

Baker's next task was to add additional capital to that endowment. Here he was playing to his strengths: knowledge of the law, experience as a trustee, and a broad range of contacts through clients and correspondents. The last was an especially useful resource in still-remote Houston. In handling the trust funds, Baker drew on the expertise of such clients as Stone & Webster, the Boston engineering and financial consultants.[15] He could turn as well to his numerous friends in Houston, people he knew and trusted, for matters such as insurance and securities brokerage, and most important, clients to whom he could lend the trust funds.[16]

As with most such trusts, the board planned to build the endowment by lending money at interest to local enterprises. Such arrangements had their pitfalls. If abused through favoritism and insider dealing, they would harm the endowment and violate the trusteeship. For this reason, selection of honest and capable directors was crucial. Yet in a world as small as turn-of-the-century Houston, a man as active as Captain Baker could not eliminate all potential conflicts of interest. In making loans to increase the endowment, Baker and the board had to exploit their numerous contacts in and knowledge of business in the region while making careful, conservative choices. Such choices would build the fund while funding the building of Houston.

The decisions made by the board had wide economic ramifications for the city. The Rice trust was probably the largest local source of capital available to developers in early-twentieth-century Houston. It was also less constrained by regulations than the city's major banks. In lending these funds Baker and other board members actually performed the functions of a bank loan and discount committee; that is, they evaluated requests for money and then decided how best to lend the trust's funds so as to maximize returns and minimize risks. At least three members of the board—Baker, McAshan, and William M. Rice, Jr., who joined the board in 1899—regularly made similar decisions in their capacities as bank officers and directors at Commercial, South Texas, and Union banks, respectively.

Early in their deliberations, the trustees decided to focus their lending on real estate and commercial construction loans secured by land and property, a choice that proved sound in a booming city. While this focus reflected Baker's long involvement in real estate development, the resources available from the trust now allowed him and his board to finance large downtown office buildings of a scale previously beyond the capacities of local financial institutions. Conservative, yet profitable, such building loans dominated the lending activities of the trust in the years before World War I. Builders such as the young Jesse Jones found the Rice endowment a valuable source of local capital. Jones used financing supplied in part by this source to construct several of his early projects, including a new office building for the Houston *Chronicle* and a rebuilt eighteen-story Rice Hotel, which opened in 1913 and became for many the symbol of Houston's aspirations as a modern city. In directing Rice funds toward the financing of much of the new generation of office construction downtown, Baker and his friends literally helped build the city. The lending of the Rice trust, loans from the Guardian Trust Company, and credit extended by the First Texas Joint Land Bank meant that Baker was involved in almost ten million dollars in real estate loans by the early 1920s.[17] This activity helped bind Baker & Botts's expanding circle of influence with one of the strongest of all glues, money.

The close ties between the Rice board, major local banks, and the law firm of Baker & Botts were most evident in 1912, when the Commercial National and South Texas National banks merged. This financial marriage brought together Commercial— a Baker & Botts client that included as directors Baker, Parker, and former partner Robert Lovett—with South Texas, which was managed by Baker's second-in-command on the Rice board, James McAshan. The unification ceremony occurred under the supervision of Baker & Botts at a meeting of the Rice board of trustees, since the merger could not go through without the approval of South Texas's major stockholder, the Rice trust. The newly created bank was chaired by Baker, managed by McAshan, and represented by Baker & Botts.

With the Patrick case settled, Mrs. Rice's heirs satisfied, and the trust expanding, the board could get down to its real business, creating an educational institution "of the first magnitude" in Houston. Under Baker's leadership, the Rice endowment grew from $4.8 million to $9.8 million between 1904 and 1912. These resources made the Rice Institute one of the first educational institutions in the South to have both a large amount of money and a free hand to use it.[18] As trustee, Baker was responsible for using these resources to build the quality school his client had envisaged and Houston needed. Such an institution would link Houston more firmly to the outside world and provide invaluable intellectual resources in an economy that would increasingly need university-trained managers, technicians, and professionals.

The Rice charter combined two almost irreconcilable missions. On the one hand, William Marsh Rice had wanted his endowment to provide Houston and the region with a public library and polytechnic school. Part of his intention was to train youths from the region in practical skills, giving them a chance to advance materially. This noble ambition was in line with those of similar organizations such as Cooper Union in New York, which Rice greatly admired. But he also recognized the importance of liberal arts education and sought to create a respected seat of higher learning. The second half of the charter called for an institute of literature, science, art, and philosophy. Blending this goal with that of a school of technical training in turn-of-the-century Houston required all of the expertise and finesse that Captain Baker and the other board members could muster.[19]

Baker oversaw the building of the school, both physically and conceptually. Through correspondent attorneys in New York, he and the trustees sent out questionnaires to a wide variety of universities, colleges, and technical schools: Stanford, Brown, and Johns Hopkins universities, Colorado College, University of Cincinnati, Fisk University, as well as technical institutions such as Cooper Union, Girard College in Philadelphia, Armour Institute of Technology in Chicago, and the Tome Institute of Maryland.[20] Questions ranged from mundane ones about endowments, bequests, and grounds, to matters of educational philosophy.

In all aspects of the building of Rice, down to the design of laboratories, purchase of equipment, and the laying out of the grounds, the trustees made good use of the evolving professional network of academics and administrators in U.S. education. H. H. Harrington, president of the Agricultural and Mechanical College of Texas (now Texas A&M University), advised them that the best models were universities with technical schools attached to them.[21] Taking this advice to heart, Baker and the board selected a faculty and president who would move the Rice

Institute away from a restricted technical orientation toward that of a modern university.

Attracting first-rate faculty members and administrators for this ambitious project presented difficulties. At its opening in 1912, the institute consisted of one completed building set in an open field served only by dirt roads. Ambitious as were the trustees' goals and as generous as was Rice's endowment, it took some doing to persuade competent professors and administrators to journey to Houston and settle at Rice. Beginning in 1907 Baker headed the search for a president. Resisting the pressure to appoint a local, or at least a southern, man, he and the board looked outside the community.[22] They solicited recommendations from the likes of David Starr Jordan, Stanford's president; Nicholas Murray Butler of Columbia University; Harry Judson of the University of Chicago; Pres. Theodore Roosevelt and former president Grover Cleveland. They then selected A. Ross Hill, the respected president of the University of Missouri. Hill satisfied those who wanted a Southerner and was also an experienced man, well respected in the academic world. When Hill rejected the offer, the trustees did not fall back on a safe second choice. Instead, they offered the position to Edgar O. Lovett, a young mathematician from Princeton.

Lovett accepted the offer and quickly set Rice on a path that would eventually make it a nationally respected center of higher learning. Only thirty-eight at the time of his appointment, the new president came strongly recommended by Woodrow Wilson, at the time, president of Princeton University. Lovett had strong ideas about the best uses for Rice's endowment. Moving a step away from the idea of an institute, he selected a well-trained, cosmopolitan faculty. It included Harold Wilson, a Royal Society Fellow and member of the faculty at Trinity College, Cambridge; Thomas Lindsey Blayney, a German-trained professor of European literature and art; and Julian Huxley, biologist and grandson of Thomas Huxley, the famous defender of evolution. These and others with similarly impressive backgrounds ventured to Houston for the start of classes in 1912.

Blending a cosmopolitan faculty and a burgeoning Texas commercial center was not always an easy task. When Julian Huxley spoke on biology and humanity in 1916, his statement that human beings were the products of evolution provoked letters to the local newspaper protesting this "anti-christian" doctrine. Baker himself received angry communications condemning the teaching of antireligious ideas at the institute. In 1918 a group of local ministers approached Lovett and asked if he supported the teaching of agnosticism and atheism.

In these instances, the trustees and administration remained firm, arguing that the institution needed to grant free expression to all ideas and special preference to none. With full support from Baker and the trustees, Lovett composed a well-reasoned defense of academic freedom that apparently soothed the agitated local clergy.[23]

A few years later, another controversy, this time concerning faculty members' profession of socialistic or communistic beliefs, was not settled with such ease or grace. In this instance the trustees performed less admirably, compromising the integrity of the institution by asking for the resignation of Lyford P. Edwards. In an address to a Sunday school class, "Ideals of Social Justice," Edwards compared Lenin and Trotsky favorably to Washington and Jefferson.[24] Irate citizens, ignited during World War I by fears of communism, called for action against these "treasonous" assertions. As head of a committee investigating the matter, Baker again defended academic freedom and found no evidence of disloyalty in Edwards's words. But Edwards was nonetheless asked to leave Rice.

The Edwards case, as well as several other matters that came up during the war, raised thorny issues for an institution simultaneously trying to gain acceptance in Houston and respect in the academic world. Houston was as yet a small southern city with limited exposure to "modern" ideas that seemed to challenge traditional views on God and country. In the charged climate of World War I and the subsequent Red Scare, Houstonians and many other Americans rushed to attack views perceived as either socialist or un-American. The temper of the times was not conducive to sober, reflective action, and there was direct pressure from the government and the community to override the needs of the university. Concerning a split with students during the war over compulsory military exercises, for example, Edwin Parker, then serving in Washington on the War Industries Board, wrote to his law partner: "I have every confidence in your ability to pour oil on troubled water."[25] While Baker found it hard to calm these seas, he and the rest of the trustees worked hard to turn aside charges of disloyalty directed at the students, as well as nativist insinuations against two foreign-born members of the faculty. They were careful to shield the school from the worst side of the Red Scare while not isolating it from the surrounding community.

By mediating relations between the institute and its surroundings and by building the endowment, Baker helped to establish Rice as a respected southern university and a valued local institution. Its southernness was reflected in its exclusion of black students. When the trustees adopted the rules and regulations of the Astor Library for their new institute, in fact, they attached a printed copy of the rules to the Rice minutes but inserted the word *white* in the section that read "open to all men and women." Ultimately, Rice as well as Houston would be integrated, but in these years neither Baker nor the rest of the board could imagine that there was or ever would be a conflict between the school's goal of being a first-class institution and its position as a segregated southern school.

Rice Institute was only one of a variety of exercises in institution building in Houston that Baker and his partners participated in during the first two decades of the twentieth century. Edwin Parker, like Baker, held a variety of corporate offices growing out of his legal work—president of Houston Lighting & Power Company; vice-president of Guardian Trust Company; vice-president of South Texas Commercial Bank. More than any other partner, he developed strong connections at the national level, particularly through his service during World War I on the government's War Industries Board. After a number of public appointments, he finally became chief counsel of Texaco in New York in 1921. Though Parker's expanded orbit took him out of the firm altogether in 1926, he continued to be a vital link between Baker & Botts in Houston and the world of eastern business.

Other members of the firm, either by themselves or through their wives, concentrated on a wide array of local charitable, cultural, and church-related activities. Baker himself was a long-time and active member of First Presbyterian Church, while his wife, Alice Graham Baker, worked with Faith Home for Orphan Children and the Rusk Settlement House.[26] Walter Walne dedicated ten years of his life to building up the Houston Symphony, a symbol of cultural progress to the upper class. Convinced by his wife, Margaret Butler Walne, and other "civic minded ladies" that the languishing symphony had to be supported, he put into the project all the zeal of a lawyer defending an unjustly accused client. Though "only mildly interested" in music, he took it on himself to solicit advice from the directors of other leading symphonies in the country and to enlist the support of his partners, friends, and associates. He served as president of the symphony for six seasons at a pivotal time in its development.[27]

Participating in civic and cultural activities gave Baker & Botts a strong presence in the life of the city, and personal and family ties extended the firm's reach in the city's elite. A number of partners and associates were related by ties of blood or marriage. Captain Baker brought one of his sons, James A. Baker, Jr., into the practice, while a nephew, Alvis Parish, joined the firm in the 1910s and stayed on for a long career. Another of Captain Baker's sons, Walter Browne Baker, married E. O. Lovett's daughter Adelaide. Other partners spun similar family webs. Walter Browne Botts left a legacy in his children. One daughter married into the Rice family, while another married a high-level official in the Southern Pacific Railroad. Botts's son Thomas became a partner in Baker & Botts.

While Baker & Botts's partners were not inclined to participate in politics, family and marriage ties offered them entry into that world as well. Captain Baker's daughter Alice married Murray Jones. Jones, who practiced with Baker & Botts a short while, was the son of Sarah Brashear Jones, the sister of one-time Houston mayor Samuel Brashear. Partner Palmer Hutcheson's brother Joseph was mayor of Houston from 1917 to 1918, and then a federal judge. Joseph Hutcheson's son, J. C. Hutcheson III joined Baker & Botts in 1931.

Over time, however, family ties became less of a factor in shaping the firm's circle of influence. Professional contacts increasingly replaced personal ones in Houston, much as they did in other urban centers. The firm's institution of an antinepotism rule in the 1930s signaled its allegiance to this new world. Thus while Captain Baker's son James A. Baker, Jr., spent his career at Baker & Botts, his grandson, James A. Baker III, made his legal career at Houston's Andrews & Kurth before going to Washington to work in the Ford, Reagan, and Bush administrations. Instead of depending on familial relations, firm members cultivated professional and business ties. Captain Baker was elected president of the Houston Bar Association, Clarence Carter, of the Harris County Bar Association in 1908. Later, partners rose to prominence in such national professional organizations as the American Bar Association.

In these ways, members of the firm became increasingly linked to national business and professional elites that served the large-scale corporations at the heart of the nation's growing economy. Over the next several decades, as the regional economy matured, Baker & Botts would forge more and more of these ties. Following the lines of transportation laid by the railroads, other new national organizations began penetrating the Gulf Coast economy, offering new challenges and new opportunities to the firm, its members, and the city of Houston.

Credits for Photographs

Baker & Botts: 1, 2, 3, 5, 7, 13, 14, 15, 18, 19, 20, 22, 23, 25, 26
Houston Lighting & Power: 12
Houston Public Library, Metropolitan Research Center: 4, 6, 9, 10, 11, 17, 21
James P. Lee: 16
Rice University: 8
Richard Payne: frontispiece

1. Judge James A. Baker

2. Peter W. Gray

3. W. B. Botts

4. Houston, circa 1866

5. Robert S. Lovett

6. Gibbs Building, 1893

7. Captain James A. Baker

8. Captain Baker (*second from right*) with the faculty
and board members of Rice University, 1912

9. Lovett Hall, Rice University

10. Houston ship channel, 1924

11. Houston street railway, 1902

12. Deepwater plant of Houston Lighting & Power, circa 1924

13. Clarence Wharton

14. Brady Cole

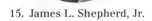

15. James L. Shepherd, Jr.

16. Houston area oil field near Humble, 1920s

21. Houston, 1926

17. Niels Esperson Building, 1927

18. Walter Walne

19. Edwin B. Parker

20. Jesse Andrews

22. Ralph Feagin

23. W. Alvis Parish

24. Dillon Anderson

25. John T. McCullough, William C. Harvin, and E. William Barnett

26. Houston, 1980s

PART II
A REGIONAL FIRM IN A MATURING REGION, 1915–1929

Power and Politics

IN 1910 the lawyers of Baker & Botts could reflect with satisfaction on both their firm and its hometown. The partnership had been expanding steadily and net income had surged to almost $125,000 annually. At the same time, Houston was enjoying rapid progress, growing to one hundred thousand residents. The city was beginning to mature as an important urban center serving a broad section of Texas and Louisiana. Apparently, the interests of elite civic organizations like Baker & Botts and the interests of the city meshed well, each reinforcing the other.

Self-satisfaction, however, could not hide the fact that growth was generating often-fierce political struggles over public policies, struggles that drew in Baker & Botts. The basic infrastructure for a growing city, including its transportation, communication, and power systems, had to be built. These tasks required political choices, particularly as the pace of development quickened after 1920. Previously, Houston had behaved much like other provincial cities. It had kept a tight rein on the public purse and battled fiercely with its rivals—mainly Galveston to the south—for trade and commerce. Successful industrialization, however, required a different approach. Industries needed expensive and complex urban services. Oil refineries required vast quantities of electric power and a readily accessible port and maritime facilities; workers needed cheap, rapid transit from home to work; a growing urban population demanded light, heat, and shelter.

In the decades before World War I Houston's business elites used public policy to promote the expansion of urban services—and of the city—primarily through privately owned companies, often controlled by eastern financiers. As the center of one important elite group, Baker & Botts played a major role in policy

68

Part II
A Regional
Firm in a
Maturing
Region,
1915–1929

formation during this era. The firm's general stance on such activity, articulated by Captain Baker, was "work hard and stay out of politics." True to his word, Baker never held public office, but he and his partners nonetheless wielded considerable power. Baker & Botts's partners worked in the way they were most comfortable and effective: behind the scenes, among friends and associates, through private bodies such as the Rice board. In this way, they constituted a strong voice for rapid development led by largely unfettered private enterprise.

Opposed to Baker & Botts and the other devotees of rapid growth were Houston's powerful civic populists.[1] They also desired growth, but they had other concerns on their agenda. Like their rural counterparts, urban populists felt a profound ambivalence about the city's increasing economic dependence on eastern capital and business. Local control of key institutions lay at the center of their platform. Many were small, local business owners, who wanted to promote development by reducing the price of public services and blocking private monopolies. Appealing to these sentiments, Mayor Samuel Brashear in 1898 had gained strong support for a program that included thoroughgoing regulation of utility rates and control of important urban services so as to benefit a broad cross section of the public.[2] Hardly a radical, Brashear was a successful local attorney and, as we have seen, a relative through marriage of Captain Baker. Under his leadership, nonetheless, the city seriously debated such policies as the municipal ownership of utilities.

After the turn of the century, Brashear's administration and its reform platform went down to defeat as the Baker & Botts–backed wing in local politics gained control. Its ascent to power was eased by Jim Crow legislation that deprived most blacks and many poor whites of the franchise. Disenfranchisement stripped Brashear and his supporters of an important group of patrons and solidified the political power of those who favored rapid development with a primary emphasis on private capital (from outside the region when necessary).[3]

Typical of the approach of these leaders—including Captain Baker and other members of his firm—was the manner in which they provided for such ambitious, broad-based projects as the ship channel. In the wake of the devastating Galveston hurricane of 1900, a well-organized municipal elite convinced Congress to appropriate funds to dredge Buffalo Bayou for navigation. In 1906 the city contributed $50,000 of its own money and continued to lend funds and municipal authority to the effort.[4]

Few citizens objected to the passage of a $150,000 bond issue the
next year to finance a navigation district, complete with wharves
and other maritime facilities. With such backing, Houston's deepwater ship channel was able to open in 1914 at a ceremony presided over by Capt. James A. Baker. The city then quickly sur-
passed its longtime rival, Galveston, as the area's major port.[5]

More controversial than the ship channel were policies concerning the city's power, light, and transportation utilities. Building them required compromises that served the needs of both
the large outside corporations that dominated these industries
and the "property-holding" public, which now composed the
electorate. Baker & Botts attorneys, particularly those with deep
roots in Houston society, were instrumental in forging such accords. They entered the debate as representatives of their clients, the large eastern utilities. These corporations feared the
threat of public ownership and the prospects of rate regulation,
which would prevent them from earning an adequate return on
their investment. They looked to Baker & Botts to foster cooperation with the city in order to "promote economy and efficiency
in the provision of service."[6] In response to their clients' needs,
Baker & Botts attorneys worked out several key compromises in
the early twentieth century.

The first of these involved urban rail service and was implemented between 1901 and 1903, when the urban populists still
held sway in city politics. Conflict had arisen after new owners
bought the Houston Electric Street Railway Company from receivers and placed it under the management of Stone & Webster,
a Boston-based consulting and engineering firm.[7] Concerned
about the uncertain legal standing of their property, the new owners wanted to settle matters quickly with the city. While in receivership, the railway had run up a debt of some eighty thousand
dollars in back assessments, which the city was now trying to collect. The company offered a compromise that was promptly rejected, bringing Baker & Botts partner Robert Lovett into the dispute. Lovett advised a second attempt at compromise, in which
the railway agreed to pay ten thousand dollars on its city debt.
Once again, the city council refused to accept the offer.

Lovett persisted, advancing still another offer. He met with
council members and proposed that they exempt the railway
from assessments in exchange for a 1 percent tax on gross receipts. To placate those desiring low fares, the railway would

70

Part II
A Regional
Firm in a
Maturing
Region,
1915–1929

agree to set a maximum rate of five cents and create a system of free transfers for riders. To satisfy those interested in expansion, it also promised to extend service at least two miles per year.[8] If council would appease the railway's owners and bondholders by agreeing to add an additional ten years to the company's franchise, the whole dispute could be solved.

Neither the railway company nor many members of the city council were prepared at first to sign this accord. Houston Electric found the limit on rates unacceptable, while the city attorney pointed out significant problems with the gross receipts tax.[9] The prime issue of contention, however, was the franchise extension. The city's power to issue franchises to use city streets was a strong regulatory tool. Houston Electric's original charter still had twenty-three years to run, and more radical members of the council feared that a ten-year addition would severely curtail the city's leverage over the railway. They demanded that this portion of the compromise be put to a vote of the citizens.[10]

Lovett took the lead in breaking the franchise deadlock. Before the close of the year, the railway and the city had a workable agreement.[11] The railway paid the city the eighty thousand dollars in back assessments and agreed to provide 1 percent of its gross receipts annually in lieu of future assessments. While it also agreed to set up a system of free transfers for riders, it was not bound by any rate maximum. The city, in turn, ended efforts to revoke the railway's franchise and license a competing company while extending the old Houston Electric franchise the additional ten years.[12] Lovett's mediation between the city and its urban railway produced a compromise that lasted with little change for the next twenty years.

As the business-oriented elite came to power and Oran Holt replaced Samuel Brashear as mayor, more and more problems were solved by compromises like those negotiated with the street railway. In 1903 Houston accepted terms with the interurban railway very similar to those negotiated with the Houston Electric Street Railway Company. Later, Baker & Botts attorneys reached similar compromises on behalf of Houston Lighting & Power (HL&P) and the Houston Gas and Fuel companies.

For Houston Lighting & Power, the city's primary electric company, Baker & Botts performed the difficult act of balancing local interests with those of an "alien" corporation. In 1911 Bertron Griscom and Company, an eastern holding company, arranged for the sale of American Cities, a New Orleans–based

company that had acquired Houston Lighting & Power in 1906.
The new owners made Baker & Botts their local representatives
and appointed Edwin Parker president of the Houston property.
He and the law firm soon had to deal with new efforts by the city
to control rates, regulate construction, and oversee financing.

Those regulatory intentions received a boost from the "home rule" law of Gov. O. B. Colquit. In 1911 the state's chief executive successfully sponsored legislation that allowed cities of over five thousand to adopt their own charters. Houston wasted little time in taking advantage of the new law. In 1913 it passed a series of amendments, many of which affected utilities. The new charter required all service providers to report their accounts to the city, which claimed explicit right to regulate rates, service, and extensions. Like the street railway, HL&P was concerned that rate restrictions would reduce profitability and restrict growth. The power company had been buying, refinancing, and consolidating a number of local and regional power companies in the vicinity of Houston, and it feared that a return to local rule would block further expansion.

While the city clearly had a right to pass regulations, the lawyers pointed out that HL&P also had countervailing powers at its disposal. In 1882 the city had granted its original power and light company a "perpetual" franchise, which HL&P had acquired when it came on the scene. Unlike other utilities, HL&P thus was not subject to the threat of franchise revocation. Unless the city could show cause why the franchise should be rescinded, the lawyers argued, the utility had a valid right to use municipal streets, byways, and thoroughfares in perpetuity. If this line of reasoning held, then the city's main regulatory lever against HL&P was virtually useless. The constitutionality of the perpetual franchise was in doubt, however, and that prompted Baker & Botts to seek a compromise.

Both HL&P and the city had strong incentives to settle these disputed matters. Drawing on their long experience in railroad rate disagreements as well as the 1903 railway company settlement, Clarence Wharton and Edwin Parker, in conjunction with Mayor Ben C. Campbell and city attorney J. C. Hutcheson, drafted a mutual accord. At Wharton's suggestion, the city abandoned the idea of a maximum rate and agreed instead that the price of service would be linked to an 8 percent return on a fair value of investment. In exchange, Houston received 50 percent of the net profits of HL&P (in lieu of taxes or assessments) over the 8 per-

72

Part II
A Regional
Firm in a
Maturing
Region,
1915–1929

cent, as did other municipalities and suburbs served by the company. To protect its interest, the city was also allowed to place two representatives on the company's board of directors.[13]

The compromise was advantageous to both sides. By replacing strict rate control with a rate-of-return approach and providing the city with a share of the income, the plan gave both parties incentive to expand service in an era of rapid growth. About a decade later, utilities in other localities would come to see the strength of this sort of arrangement. At the same time, the fixed rate of return provided the city with protection against unreasonable price increases, while the excess profits tax proved an easy means of financing the budget in a time of expansion. Houston's solution proved a remarkably durable approach to regulation. It lasted until 1945, during which time the company paid out three million dollars in profits to the city.[14]

Baker & Botts played a similar role in bringing together local interests and corporate owners in Houston's third major utility, gas. Houston Gas, which was chartered as a small gas lighting concern in 1866, subsequently underwent a series of reorganizations and was absorbed in 1905 by American Cities, the New Orleans–based holding company that also owned HL&P. In 1911, Bertron Griscom and Company arranged for the sale of Houston Gas to United Gas and Electric.[15] As representatives for Bertron Griscom, Baker & Botts presided over the transfer of the gas company. United Gas and Electric acquired title to two properties, Houston Gas, an illuminating company whose profits were dwindling in the face of competition from electricity, and Houston Fuel. Merging the two into Houston Gas and Fuel, the financiers created a larger, stronger entity whose major concern was the provision of gas for heating.[16]

The new structure operated smoothly until World War I. In the wake of a postwar depression HG&F found itself in a temporary financial bind. As part of the 1911 acquisition, HG&F had obligated itself to pay the bonds of its predecessor, Houston Gas, which were coming due. Captain Baker went to New York to find funding for this obligation. Meeting with the Harris-Forbes Company, he arranged the refinancing (though at high postwar interest rates) while other members of his firm worked out an agreement with the old bondholders.[17]

Baker & Botts also worked with public officials in charge of gas regulation. During the turbulent 1890s the city had moved to reduce rates, in keeping with Mayor Samuel Brashear's brand of public policy. Offering an extended franchise, the council demanded a maximum rate of $1.50 per 1,000 cubic feet of gas, as well as free illumination for city buildings and offices.[18] Captain Baker, then a director and principal stockholder, and another director, T. W. House, offered a compromise. A majority of the council immediately rejected their offer, but Baker and House found a sympathetic minority. This group wanted lower rates but feared that continued wrangling over the issue would discourage outside investment. They moved for settlement.[19] Bolstered by the city attorney's opinion that the council could not change rates after having set them in 1891, the minority view eventually prevailed, resulting in a settlement that lasted another twenty years.

Baker & Botts's utility work did not always proceed this smoothly or draw to a mutually acceptable compromise. Conflicts frequently erupted between local business owners and the large corporate organizations that were playing an increasingly important role in Houston's economy. The law firm stood squarely in the middle of these heated exchanges, as was the case when the traction company set out to eliminate competition from the so-called jitneys. Jitneys were private cars that competed with the trolley for riders. Owned primarily by small local entrepreneurs, they proved no match for Houston Electric Railway and its corporate counsel. Bringing in outside financial experts, Clarence Wharton first secured a rate increase for the railway in federal court to offset profits lost to the jitneys. He then offered the city a compromise in exchange for a ban on jitneys. Finally, in 1924 Wharton mobilized voters behind a referendum that sanctioned the accord and ended jitney service.[20]

The struggle between the trolley corporation and its small competitors was protracted and painful. It convinced many citizens that when client interest ran up against that of locals, the lawyers would always choose their well-paying clients. Although Baker & Botts finally won a statutory victory for its client, it proved a hollow one. Cars, buses, taxis, and motorized service eventually replaced railways in municipal transportation. The effort to ban jitneys only temporarily staved off the decline of the street railway while depriving Houston's citizens of a valued form of transit.

In these early years of the twentieth century, however, most of the compromises Baker & Botts negotiated were, on balance, successful and served the needs of both client and city. The firm's work exemplified the style of policy making by private action

74

Part II
A Regional
Firm in a
Maturing
Region,
1915–1929

common at the time in many small and midsized cities, particularly in "frontier" regions, where the contending interests were not very diverse. Employing their expertise in matters such as rate making and property valuation, the lawyers settled controversial disputes privately; drawing on clients and personal acquaintances, they worked behind the scenes to negotiate settlements. The result was a strong progrowth commitment throughout Houston society that generally rolled over all objections and differences.

The effectiveness of this brand of policymaking faced a strong challenge after World War I, as Houston's economy became more complex and the city grew increasingly dependent on national utility systems. In this period compromise proved more elusive. Huge national holding companies entered the region, bringing new capital, new technology, and new legal problems. Like the railroads before them, these concerns called on Baker & Botts to represent them before regional political bodies in often-heated exchanges over the control of the urban infrastructure and the direction of public policy.

Utility consolidations were driven by a number of forces. In industries such as electric power, economies of scale motivated expansion and merger. As industry developed in Texas, demand for electric power and other utility services grew apace, particularly as the first generation of oil refineries were built along the Gulf Coast. Large generators serving a wide area proved more efficient than small generators in meeting this demand. Efficient use of these large generators required a balanced load so that capacity was fully employed at all times. By serving a variety of places and industries, particularly energy-consuming oil refineries, large power companies were able both to take advantage of the technology of large-scale generation and to make efficient use of their equipment by building a balanced load. These considerations induced local power companies to reach out beyond their original service area and bring other towns into their scope.[21]

Such efforts at expansion, though vital to growth in the region, required both financial and technical resources unavailable within the region. Consolidation, larger-capacity plants, new equipment, and expansion in the wake of population growth and economic development all demanded capital that could be supplied only by huge national holding companies. The national market for utility securities did not yet reach into eastern Texas, or indeed into most other parts of the South and rural West. As a result, the mortgage bonds used to finance utility operations could only be sold at high interest rates, leaving little surplus for operations. Common stocks of local companies whose names did not command widespread public recognition also proved difficult to market. Houston companies thus had to depend on larger organizations, which could mobilize capital from money centers and send it to the Southwest. Holding companies were able to provide this vital financial service and maintained a diversified portfolio of regional utility company securities that were difficult to sell individually. Against these assets they issued their own stocks and bonds, which were more readily taken by New York and Chicago investors. In this way, they supplied regional utilities such as HL&P and HG&F with much-needed funds.

Holding companies also provided a variety of technical and managerial services that isolated Texas utilities could not yet easily obtain on their own. Through service contracts, the holding companies sent out managers and technicians to assist local managers in the construction, installation, and use of equipment, and to help them institute managerial, financial, and accounting practices to run their enterprises efficiently. This service was not free—generally, it cost 1 to 3 percent of the local company's gross income—and it was not provided for altruistic reasons. The large holding companies, often themselves subsidiaries of important manufacturers such as General Electric, wanted their operating companies to use the equipment made by their own manufacturing concerns. Still, Texas utilities had much to gain from these services, which hastened the development of local power, light, and gas companies and allowed them to realize scale economies that they otherwise might have missed.

Whatever the advantages of holding companies, many Texans greeted their arrival with skepticism and even outright hostility. The entry of these corporations into the state provoked long debates over the costs and benefits of dependence on outside capital. Critics attacked the service contract and fee system as a drain on local income that enriched the parent corporation at the expense of Texas utility consumers; supporters argued that it was well worth the cost. Throughout the 1920s and 1930s, the two sides would keep the debate going.

As the legal representative of such companies, Baker & Botts

76

Part II

A Regional
Firm in a
Maturing
Region,
1915–1929

came down squarely on the side of the developing national systems. As it had done earlier for the railroads, the firm worked to deflect local challenges. To overcome stringent state antitrust and regulatory laws, the lawyers employed a variety of means, ranging from constitutional arguments in federal courts to lobbying before the state legislature. As in the railroad era, though, most of their efforts involved more mundane work: skillful application of state law to permit new business endeavors; careful study of legal precedents from other, more advanced states for ways around Texas prohibitions; protracted negotiations with regulators.

Work of this sort began in the years just before World War I. Baker & Botts established contact with consolidators such as A. E. Fitkin & Company, who drew on capital from New York, Chicago, and Saint Louis to acquire a number of East Texas utilities.[22] The firm also represented the Boston company of Warner-Tucker, which in 1914 acquired and consolidated local gas, electric, water, and ice companies in Victoria, Del Rio, Wharton, and Beeville.[23] Baker & Botts attorneys handled the local work arising out of these acquisitions, while the old-line Boston firm of Gaston, Snow, Saltonstall and Hunt acted as general attorneys for the owners. In this way, Baker & Botts forged important contacts with the Boston legal and financial community, contacts that would prove valuable later.

The post–World War I depression toppled many small local utility concerns, forcing them into receivership and bringing still more new capital into the industry. Baker & Botts worked with Chicago entrepreneur A. E. Pierce, who reorganized People's Gas of Port Arthur and placed it in the hands of his Central Public Service Corporation.[24] Pierce relied on Chicago attorneys Cutting, Moore & Sidley (predecessors of Sidley & Austin) as general attorneys, but Baker & Botts again handled the local representation, thereby establishing another relationship with outside legal and financial institutions.

Though subordinate to the outside counsel of the large utility financiers, Baker & Botts nonetheless played a crucial role on the local level, permitting the restructuring and refinancing to take place in the face of often-difficult local problems. In 1920, for example, Captain Baker helped to refinance the Warner-Tucker enterprise. Samuel Bertron, president of Baker & Botts client HL&P, agreed to act as receiver. The new owners—Morrison

& McCall—agreed to take on the ailing company's property.[25]

Although local lienholders, mainly merchants owed for materials, at first objected to the terms of the settlement and threatened legal action, Baker & Botts settled the dispute and the property was either sold or refinanced to the numerous creditors'
satisfaction.

The firm's strong ties both within and outside of the Texas
economy made possible this solution. The Houston lawyers had
already established contact with the new investors. A. W. Morrison resided part of the time in San Antonio and Edwin Parker,
full-time counsel of Texaco at this date, had also met him in New
York through his banking correspondents. Adding the Warner-
Tucker properties to Morrison & McCall's holdings proved tricky,
because of the state's limits on capitalization. But Baker & Botts
helped these Saint Louis financiers organize a subholding company under Texas law, thereby permitting the consolidation to
go through.[26]

Throughout the 1920s similar consolidations and reorganizations took place. Baker & Botts again and again played a pivotal
role in this process. Northern banks engaged northern attorneys
to complete the legal instruments for these transactions; these
law firms in turn depended on Baker & Botts to examine the
titles, draw up the conveyances, check the franchises, and organize the new corporations that would take ownership of the consolidated property under Texas law.[27] Besides facilitating the
flow of capital in this way, the firm also provided vital local representation before state agencies and municipal councils, which
sought to regulate the increasingly important public utilities industry. Baker & Botts's knowledge of Texas law and influence
within the state was a key factor in linking Texas into the na
tional power industry.

The most important of the clients the firm represented in these
matters was the giant Chicago-based Electric Bond & Share
Company (EBASCO). Baker & Botts's connection to EBASCO began in the post–World War I depression, when HL&P experienced a financial crisis.[28] American Cities, the smaller regional
holding company that had owned HL&P since 1905, found that it
could not place the Houston power company's securities in the
depressed market of 1921.[29] As a result, HL&P lacked capital
sorely needed to keep pace with Houston's surging demand
for electricity.[30] When Captain Baker and Edwin Parker went to

78

Part II

A Regional

Firm in a

Maturing

Region,

1915–1929

New York in search of investment capital for HL&P, EBASCO responded to their entreaties, introducing a new era in the history of Houston utilities.[31]

The lawyers did not have to wait long for their first assignment from the new client. In taking over HL&P, the largest power company in the Houston region, EBASCO immediately confronted renewed debate on the issue of a city franchise. Before the holding company could market the securities of its new subsidiary, it needed assurance that it had a valid right-of-way franchise to operate in Houston and that its relations with the city would remain smooth and amiable.

The franchise issue had resurfaced when the city and HL&P began renegotiating the profit-sharing plan in 1922. Of prime concern in these negotiations was the continued validity of HL&P's existing franchise and the city's power to regulate the company. Any effort by HL&P to gain a new franchise would inevitably raise political and legal difficulties for the company. Franchise grants of more than thirty years had to pass a referendum vote, which would no doubt turn EBASCO's recent acquisition of HL&P into a hot political issue. Franchises of less than thirty years could also be forced to a vote if enough citizens petitioned to do so. In any case, the maximum allowable franchise was fifty years, and by city charter all new franchises were subject to a fixed annual fee.[32] The lawyers claimed that they had been able to "draw the teeth" of most of these provisions for other clients, and that a franchise for less than thirty years would present no problems.[33] But with EBASCO planning to issue substantial long-term obligations in order to undertake expensive new construction, even a thirty-year franchise might not be sufficient, particularly if relations between the city and the company turned sour over time or if a new administration with a new agenda took office.

As it had done before, Baker & Botts advised its client that the original franchise was valid in perpetuity, so there was no need to raise the issue at all. For the holding company, this meant that its expansion into the Houston region turned on a fine legal point. If the franchise was valid, then EBASCO had little to worry about; if, on the one hand, the 1882 franchise were declared void, the corporation would have to seek approval from the city before it could begin its ambitious plans along the Gulf Coast. Baker & Botts's legal opinion on the validity of the franchise was thus crucial to EBASCO as it planned its strategy for expansion in the Houston area.

Although the senior partners agreed that the franchise was valid, there was no way of knowing for certain that their opinion would stand up in a court of law.[34] Clarence Wharton, who had perhaps more experience before the Texas bench than any other Baker & Botts attorney, was especially uneasy. He knew from experience that clear reasoning and strong legal precedent did not necessarily carry the day when a powerful northern corporation came before a Texas court.[35] According to Wharton, anyone wishing to overturn the franchise had two lines of attack. They could argue that it was invalid either because it was a perpetuity or because it was a monopoly grant.[36] Strictly speaking, the HL&P franchise was neither.[37] But words like *monopoly* and *perpetuity* were highly charged political shibboleths, frequently invoked against any large corporation or vested interest.[38] In popular usage if not strict legal definition, these words still called forth the image of powerful, abusive corporate interests, and Baker & Botts attorneys feared that this definition would be the one to stand in the courts.

Although Electric Bond and Share could not be absolutely sure of its position, it took the advice of its attorneys and went ahead with the issue of bonds to fund HL&P.[39] The fears of a legal challenge to the franchise proved unfounded, and EBASCO enjoyed amiable relations with the city throughout the decade. But the potential dangers of a flare-up of local resentment and legal challenges were real, and EBASCO needed expert local counsel capable of providing much-needed guidance through a thicket of legal and political uncertainties. The holding company continued to rely heavily on Baker & Botts for advice, opinions, and general representation before the citizens of Texas.

Since EBASCO was an innovative company with new and, for Texas, alien ideas, its demand for Baker & Botts's services was heavy. To finance expansion in the Gulf Coast, the Chicago-based holding company introduced the open-ended mortgage to Texas.[40] Though the open-ended mortgage offered important financial advantages in an era of rapid growth, it ran counter to Texas's traditional concern with close financial regulation of corporations, and the attorney general looked with suspicion on it. Given such legal, financial, and political uncertainties in the state, Baker & Botts worked closely with Electric Bond and Share

80

Part II

A Regional
Firm in a
Maturing
Region,
1915–1929

on a day-to-day basis to gain acceptance of this "alien" capital in Texas.[41]

Baker & Botts also helped to get other laws changed. The firm represented EBASCO before the Texas legislature, lobbying for passage of a No Par Value Stock Law in 1925. The new law permitted corporations to issue common or preferred stock with no set value or dividend, something common in other states. Under the statute, EBASCO would be able to vary the dividend on issues as conditions dictated. Baker & Botts helped shepherd the No Par Value Bill successfully through the state legislature.[42] Experienced lobbyist Hiram Garwood "prepared, introduced and piloted" the bill through, steering it to a friendly committee and helping to defeat hostile amendments. This experience gave Baker & Botts more knowledge of the new law than any other firm in the state. Thus when EBASCO took advantage of it and had HL&P issue some two million dollars more in securities, Baker & Botts oversaw the issue.[43]

Electric Bond and Share also sold the preferred stock and bonds of its operating companies in the local market to give local parties a greater stake in the utility properties and to reduce the "alienness" of the capital that financed them.[44] Guardian Trust Company, a Houston bank with strong ties to Baker & Botts, handled these preferred stock issues for HL&P. Captain Baker and Edwin Parker helped to tighten relations between Guardian Trust and the outside financiers by arranging for Guardian to market some of the new mortgage bonds being underwritten by Halsey, Stuart as well.[45] Besides serving EBASCO's needs, this financing boosted the Houston financial community and increased the capacity of Baker & Botts and its circle to shape economic development in the city.

Like finance, corporate reorganization involved Baker & Botts in a delicate balancing act between the needs of the holding company and the fears of local citizens and politicians. Though Texas had fewer formal laws regulating outside utility companies than railroads, its fierce antimonopoly tradition posed potentially explosive challenges to large-scale consolidations in any industry. Such sentiment became a prime concern for EBASCO as it moved beyond Houston and began to acquire local power and gas companies in eastern Texas.

In this work, the firm's many contacts in the regional economy proved vital. Through A. P. Burnett, a close friend of Baker & Botts partner Walter Walne, HL&P was able to bring a number of small nearby utilities into its grid.[46] Negotiating settlements with old bondholders, Walne and Burnett worked to clear the path for these mergers, thereby appreciably shrinking the number of local companies and greatly increasing HL&P's market.[47] Later, Baker & Botts helped EBASCO organize the South Texas Utilities Company, a small subholding company that acquired other utilities in the Houston region.[48] Carrying on multilateral negotiations with local parties, the lawyers brought together the interests of their clients and the communities this company served.

Drawing on the considerable power and influence they had acquired in the Houston region, as well as their legal expertise, the lawyers also worked to block municipal attacks on acquisition and consolidation. In 1924, when nearby Pasadena grew enough to incorporate under the provisions of the home rule law, HL&P became alarmed that its Deepwater power station, now in the new city's corporate limits, would come under the municipality's control. More generally, the power company feared that the assumption of home rule by other places would threaten its efforts to integrate the different towns in the Houston metropolitan region into one large power system. Accordingly, the utility turned to Baker & Botts for help, and the lawyers succeeded in getting Pasadena's incorporation charter declared null and void. In 1929, however, the suburb again moved to incorporate, now with more determination. This time the lawyers worked out a compromise that gave HL&P a long-term franchise to operate in the city.[49]

In a similar case, Baker & Botts used its expertise and national contacts to counter a threat by the city of Goose Creek to abandon HL&P service and purchase its own generating equipment. Presenting information from engineering experts showing that the cost of independently generated power would exceed the cost of HL&P service, the firm convinced a citizens' committee to force the city council to reconsider the new policy. The committee had some leverage because the city had violated its own charter by not arranging for competitive bids on the new power equipment, which suggested a close connection between the proponents of local power and the manufacturing concern trying to sell Goose Creek equipment. The citizens' committee prevailed, providing Baker & Botts with a model to use in other cases where municipalities threatened the same action.[50]

In these cases, Baker & Botts's political skills were an important factor in building the power system of the Gulf Coast.

82

Part II
A Regional
Firm in a
Maturing
Region,
1915–1929

Economies of scale made large, interconnected power grids the cheapest way to supply urban power needs, but this technology frequently ran against strong traditions of home rule and entrenched local interests. City leaders, often with support from small-scale equipment manufacturers eager to find markets for their products, searched for ways to achieve independence from large corporations such as EBASCO. With its growing influence in the Houston metropolitan region, Baker & Botts brought to bear legal and political pressure to break down this localism and permit power systems to develop.

Other holding companies that entered Texas also sought Baker & Botts's services. When Stone & Webster, a Boston-based consulting and engineering firm, expanded its operations in the state, it, too, ran into legal and political difficulties that required the lawyers' assistance. Stone & Webster had been a Baker & Botts client since the turn of the century, when it took over the Houston Electric Railway, as we have seen.[51] In later years it expanded its holdings of utilities in the region.

Stone & Webster eventually consolidated its Texas interests under a holding company—Eastern Texas Electric. As local counsel, Baker & Botts participated in the formation of this enterprise, which was chartered in Maine.[52] Stone & Webster added more light and power properties, and in 1924 organized Eastern Texas Electric Company of Delaware. The following year Stone & Webster formed Engineers Public Service Corporation, which took overall control of its many regional holding companies such as Eastern Texas Electric. Engineers Public Service became the capstone of Stone & Webster's expanding holding company operation, and the company picked up properties across the nation and sold its own securities in the East much as EBASCO did.

With the Stone & Webster holding company structure in place, Baker & Botts began to take on a host of new responsibilities. The Boston firm employed eastern lawyers for top-level legal matters affecting the entire holding company. Baker & Botts, however, continued to provide local counsel to settle the numerous disputes and conflicts generated by consolidation. The Texas lawyers worked out the acquisitions of local utilities, settling matters with private parties and municipal governments. At the same time, they performed certain managerial functions for Stone & Webster, whose decentralized operations were in sharp contrast to the tight, hierarchical management structure of EBASCO.

Baker & Botts's special expertise in Texas corporation law gave it a great advantage over law firms from outside the state in these matters. In 1926 Stone & Webster wanted to simplify its corporate structure by consolidating its electric, gas, urban, and interurban railway properties into a new corporation and refinancing the entire operation. Baker & Botts attorney Palmer Hutcheson, however, advised that this could not be done under existing Texas law, for the state's corporate statutes made no provision for licensing a single corporation to perform such a combination of services. Hutcheson instead recommended that Stone & Webster form a new company to hold all of the utility properties except the railways. Though formally separate, the stock of this new concern would be owned by Stone & Webster's Eastern Texas Electric.[53]

The new company formed on Hutcheson's advice was Gulf States Utilities, destined to become a major power supplier for a broad section of southeastern Texas and southwestern Louisiana that contained several medium-sized cities and numerous giant petroleum refineries. Baker & Botts played a prominent role in the organization of Gulf States. Palmer Hutcheson served as one of the corporation's original incorporators and its first president.[54] Gulf States had been organized as a Texas corporation, but its stock was quickly transferred to Stone & Webster's Eastern Texas Electric Company (Delaware), and Hutcheson and the other local executives were replaced by Boston men. Nonetheless, whenever special stockholders' meetings had to be called—as when Stone & Webster wanted Gulf States to issue more securities—they were held at Baker & Botts's office, with Hutcheson serving as temporary president.[55]

To finance Gulf States, Stone & Webster authorized the issue of some nine million dollars in bonds against its light and power properties. This issue was underwritten by Chase Manhattan Bank, with the assistance of Stone & Webster's eastern lawyers. Here, too, however, Baker & Botts provided crucial advice on Texas securities laws.[56] Particularly important was the firm's opinion that in the event of a foreclosure, Chase could operate utility properties in Texas as a trustee, even though the bank did not have a permit to do business in the state.

While Baker & Botts could not make laws that satisfied out-

84

Part II
A Regional
Firm in a
Maturing
Region,
1915–1929

side financiers, it could give legal opinions based on its long experience with Texas laws, courts, and public officials. As the state's premier corporate law firm, Baker & Botts had gained considerable experience dealing with these issues since the 1890s. The firm's opinion that the bank could take possession in event of a foreclosure was based on this experience, as well as its knowledge of Texas judges and confidence in its own ability to make a successful argument in court. These reasoned judgments of skilled lawyers were crucial factors in entrepreneurial decision making. They allowed companies such as Stone & Webster and the Chase Manhattan Bank to plan strategies of expansion into Texas with the clearest possible understanding of both the immediate and long-term implications of the different choices available to them.

Making use of Baker & Botts's advice, Stone & Webster went ahead with the reorganization. In 1926 Gulf States acquired Eastern Texas Electric's utility properties and became Stone & Webster's main operating company in southeastern Texas. Like HL&P under Electric Bond and Share, Gulf States began to consolidate small properties and build a regional power grid. It extended transmission lines from its plant in Beaumont to HL&P's Deepwater generating station along the ship channel in order to share capacity efficiently. Over time, Gulf States made connections with other utilities in surrounding areas, further extending the eastern Texas power grid.

To finance its expansion, Gulf States wanted to raise capital through no par value preferred stock. The company's charter contained no reference to preferred stock, however, and Texas securities and financial laws were unclear about whether the company could issue any. Baker & Botts advised, therefore, that Stone & Webster amend Gulf States' charter to permit the issue. This move was quickly blocked by Texas's secretary of state, who forbade such an amendment. Baker & Botts worked within his ruling to get "something as near the purposes desired as could be done under the statutes as construed by the Secretary of State."[57] The lawyers submitted a substitute amendment to the secretary that satisfied both him and their client.

Work for the giant utility systems frequently carried Baker & Botts attorneys beyond the courtroom and the boardroom and into the halls of the state legislature. In 1929, for instance, the Texas legislature introduced several corporate tax bills, as well as a proposal to start a state public utility commission. Hiram

Garwood of Baker & Botts was instrumental in defeating or blunting all of them.[58] Returning to the familiar theme of outside economic domination, the legislature proposed heavy franchise and gross receipts taxes, as well as a corporate and personal income tax. Striking up an equally familiar refrain, however, Garwood mounted an effective antitax campaign on the argument that higher taxes would discourage investment in the state. He also argued convincingly that the burden would fall as heavily on local as on outside businesses.

Similar arguments went into Garwood's efforts against the proposed public utilities commission bill.[59] With the increasing control of utilities by large holding companies based outside of the state in the 1920s, Texans looked with renewed interest on the creation of a utilities commission. But the House and Senate versions of the bill exempted "all cities and towns with regulatory powers" in an attempt to keep support for the law by bowing to Texas traditions of home rule. Garwood made use of this exception to argue that the bill was prejudicial to smaller towns and cities, which could not pass their own charters to regulate utilities. By playing on the rivalries and jealousies between places, he helped prevent a solid majority from forming in favor of a utilities commission, thus ending the threat.

In work ranging from business advice to lobbying, Baker & Botts's lawyers helped to open up new opportunities for investment in the state by outside utility corporations. Members of the firm also helped to define the scope and limits of state regulation, thereby frustrating those who wanted tighter control of big business. They did not win every case. Sometimes federal judges, supposedly friends of big business in this period, failed to sustain their arguments.[60] Other times, local political interests won out. But through their relentless pursuit of their clients' interests in court, in private consultation, and in the legislature, they gradually reshaped the political economy of Texas. The resulting business style was largely one of powerful private interests keeping public regulation at bay. Pushing aside old agrarian values, surmounting small-town traditions of local control, actors like Baker & Botts worked to create the "good business climate" thought necessary for economic development.

This work at times generated intense controversy. Such was the case when the firm fought against jitney service and when it negotiated with the state over utility consolidations. Often the results were difficult for certain groups to accept. In represent-

86

Part II

A Regional
Firm in a
Maturing
Region,
1915–1929

ing big eastern businesses, the firm had to walk a fine line between several powerful sets of interests in Texas. When changing circumstances made interurban rail service unprofitable for Baker & Botts client Stone & Webster, for example, the firm had to present the case to the public for ending this service. Citizens who only decades before had heard Baker & Botts argue that the interurban lines deserved incentives from government now listened with skepticism as the firm proposed that the lines should be abandoned.[61]

In cases such as these it was difficult to determine when the firm's defense of its clients' interests yielded results in the best interests of society as a whole. Undoubtedly, Texas's stringent laws prohibiting consolidation at times ran counter to the economic logic of modern industrial enterprise, and the traditional nineteenth-century fear of bigness threatened industrial development.[62] On the other hand, not all aspects of government regulation were uneconomic and not all consolidations were for the good. Baker & Botts applied the same legal acumen to the cases of all of its clients, regardless of the social value of their actions. The firm was in the business of facilitating corporate expansion. Its members went about their work with confidence that the voice of their populist critics was the voice of the past. The future, they felt certain, belonged to big business. In Texas in the early twentieth century, the rising new business was oil, and Baker & Botts became deeply involved in the legal, political, and regulatory debates surrounding this crucial industry.

Oil-led Developments

Oil gave Texas its identity in the national economy. With the rise of its petroleum industry, the state began to shed its colonial status and to emerge as a region of national, even world-wide, significance. Cotton, timber, and other traditional industries remained important well into the twentieth century, but oil was the primary engine of development as the state surged into national prominence in the 1920s and 1930s. The production, transportation, and refining of petroleum products spun a web of new economic activities, with Houston at the center of a system of pipelines reaching out into the major producing fields of Texas, Oklahoma, and Louisiana.

As this industry grew in importance, so did Houston. In the decade after World War I, the gasoline-powered automobile became the nation's primary means of transportation, and the future of the city, the "oil capital" of the United States, was secure.[1] And like the railroads before it, the oil industry advanced the fortunes of Houston and its major law firm together. For Baker & Botts, seeking prominence at the national level, oil provided a key stepping-stone upward.

After the first big strike at Spindletop in 1901, Houston's leading corporate law firm found ample opportunity for involvement with the oil and gas industries. Many of the large corporations that developed these natural resources relied on Baker & Botts's special knowledge of the law in Texas, a state still uncomfortable with modern corporate enterprises. Because Texas had become one of the largest producing states for oil and gas, the largest petroleum-refining complex in the nation grew up on the Texas-Louisiana Gulf Coast. Thus, many of the major oil companies chose to maintain administrative offices in Houston, and Baker & Botts found itself by a fortunate accident located in one

88

Part II
A Regional
Firm in a
Maturing
Region,
1915–1929

of the fastest-growing markets for oil-related legal services in the nation.[2]

The work required by major oil companies was not quite like the legal services the firm had supplied to the Southern Pacific and other northeastern-based companies. In patent law, antitrust, and corporate organization, the dynamic oil industry created some of the most challenging questions facing the entire legal profession. The issues raised by the operations of these companies in Texas were critically important to the nation as a whole. Involvement in the legal affairs of the major oil companies active in and around Houston thus elevated Baker & Botts at least a step above its former standing.

While the firm had been gradually moving toward greater national prominence by providing legal assistance to outside firms adding operations in the Southwest, oil reversed this equation. This booming industry was reaching out from Texas to the remainder of the nation, and Baker & Botts and other leading Texas law firms had the opportunity to perform at the cutting edge of legal developments in a vital industry. In oil and gas law and in aspects of corporate law relating to oil and gas companies, Baker & Botts now had regular opportunities to handle cases of national significance.

The impact of the oil and gas industries on Baker & Botts was first evident in the firm's traditional areas of strength, its railroad and utility work. The Southern Pacific Railroad quickly became involved in many aspects of the oil industry, which created additional work for its general attorney in Texas. As a major landowner, the SP needed legal assistance in defending its claims to oil-producing lands. And as a central part of the state's transportation system, it carried much of the oil produced on the Texas Gulf Coast to refineries and to markets, particularly in the years before the completion of an adequate pipeline system. Disputes over rates for these shipments found their way into the regulatory system, where Baker & Botts argued its client's cases. The SP also became a major user of petroleum, as it converted its engines in the Southwest from coal to fuel oil.

The railroad's deep involvement in the oil industry led to the formation in 1903 of a subsidiary, the Rio Bravo Oil Company, to coordinate its petroleum-related activities. Rio Bravo's primary mission was to supply the fuel oil needed by the Southern Pacific in the Southwest.[3] The charter under which Rio Bravo operated allowed it to mine, develop, use, store, sell, and transport oil, gas, and other minerals, as well as to contract to purchase and use them. It could not, however, enter into the market for already-developed minerals and thus could not simply become an oil distribution firm. Rather, it was tied to the developmental activities that might legitimately be considered the province of a transportation corporation that desired to build up a business carrying oil.[4] Within these legal boundaries, however, Rio Bravo undertook a host of ventures. Among other things, it acquired coal lands, drilled wells in the Saratoga field, and purchased water plants and pipelines. It also built its own pipeline from existing oil fields to nearby railroad tracks.[5]

Rio Bravo depended heavily on Baker & Botts, and several members of the firm served as directors. Nominally, Southern Pacific executive Robert Lovett ran this subsidiary, but local SP officials actually directed operations.[6] To finance its activities, Rio Bravo drew on SP resources, especially the railroad's vast holdings of land. The oil company acquired mineral rights to land from the various SP lines in Texas in exchange for its stock. Because this land also secured the railroad's mortgages, it could not be transferred easily to Rio Bravo. Yet, given the increasing mineral value of this land, as well as the oil company's need for collateral for its own notes, the transfer would benefit the SP enterprise as a whole. Baker & Botts worked out the legal details of these transfers, enabling the Southern Pacific to make full use of these resources. This business gave the law firm its first important client in the new leading sector of the regional economy.

Other clients also pulled Baker & Botts into oil-related business. As Houston Lighting & Power expanded, it became a major purchaser of fuel oil and natural gas. Baker & Botts negotiated the substantial oil and gas contracts required by HL&P and handled the process of accounting for these purchases in rate making. Another client, Houston Gas and Fuel Company, became a major supplier of natural gas and fuel oil in the region, and the law firm maintained close ties with this concern and with the holding companies that subsequently acquired it. Baker & Botts's longtime client, South Texas Commercial National Bank, one of the city's largest financial institutions in the early twentieth century, had a client list and a board of directors that included many individuals and companies from the oil industry. The bank and its attorneys quickly developed a growing interest in oil-related activities.

The first major oil company with which Baker & Botts was in-

90

Part II

A Regional
Firm in a
Maturing
Region,
1915–1929

volved was the Texas Company (Texaco), which paid a retainer to the firm from 1914 through 1954.[7] Although Texaco's original oil deposits and its first refinery were located in Texas, soon after its founding in 1902 it grew into a vertically integrated corporation active throughout the nation and around the world. Baker & Botts handled much of the company's legal business in Houston and in the Texas oil fields. This work moved the firm a long step away from its traditional role as the local representative of eastern companies. Yet at the same time, Baker & Botts's representation of Texaco also suggests the limits of the firm's development in this era. Although playing an important part in nationally significant patent litigation for the company, Baker & Botts remained largely a specialist in Texas law, a regional law firm not yet the equivalent of the leading Wall Street firms or of Texaco's in-house counsel in matters of corporate organization and financing or in national regulatory matters.

Baker & Botts's new client had been born at Spindletop, the offspring of Joseph Cullinan, who had learned the oil business in Pennsylvania before migrating to Texas. He had joined forces with a group of eastern investors who found opportunities in the Texas oil industry attractive. Beginning with only fifty thousand dollars, Cullinan and his operating officers built a major oil company by combining considerable skill and hard work, a healthy dose of good luck, and the generous financial backing of wealthy investors centered primarily in New York City. In 1908 Cullinan moved Texaco's headquarters from Beaumont to Houston, although much of the company's marketing was done through offices in New York.[8]

Led by Cullinan and the company's attorney, Houstonian James L. Autry, the "Texas group" primarily responsible for finding and refining the petroleum became increasingly impatient with what they saw as eastern investors' interference in daily management. Cullinan resented the conservative impulses of these investors and protested that the "New York tail was wagging the Texas dog." Chafing under what he felt were unnecessary constraints imposed by people who had little knowledge of the oil business, Cullinan put the issue of control to a stockholders' vote in 1913. When he lost this showdown, Cullinan left Texaco, taking Autry with him. Houston newspapers reported this confrontation as "the culmination of a contest that has been on between the eastern and Texas interests of the Company"

and suggested that Texans should reexamine the laws that allowed a Texas corporation to be "administered and governed
beyond the convenient reach of her authority and responsibility." Here was a ready symbol of dominance by outsiders. Control of the Texas Company had been wrested from some of Houston's leading citizens by a group "composed largely of New York
capitalists."[9]

As the uproar gradually subsided, the directors of Texaco
looked within the ranks of their company for new management;
at the same time, they looked to Baker & Botts to replace the
knowledge of Texas law previously provided by Autry. Texaco's
choice of Baker & Botts as its primary Texas counsel reflected the
firm's growing reputation in the East. From the perspective of the
Houston business community, this episode reinforced Baker &
Botts's image as the "New York" firm in the region.[10]

In a letter to Edwin B. Parker of Baker & Botts, Texaco's general counsel, Amos L. Beatty, outlined the terms of the retainer
agreement, which became effective on 1 January 1914:

> The Texas Company will employ you as counsel at a salary of
> $6,000 per annum. . . . Our desire is that you will advise with
> the officers of the Company, with the heads of its departments,
> and with the members of the legal staff on all questions of a
> legal nature that may arise, giving written opinions when de-
> sired; that you will also let us have the benefit of your judg-
> ment on matters of policy and business expediency, as they
> may arise and be submitted to you from time to time, though
> they may be only quasi-legal in their nature; and that a trial
> lawyer of your staff will actively participate with one or more
> of our staff in the preparation and trial of our cases in the
> District Courts of Harris County and the Federal Court at
> Houston.[11]

Baker & Botts eagerly accepted a proposal that promised exciting new work on the legal issues and policy questions facing
what had already become one of the world's leading petroleum
companies.

In its early relationship with Texaco, Baker & Botts provided a
wide range of legal advice and consultation, from handling local
damage suits to trying important cases that helped shape the development of modern leasing laws in Texas. Baker & Botts attorneys Clarence Wharton and Brady Cole also played prominent
roles in trying a series of important patent infringement cases
involving Texaco. Although the firm's work was closely super-

92

Part II
A Regional
Firm in a
Maturing
Region,
1915–1929

vised by Texaco's growing in-house legal department, Baker & Botts nonetheless enjoyed the opportunity of participating in significant, highly visible litigation.

During the early years of Baker & Botts's representation of Texaco, the state revised the basic laws under which all oil companies operated. Texas's turn-of-the-century incorporation laws and antitrust statutes contained language that—if strictly interpreted—limited the scope of an oil company's operations in several significant ways. These laws embodied the strong populist sentiments of an era before oil was discovered in Texas, and one of their purposes was to block the entry into the state of John D. Rockefeller and the Standard Oil Company.

Growing companies such as Texaco and the Gulf Oil Corporation soon found their activities sharply constrained by these laws. Corporations chartered in Texas could, for example, legally engage in only a single phase of the oil industry. Under a strict interpretation of Texas law before 1917, vertical integration—the structure perfected by Rockefeller to coordinate the production, transportation, refining, and marketing of oil in a single organization—was illegal in the state. Also forbidden at this time were holding companies—in which one corporation owned stock in another—and the operation across state lines of a company chartered in Texas. Thus to remain in strict compliance with state law would have required an oil company to refrain from using several of the organizational devices employed by Rockefeller to build the modern oil industry at a time when the young Texas companies were struggling to survive in competition with Standard Oil. The management of Texaco recognized this dilemma and spent considerable energy seeking to change the state laws.

These laws embodied agrarian fears of industrial combinations and they represented challenging barriers for corporate lawyers attempting to give their clients as much freedom of action as possible. Commenting on the strict limitation on corporate actions and the severe penalties set forward in one of Texas's early antitrust laws, Baker & Botts attorney Clarence Wharton observed that the law was "evidently drawn with an intent to terrify."[12] This was not surprising, since many Texans were themselves terrified by the size, the power, and the outside control of the large corporations that were moving into their state. The discovery of oil brought a new urgency to the question of antitrust by raising widespread fears that "foreign" companies, led by the infamous Standard Oil, might take control of this vital Texas resource.

In the first decade of the twentieth century, state officials focused primarily on two oil company attributes to determine whether they were violating the law. First, did a company combine oil production with other oil-related activities? Second, was it directly or indirectly tied to Standard Oil? Texaco avoided problems on the first count by organizing its production under the Producers Oil Company, which was owned by individuals closely connected to Texaco's management and operated in coordination with the remainder of the company's holdings. This was not an ideal arrangement, since it was based on the legal fiction that a subsidiary vital to the smooth functioning of the company was an independent concern. The second count was equally uncomfortable for Texaco, which had a variety of close ties to Standard Oil, ranging from a president who had learned the oil business as an employee of Standard to the sale of large amounts of oil to the company that was a symbol of monopoly in Texas.

Texaco argued that a law discriminating against a specific company was "an extremely dangerous precedent" and represented "a very low order of legislative sentiment" that should be "frowned upon." The company's representative feared "that bills would be introduced with reference to their application to other corporations singled out where popular prejudice can be aroused." [15] Instead of using the prevailing anti-Rockefeller sentiment against its larger rival, Texaco took the long view, lobbying to alter the laws that limited the operations in Texas of modern, vertically integrated oil companies.

This was no easy task, and it ultimately required almost fifteen years of efforts by Texaco and its representatives in the state, including Baker & Botts. As one of the largest Texas based oil companies, Texaco enjoyed considerable leverage at Austin, but it also faced concerted and effective opposition from independent oil producers who had little interest in seeing the legal powers of vertically integrated companies expanded. In 1913 Texaco threw down the gauntlet by announcing to the independents and the state government that it had formally absorbed the stock of its production subsidiary, Producers Oil. Texaco challenged the state either to change its restrictive laws or to enforce them.

Texaco lobbyists pushed their case before the legislature,

94

Part II
A Regional
Firm in a
Maturing
Region,
1915–1929

even taking out full-page advertisements in Austin newspapers to present their arguments to the voting public as well as its elected representatives. The company's representatives in Austin stressed the fact that Texas laws reflected conditions in the state before large corporations were common and were more restrictive than those of many other states. As a result, a charter in Texas was "a serious handicap to the company on account of the territorial restrictions, lack of authority to own subsidiary corporations, and an absence of power to explore for and produce oil." [14] Texaco wanted "such legislation as will remove the handicap and accord it those lawful corporate rights that are enjoyed by companies organized in such states as California, Oklahoma or Louisiana." [15] Texas could no longer afford to cling to laws, the oil company said, suited to the nineteenth century. Texas could not alter the organization of the modern oil industry; it could only assure that leading companies would obtain charters in other states. Possible corporate abuses need no longer be feared, since federal laws afforded ample protection.

Although Baker & Botts's client had the logic of modern industrial organization on its side, the opposition had history and emotion on its. Representatives of groups of independent oil producers bristled at Texaco's arguments and lobbied aggressively against changes in the law. Companies engaged primarily in the production of oil within the state feared that larger companies such as Texaco would gain added market power. Their objections were couched in the strong language of an earlier era. Witnesses before the state Senate proclaimed that the "Texas Company is a Texas organization only in fancy rather than in fact," since its headquarters was in New York. They decried the company's "powerful lobby"—including Baker & Botts—and its effort to secure passage of a new law that would "give the company a chance to crush out all independent oil production in Texas." One leader of the opposition predicted that the proposed changes would "overturn every public policy that underlies the corporation laws of this state." [16]

For four years lobbyists from Baker & Botts joined other Texaco representatives in Austin in a determined campaign for a more permissive incorporation law. Their efforts finally paid off in February of 1917 with the passage of two important acts. The first provided that corporations formed for the purpose of storing, transporting, buying, and selling oil and gas and other products "may also engage in the oil and gas producing business,

prospecting for and producing oil and gas and owning and holding lands, leases and other property for said purposes; provided
that no corporation shall exercise these powers while owning or
operating oil pipelines in this state." The companion act declared pipelines to be common carriers and placed them under
the control of the Texas Railroad Commission.[17] This compromise suggests that by 1917, independent oil producers in Texas
were more concerned about the practical matter of access to
markets through pipelines than about the more abstract question of the monopoly power of big oil companies. By 1917 Texas
stood poised to enter a new era in its economic development, one
in which its leading economic institutions would be absorbed
into the national economic matrix. The Texas Company Act of
1917 was the important symbolic end to traditional nineteenth-
century constraints on vertically integrated businesses. Symbolic of the dawning era was the ironic fact that, despite its
hard-won victory in Austin, Texaco decided in 1926 to move its
charter to Delaware, a move assisted by its legal advisers at
Baker & Botts.

With the emergence of Texaco as a fully integrated oil company, the value to Baker & Botts of its close relationship to the
corporation increased manyfold. It seemed as though that relationship was about to pay impressive dividends in the early
1920s, when Edwin B. Parker was appointed general counsel of
the company. He had worked with Texaco officials before the
war, and on the completion of that work, he accepted Texaco's
offer of the office of general counsel and memberships on the
board and executive committee.[18]

In announcing Parker's new affiliation with Texaco, Baker &
Botts stressed the fact that "our Firm itself will continue to represent the Company locally on the basis which has existed for
several years," and that "Mr. Parker *personally* became General
Counsel and will have entire charge of all of its legal work." The
appointment was obviously a point of pride for a regional law
firm such as Baker & Botts: "This new and closer relationship
with its [Texaco's] business marks a decided step forward in
the progress of our Firm—an advancement which comes very
largely as a recognition of Mr. Parker's influence and ability, but
which, nonetheless, redounds to the benefit of the Firm as a
whole."[19]

As long as Parker remained part of both the firm and a major
New York–based oil company, Baker & Botts maintained a high

96

Part II
A Regional
Firm in a
Maturing
Region,
1915–1929

profile in the heartland of the corporate economy. But in 1922 Parker resigned from Texaco, and thereafter the firm's working relationship with the company became somewhat less glamorous. The original retainer had stipulated that the law firm would try the company's cases in the district courts in Harris County and the federal court at Houston. This was a logical arrangement, similar to the one Baker & Botts maintained with the Southern Pacific and numerous insurance companies. The firm had developed an excellent reputation for its trial work, and its expertise was of considerable value to a company based outside the state. Yet this was seldom prestigious or particularly remunerative work, and it at times included a large helping of the sort of personal injury suits that Baker & Botts would have been all too happy to farm out to local attorneys.

A sampling of the firm's case load for Texaco in the early 1930s suggests that most of its work was of this routine variety. There were suits for personal damages from an accident in the oil fields, for damages to property as a result of the construction of a pipeline, for damages from breach of contract in drilling an oil well, and for personal injuries suffered by a customer who slipped and fell in front of a service station. Although such cases helped pay the bills and provided training for young trial lawyers, they were hardly the "decided step forward" that the firm had envisioned when it signed the original retainer.[20]

Local trial work did not prove sufficient to justify a substantial retainer. In 1924 the company cut the retainer in half. It explained the reduction by noting that "you will recognize that the number of ordinary cases on the docket in Harris County does not justify us in maintaining the schedule heretofore existing."[21] This came as no surprise to the partners, who were aware that Texaco was not using their services in matters of overriding importance. Even when faced with a controversial Texas antitrust suit in the 1920s and 1930s, the corporation relied on its in-house lawyers instead of Baker & Botts. Individual members of the firm maintained close personal ties to individuals within Texaco, particularly with Harry T. Klein, who had been brought into Texaco's Legal Department by Edwin Parker and who subsequently became general counsel and then president of the company. But, in general, the promise of high-level corporate work for this important client was never quite fulfilled.

The one important exception to this rule was Baker & Botts's contribution to a series of nationally significant patent cases involving Texaco. In this highly specialized area of law, Clarence Wharton and his protégé, Brady Cole, became significant members of the team of attorneys that tried a set of cases with far-reaching implications for the company and for the entire industry. Cole, who came to Baker & Botts in 1923 and remained until his death in 1953, spent much of his career traveling the nation to prepare and try patent cases for Texaco.[22] These arose as a result of the rapid improvement that took place in the technical processes used to find and refine petroleum in the interwar years. Technological progress bred patent disputes that required great skill and technical understanding to resolve. Cole—and Baker & Botts—were able to provide Texaco with the right combination of legal skill and technical knowledge, and this patent work was a significant step up the legal ladder from the firm's "Texas" cases.

The Texaco patent work grew out of Baker & Botts's earlier involvement in patent litigation in a local case. Hughes Tool Company, the leading manufacturer of drilling bits for oil wells, owed much of its success to a series of innovations in the design of oil tools. It naturally sought to defend itself against any infringement on its patents. When another growing oil tool company, Reed Roller Bit, seemed to be guilty of patent infringement, Hughes Tool assembled a formidable team of attorneys to try its case. Clarence Wharton's reputation as one of the state's leading trial lawyers made him a key part of this team, which won a much-publicized victory for Hughes Tool.[23]

As a result of his success, Texaco retained Wharton to help try one of its patent infringement cases. *Gray & The Texas Company* v. *McAfee and the Gulf Oil Company* pitted two rising giants of the oil industry against each other in a dispute over patents covering the aluminum chloride process for increasing the yield of gasoline from crude oil.[24] Wharton, who entered the case on appeal as a trial lawyer, worked closely with both the Legal Department of Texaco and its special patent counsel, Gifford & Bull. Wharton was assisted by Brady Cole, fresh out of law school and with little inkling that he was beginning a "detour" into patent litigation that would dominate the rest of his career. According to one of Cole's contemporaries, "the field of patent law seemed to call especially for the exercise of the talents he [Cole] possessed. It called for almost endless technical research and investigation—research in widely separated domains of knowledge."[25] Into this work Cole threw himself with a vengeance. Al-

98

Part II
A Regional
Firm in a
Maturing
Region,
1915–1929

though he subsequently engaged in a general practice, he would devote most of his time to complex patent cases, becoming a specialist in this highly technical field at a time when few Baker & Botts lawyers had such a technical specialty.

Wharton and Cole's timing could not have been better. In the decades after World War I, the basic processes used to find and refine oil spawned hotly contested patent suits. Taken together, these cases were among the most significant ever litigated in the evolution of patent laws covering basic manufacturing processes.[26] These patent cases helped shape the evolution of the refining industry, the leading edge of industrialization in Houston. New methods for increasing the yield of gasoline from crude oil revolutionized refining and provided strong incentives to construct new plants employing the most modern technology. For most large U.S.-based companies, the location of choice for these giant manufacturing plants was the Texas Gulf Coast from Houston to Port Arthur. But to develop these plants fully, the companies had to settle the patent cases involving the rights to various cracking processes.

After Wharton and Cole helped bring the case against Gulf Oil to a successful conclusion, Cole participated in a variety of other cases that involved the most modern processes for extracting final products from both oil and natural gas. The most important of these disputes were over the combinations of heat, pressure, and catalysts used in petroleum cracking to increase the yield of gasoline. Over the years, Cole developed impressive technical knowledge and personal contacts, which made him a uniquely valuable resource in patent suits. In finding expert witnesses and building effective cases around their testimonies, Cole regularly visited the nation's leading universities, notably Massachusetts Institute of Technology and the University of California at Berkeley. There he familiarized himself with the research of prominent scientists in a variety of fields. He had a talent for reconstructing the evolution of new technologies through extensive interviews with scientists and refinery operators. He was able, moreover, to present this information in a straightforward way that proved effective with judges and juries.[27]

The refinery cracking cases led naturally to other oil- and gas-related patent suits. One of Cole's major victories came in *Carbide & Carbon Chemical Corporation* v. *The Texas Company,* which was decided in 1927. This case involved processes used to extract gasoline from natural gas through "rectification."[28]

When Texaco sought to employ a form of rectification in its operations, it was sued by the Carbide & Chemical Corporation, a subsidiary of the Union Carbide & Carbon Company established to exploit what that company thought was a patent monopoly on this vital process. As Clarence Wharton explained to his partners, "The amount of damages that would have been assessed had plaintiff prevailed would have been very large." Cole, however, successfully attacked the validity of Carbide & Chemical's patents. According to Wharton, "Cole had the entire supervision of preparing this case for trial," a fact that testifies to the excellent reputation of a young trial lawyer who was not yet even a partner in his firm.[29] In subsequent years, Cole's meticulous research enabled him to defend patents covering both cracking processes and the use of specialized seismological techniques for oil exploration. In these and other cases, he worked closely with leading patent specialists throughout the nation. Large fees and considerable publicity within the national legal profession—especially in the growing specialty of patent law—flowed to Baker & Botts from these activities.

This high-profile, high-pressure work helped the firm solidify its national reputation, but it also exacted a heavy toll on those responsible for preparing and trying the cases. The trial work required long and often tedious research. These efforts were made more difficult by the fact that the Houston offices of Baker & Botts were far removed from the centers of research and litigation in the East. Brady Cole kept a diary during his years as a partner at the firm, and it yields sobering insights into the personal and emotional sacrifices he made in his efforts to win his never-ending round of patent cases. There were constant struggles to make connections between the available trains and planes moving between Houston and the Northeast. Air travel was uncertain at best in this era. Trains forced him to spend days away from the office and away from home. Cole logged week-long and even month-long research trips that concluded with an all-night train ride back to Houston, a brief breakfast with his family, and then a full day's work in his Houston office.

The cumulative impact of Cole's killing work schedule is evident in the pages of his diary. New Year's Eve of 1936 brings the following entry: "This was the last day of the year. I read seismic literature until midnight and then walked out into the middle of the street."[30] As the years pass, the references to "long, hard days" increase, as do his laments that he is seldom able to gain

100

Part II

A Regional
Firm in a
Maturing
Region,
1915–1929

control over his work: "I work constantly and yet I seem never to be able to catch up with all of my many obligations. As a matter of fact, I have great difficulty in finding time to devote to my next important matters because of the necessity to turn aside and handle collateral tasks that are constantly arising."[51]

Sad notes emerge: "The Bambino [his two-year-old son] did not know me when I got home." A tragedy awaited. Cole's commitment to his career and to the continued development of his firm drove him to accept unusual hardships. After several bouts with nervous exhaustion in his forties, he died of a long-neglected ulcer at the age of fifty-two. He was at once a testament to and a casualty of his firm's climb up the nation's legal hierarchy.

Representation of Texaco enabled Baker & Botts to take a half step toward the status of a national corporate law practice. If much of the work consisted of routine local damage suits, valuable opportunities in areas such as patent law also came with the package. If Baker & Botts did not regularly "advise with officers of the Company," individual lawyers did work closely with Texaco's Legal Department. Numerous lucrative cases came to the firm from individuals who had once worked at Texaco or who first became aware of the firm through personal contacts with Texaco officials. At least one major client, Schlumberger Well Surveying Company, and numerous important cases went to Baker & Botts as a direct result of the patent work of Brady Cole and others.[32] In meeting some of the legal needs of an international oil company with strong ties to the Houston area, Baker & Botts gained status as well as experience.

The law firm also drew great strength from its representation of other oil-related concerns. It established close ties with other large, vertically integrated oil companies, most of which had extensive exploration and production in Texas. They usually had refineries along the Gulf Coast and administrative offices in Houston and Dallas, under the guidance of a central office in New York or Chicago. Such clients were Baker & Botts's comparative strength in the Houston legal market. Another Houston firm that became a major competitor after the 1930s, Vinson & Elkins, was known as the representative of choice for many of the Texas independents—that is, oil-producing companies whose business consisted primarily of finding oil, producing it, and then selling it to large, vertically integrated companies. Still another, somewhat older, Houston firm, Andrews & Kurth, became the lead attorneys for the Hughes Tool Company, the dominant oil well drilling equipment manufacturer. In practice, these distinctions did not always hold. Thus, Baker & Botts represented independents in a variety of cases, as well as Hughes Tool in a patent infringement suit, as we have seen. But each of the leading firms offered a somewhat different package of services and each tended to represent an identifiable type of client.

By the early 1920s Baker & Botts had already begun to develop its distinctive oil industry clientele. In addition to Texaco, several growing oil companies established retainers with the firm. The first was the Sinclair Oil Company,[33] which placed Baker & Botts on retainer in 1918. Although its general offices were in New York and its sales and refining departments in Chicago, this company had producing properties throughout the Southwest and a major refinery on the Houston ship channel. Two years later, Baker & Botts signed a retainer contract with the Atlantic Refining Company,[34] a Philadelphia-based concern whose Texas oil production was concentrated in West Texas and the East Texas field. Continental Oil Company generated a large volume of work for Baker & Botts for a time after it established administrative offices in Houston in the early 1930s.[35] Similarly, Standard Oil Company of Texas, a subsidiary of Chevron, became an important client after it began in the late 1930s to develop significant properties on the Gulf Coast and offshore in Galveston Bay and the Gulf of Mexico.[36] Numerous other oil companies called on the services of Baker & Botts from time to time, but Sinclair, Atlantic, Continental, and Standard of Texas remained among the firm's major oil industry clients for decades.[37]

The retainer agreements with all of these companies were similar to the one with Texaco. Far and away the most common work involved the leasing of lands for oil exploration and production. Much of this service was routine but nonetheless quite demanding. The examination of titles, for example, required meticulous research. In this important aspect of their operations, the major oil companies had little choice but to rely on attorneys well versed in the land laws of each particular state, and Baker & Botts often had so much title work that it threatened to overwhelm the firm's ability to do it.

Even the law concerning titles and leases at times raised important legal questions. The state laws governing the conveyance of land had been enacted in the years before oil and gas were discovered, and these laws required considerable clarification before they could provide a suitable framework for the ex-

102

Part II
A Regional
Firm in a
Maturing
Region,
1915–1929

ploration and production of these minerals. The resulting legal issues were of critical importance to Texas after the turn of the century. Oil, not agriculture, now shaped the state's economic development, and oil exploration could not go forward smoothly until a commonly accepted, legally ratified system of leasing had emerged from cases tried by numerous lawyers and law firms. Baker & Botts joined other firms throughout the state in creating a body of precedents to remove as much uncertainty as possible from the law governing leases. In the process, Baker & Botts participated in several landmark cases.

One of the firm's initial forays came in its representation of the Southern Pacific Railroad, which held title to a significant amount of land and, through its Rio Bravo subsidiary, was a participant in the oil industry. Much of the land was acquired for normal railroad operations, such as easements for rights-of-way. After the discovery of oil, however, some of this land became much more valuable, prompting landholders to demand royalty payments for their mineral rights. The issues were complex. Who had title to land that also had a railroad track running through it? Did the granting of easements by landholders constitute a transfer of mineral rights as well? Either the SP or Texas landholders stood to gain a great deal, depending on how these questions were answered.

The issue was finally decided before the Texas Supreme Court in 1927, with Baker & Botts attorneys arguing for the railroad. In this case, the landowners triumphed. The railroad was forbidden to drill for oil or gas along its right-of-way and was forced to pay six million dollars in royalties.[38] This precedent-setting decision determined that local landowners would participate fully in the windfall resulting from the discovery of oil on their land. In this instance, despite the best efforts of its counsel, the SP was forced to compromise.

Other important decisions went in favor of Baker & Botts's clients. None of the victories was more significant than that in *Texas Company* v. *Davis,* which was decided in 1923. This case helped clarify the legal status of a lease while also helping to define when a lease had been legally abandoned and was therefore available to others. It also saved Texaco an estimated million-dollar judgment. The case involved a lease acquired in 1902, developed briefly, and then abandoned in 1904. Texaco subsequently leased the land in the 1910s and, by drilling deeper than the original lessee, found a valuable deposit of oil.

The lease in question was of a traditional format, its form having been borrowed from those widely used in the late nineteenth century in the Pennsylvania oil fields. Under this agreement, a lessee retained rights for twenty-five years on the condition that wells were to be drilled on the property. Fourteen years after vacating the property, the original lessee brought suit requesting reimbursement from Texaco for the value of oil produced. The lower courts supported this position, and Baker & Botts attorney Clarence Wharton took the lead in attempting to reverse the decision on appeal.

Wharton faced a difficult challenge, but he specialized in winning such battles in court during his forty-year career at Baker & Botts. He was one of the most determined and distinguished litigators at the early-twentieth-century Texas bar, and he became one of the visible symbols of Baker & Botts's excellence before juries. He was invited to join the firm in 1902, after Edwin Parker had observed him in action in the courtroom. A short, round man who used an ever-present cane to punctuate his points, Wharton quickly became a favorite of Baker & Botts clients in need of an advocate before a judge and jury.

In the *Texas Company* v. *Davis* case, Wharton found the winning ground in a common law precedent for a "determinable fee estate," one that automatically terminated by its own limitations without the necessity of any notice, demand, or suit. Under this theory of the nature of a lease, the court found an implied limitation on the continuation of the lessee's title when he or she was shown to have abandoned the development of the property. Subsequent cases amplified this ruling by holding that after the discovery of oil on a property the lessee's rights were contingent on "reasonable diligence" in continued development, a phrase that came to be legally defined as continuing to produce oil in paying quantities.[39]

According to A. W. Walker, Jr., longtime specialist in oil and gas law at the University of Texas Law School, the decision in *Texas Company* v. *Davis* and related cases "established the basic nature of an oil and gas lessee's estate in Texas." These decisions represented a compromise among conflicting interests under which local landowners retained the legal title to their lands while leasing minerals extracted from them for specific purposes under specific conditions. In Wharton's words: "Henceforth in Texas, an oil lease is a deed, and the title that it passes may be helpful to the oil industry."[40]

104

Part II
A Regional
Firm in a
Maturing
Region,
1915–1929

These decisions hastened the development of Texas oil lands by favoring active developers over passive ones. They also removed much of the existing uncertainty over the legal rights of both lessor and lessee, thereby encouraging development to proceed under more clearly defined rules known to all parties— or at least to those who had a good lawyer. More than a few landowners no doubt cursed the lawyers of the major oil companies, though as the Southern Pacific case demonstrated, the big corporations did not always win. What gradually emerged was a system of clearly defined rights to a valuable resource. By helping to resolve the many legal disputes that arose during the production of this valuable mineral, Baker & Botts and other Texas firms facilitated the flow of the state's vast oil reserves to market.

Large deposits of natural gas also were discovered in the rush to develop oil reserves, and Baker & Botts gradually became deeply involved with the corporations that grew to produce and distribute gas. The natural gas industry developed more slowly than did oil. Transportation was the major constraint. Gas was more difficult to ship via pipelines than was oil, which could also be transported easily by oceangoing tankers, railroad tank cars, and trucks. The technology needed to build and operate long-distance gas pipelines emerged relatively slowly, limiting the market. Texas had a big stake in the development of that technology and thus of the industry because the state supplied at least 30 percent of the nation's supply of this valuable fuel.[41]

In the late nineteenth century, "gas" still meant the product manufactured from coal, which is what a Baker & Botts client, Houston Gas and Fuel, distributed in the city. After the turn of the century, however, local fields quickly made natural gas available to nearby factories and homes. Each new gas field discovered in the region increased the interest of potential investors in gas pipelines, since the large expenditures required for the construction of such lines could be justified only if a large volume of gas would be available for many years. As the industry grew, Baker & Botts had occasion to represent both buyers and sellers of the resource.

The firm's early involvement in this industry climaxed when it played an important role in the creation of the United Gas Corporation. In 1930 this combine amalgamated over forty operating concerns under the auspices of Electric Bond and Share Company, the giant utility holding company based in Chicago and long served by Baker & Botts. The most important of the constituent parts of United Gas was provided by the Moody-Seagraves interests. Controlled by W. L. Moody III of Galveston and O. R. Seagraves of Houston, these properties included pipelines running from the Jennings field in southwestern Texas to Monterrey, Mexico, Austin, and San Antonio, as well as lines from Corpus Christi to Houston, and from Shreveport to Beaumont. In all, they constituted one of the largest gas pipeline systems in the country at the time. Moody-Seagraves had set out to expand its operations further by purchasing the gas properties of Texaco when that company decided to retire temporarily from the gas business. Armed with an option to purchase the holdings of Texaco's subsidiary, Magnolia Gas Company, for fifty million dollars the Galveston-based gas concern moved in 1928 to incorporate a new company for its many properties, the United Gas Company.[42]

This ambitious project needed a level of financing not easily available in Texas, particularly after the stock market panic of 1929. Up to this point, Moody-Seagraves had relied on Vinson & Elkins for legal representation. But Baker & Botts, with its numerous connections outside of the Houston economy, had access to the capital and contacts the Moody-Seagraves interests now needed. Calling on former Baker & Botts managing partner Ralph Feagin, who in 1929 had become a vice-president of EBASCO, Moody-Seagraves and associates formulated a plan whereby EBASCO would advance funds needed for the consolidation. In turn, EBASCO would become the major owner of United.[43]

Securing this loan and effecting the consolidation involved important questions of state law, particularly regarding the antitrust statutes of Texas. Feagin turned to his old partners at Baker & Botts, and attorneys Garwood and Parish journeyed to New York to meet with the EBASCO managers. They feared that the consolidation of so many gas properties, some of which had been in competition, might contravene the state antitrust laws. Based on their long experience with these issues, they suggested that Moody-Seagraves could avoid legal entanglements simply by dissolving the existing organizations and transferring their assets to a new corporation. Though critics of big business might complain that such action circumvented the existing laws, in fact, as the lawyers pointed out, the Texas antitrust statute had to be strictly and narrowly applied, lest it contravene such basic rights as the ability to dispose freely of one's property. Baker &

106

Part II

A Regional
Firm in a
Maturing
Region,
1915–1929

Botts thus found for its client a legal loophole that enabled it to consolidate the several companies in the gas industry.

After securing the contract that brought together the Magnolia and the Moody-Seagraves properties with EBASCO money, Baker & Botts lawyers went to work adding other gas interests to the new combine. Through its subsidiary, Electric Power and Light, EBASCO had itself entered the natural gas business some years earlier at the massive Monroe, Louisiana, field. In 1929 EBASCO had consolidated these properties with those of the Palmer interests from Chicago. In 1930 the EBASCO-Palmer enterprise, Louisiana Gas and Fuel, was folded into the United Gas Company, and the addition of a final piece of property, the Northern Texas Utilities Company, serving parts of the Texas Panhandle, completed the formation of United Gas.[44]

Through its holding of securities exchanged for its original loan, EBASCO's subsidiary, Electric Power and Light, became the majority owner of United Gas. The distant utility company helped to reorganize United's operations on a functional basis and simplify its structure. Over forty units were consolidated, all under one major operating company, United Gas Public Service Company.[45] Baker & Botts helped to carry out the reorganization and Ralph Feagin served as the first president of the company.

In the 1930s United Gas became one of the largest handlers of natural gas in the nation. It continued to grow by absorbing smaller companies in its region and by supplying larger and larger amounts of natural gas to customers within reach of its extensive distribution network. Baker & Botts did substantial legal work in these consolidations, investigating titles, settling claims, and conveying property.[46] As United Gas's pipeline system spread across Texas, Louisiana, Mississippi, Alabama, and Florida, Baker & Botts's name and influence spread with it. Houston and Baker & Botts were at the center of the United Gas network. In this case, the law firm was not out in the hinterlands looking to the East for guidance; instead, Baker & Botts was helping to shape a vital, rapidly expanding industry whose sprawling network of pipelines was integrating the gas fields of the Southwest with the growing complex of gas-burning factories and buildings in the region.

From oil-leasing cases in the Permian Basin of West Texas to the activities of United Gas in Shreveport, Louisiana, the firm pursued its clients' interests in a widening geographical area. The work in gas and oil provided the firm opportunities to earn large fees and to participate in nationally important cases such as those involving patents for various cracking processes. Oil and gas were the first "local" industries that allowed Baker & Botts to perform on a national stage. In these cases its familiarity with the law and the major actors in these industries made it the equal of the leading law firms in the nation.

The best measure of the impact of the energy industry on Baker & Botts's practice was the career of James L. Shepherd, Jr. He came to the firm in 1917 after graduation from the University of Texas Law School and rose to the status of name partner primarily through his work in oil and gas law. One of the first clients Shepherd worked for was the Sinclair Oil Company. Almost immediately after his arrival at the firm, he began to review all of the cases reported in the advance sheets of the entire National Reporter System and to compile a notebook that cited and analyzed every "current noteworthy decision affecting the law of oil and gas."[47] Until his death in 1964, Shepherd never really abandoned this project, and he became a walking compendium of almost a half century of developments in oil and gas law.

Shepherd's professional life coincided with the heyday of the southwestern petroleum industry, and his knowledge of the industry soon made him one of the nation's top authorities on oil and gas law. He became a leader in the early work of the Section of Mineral Law of the American Bar Association (ABA) and was elected chairman of this section in 1937. Included in his work in the section were various reports on oil and gas law for use by government officials in their efforts to bring order to the chaotic industry in the 1930s.[48] He was the editor of *Legal History of Conservation of Oil and Gas—A Symposium*, a path-breaking and oft-cited compilation of laws and court decisions.[49] In the late 1930s he was appointed to the ABA's House of Delegates and was elected chairman in 1957.

This self-described "lawyer's lawyer" became a symbol of the growing maturity of Baker & Botts, both inside and outside the firm. A tall, slender, distinguished-looking gentleman, Shepherd was known within the firm for his long cigarette holder, his soft felt hats, and his openness to his younger colleagues. A man of genuine good humor, he was a comforting presence within the firm, for he signified that the practice of law at the most demanding levels was compatible with a humane approach to life that included room for humor and friendship. These qualities made him an important figure in the internal life of the firm.

108

Part II

A Regional
Firm in a
Maturing
Region,
1915–1929

Shepherd's visible presence at the highest levels of the American Bar Association also made him an important symbol of the growing national standing of Baker & Botts. His work was backed by the efforts of numerous oil and gas specialists within the firm, and his personal reputation was matched by the firm's overall performance in this area. While oil and gas law was neither the first nor the only field of excellence developed at Baker & Botts, it involved the firm with the first locally based industries to become major factors in the national economy. Houston became the "nation's oil capital," gaining an identity as the central city in the production of a vital commodity. Baker & Botts went along for the ride, using its close connections and intimate knowledge of the oil and gas industries to advance toward a new status as a leading national law firm. With this new status came a new scale of operations—and a need to find more effective ways to manage the growing organization.

A Permanent Institution

B ETWEEN 1920 AND 1930 Houston experienced its most rapid growth. Prepared by the rail lines, utility systems, and the ship channel for its emergence as the major industrial power in the Southwest, Houston burst into the national spotlight with its spectacular oil industry. Migrants were drawn to the city from surrounding rural areas and from other sections of the nation. The ship channel made the city a thriving port and a center of national and international trade; the giant oil refineries and other factories that sprang up along the waterway turned the region into a manufacturing center. A wave of office construction produced an impressive downtown skyline visible for miles on the flat coastal plain.[1] The population surged to almost three hundred thousand by 1930, and boosters sang the praises of the "Chicago of the South." Their boasts seemed less hollow when the Democratic party chose Houston as the site of its 1928 nominating convention.

Riding this tide of economic development, Baker & Botts doubled in size between 1920 and 1940. Though it was by no means the only prosperous law firm in Houston in these years, it remained the leader in its city, region, and state. Underlying Baker & Botts's growing maturity was a more diversified client base. Work for the Southern Pacific remained important, but numerous other clients now helped shape the organization's development. The firm's annual "listing" in the legal directories of the time (fig. 1) reflected this diversity. The Martindale-Hubbell directory provided a ready reference of law firms throughout the nation, and Baker & Botts designed its listing to give those who looked through the directory in search of a Houston-based law firm a good sense of the nature of its practice. The 1927 listing— the closest thing to advertising that law firms of the day were

110

Part II

A Regional

Firm in a

Maturing

Region,

1915–1929

APPENDIX.   609

TEXAS.

Cable Address: "Boterlove"

BAKER, BOTTS, PARKER & GARWOOD

Esperson Building

HOUSTON, TEXAS

Founded in 1866

JAMES A. BAKER	HIRAM M. GARWOOD	JESSE ANDREWS
CLARENCE R. WHARTON	CLARENCE L. CARTER	JULES H. TALLICHET
WALTER H. WALNE	PALMER HUTCHESON	HOMER L. BRUCE
W. ALVIS PARISH	JAS. A. BAKER, JR.	RODMAN S. COSBY
WINSTON CARTER	BRADY COLE	RAYMOND E. DRAPER
A. H. FULBRIGHT	CALVIN B. GARWOOD	ST. JOHN GARWOOD
S. H. GERMAN	CORNELIUS E. LOMBARDI	YORICK D. MATHES
CARL D. MATZ	H. MALCOLM LOVETT	JAMES L. SHEPHERD, JR.
BARKSDALE STEVENS	FLAVEL ROBERTSON	L. G. ZINNECKER

COUNSELORS AND ATTORNEYS AT LAW

GENERAL PRACTICE IN ALL COURTS

Specialize in: Corporation Law in all its phases; Legal Supervision of Domestic and Foreign Corporations; Mortgages and Bond Issues; Real Estate Law and Title Examinations; Insurance Law; Admiralty and Maritime Law; Law of Oil and Gas; Public Utilities

Reliable Correspondents Throughout Texas
(Small Collections not desired)

REPRESENTATIVE CLIENTS FOR WHOM FIRM IS GENERAL COUNSEL:

Bowman-Hicks Lumber Co.	Houston Gas & Fuel Company	South Texas Commercial Nationa Bank of Houston
W. T. Carter & Brother	Houston Lighting & Power Co.	
Lynch Davidson & Co.	Houston Post-Dispatch	South Texas Cotton Oil Co.
Eastern Texas Electric Co	The Long-Bell Lumber Company	South Texas Imp. & Mach. Co.
El Paso Electric Railway Co.	Louisiana Central Lumber Co.	South Texas Utilities Co.
First Texas Joint Stock Land Bank of Houston	Louisiana Long Leaf Lumber Co.	Southern Pacific Lines (Texas & New Orleans R. R. Co.)
Forest Lumber Company	Magnolia Provision Company	Stone & Webster Interests in Texas
Galveston Electric Company	Merchants & Planters Oil Co.	
Guardian Trust Co. of Houston	National Bond & Mortgage Co.	Sugarland Industries
Gulf States Utilities Co.	Peden Iron & Steel Company	Texas Creamery Company
F. W. Heitmann Company	W. R. Pickering Lumber Co.	Texas Gulf Sulphur Co. in Texas
Houston Car Wheel & Mach. Co.	Wm. M. Rice Institute	Trinity County Lumber Co.
Houston Cotton Oil Mill	The Second Natl. Bank of Houston	Western Public Service Company
Houston Drug Company	Sinclair Oil Interests in Texas	
Houston Electric Company		

SOME OTHER REPRESENTATIVE CLIENTS:

Aetna Life Insurance Company	Electric Bond & Share Co.	M-K-T Railroad Co. of Texas
American Brake Shoe & Foundry Co.	Equitable Trust Co. of N. Y.	Morris & Company
American Bridge Company	Estate of Dellora R. Gates	Mortgage & Securities Company of New Orleans
American Construction Co.	Fairbanks Co.	National Biscuit Company
American Express Company	Famous Players-Lasky Corp.	National Tube Company
American Railway Express Co.	Federal Steel Company	Ocean Accident & Guarantee Corporation, Ltd.
American Steel & Wire Co.	Film Board of Trade	Oriental Textile Mills
American Sugar Refining Co.	Firestone Tire & Rubber Co.	Pacific Fruit Express Company
Anheuser-Busch Interests	First National Co., St. Louis	Prest-O-Lite Company
Appleton & Cox, Inc.	N. K. Fairbank Company	Royal Dutch-Shell Interests
Armour & Company	Ford, Bacon & Davis	Southern Casualty Company
Associated Oil Co.	Ford Motor Company	S. W. Straus & Company
Atlantic Refining Company	General Cigar Company, Inc.	Swift & Company
Blair & Company	General Electric Company	The Texas Company
Brown Brothers & Company	Globe Indemnity Company	Texon Oil & Land Company
Burton Lumber Corporation	Guaranty Trust Co. of N. Y.	Texas Pacific Coal & Oil Co.
Carnegie Steel Co.	Halsey Stuart & Co.	Texas Portland Cement Co.
Central Coal & Coke Co.	Hartford Accident & Indem. Co.	Travelers Insurance Company
Central Union Trust Co. of N.Y.	Indemnity Insurance Co. of N. A.	United Cigar Stores
Chicago Bridge & Iron Works	Insull Interests	United Fruit Company
Chipman Chemical Eng. Co.	International Paper Company	United States Rubber Company
Coca-Cola Company	Interstate Trust & Banking Co.	United States Steel Corporation
Columbia Casualty Co.	Johns-Manville Company	Western Union Telegraph Co.
Consumers Cotton Oil Co.	Johnson & Higgins	Westinghouse Electric & Manu- facturing Co.
Crane Company	Louis K. Liggett Company	Youngstown Steel Products Co.
De La Vergne Mch. Co.	Louisiana State Rice Milling Co.	
Dodge Bros.	Marland Oil Company	
	Maryland Casualty Company	

KANSAS CITY OFFICE:

The Firm also maintains offices at 1314 R. A. Long Building, Kansas City, Mo., where it is engaged in the general practice, the following—for whom it is General Counsel—being among its clients there: The Long-Bell Lumber Company and allied Companies; W. R. Pickering Lumber Company and allied Companies; Bowman-Hicks Lumber Company; Louisiana Central Lumber Company; Louisiana Long Leaf Lumber Company; Forest Lumber Company and allied Companies

Compilers of Texas Laws for Hubbell's for thirty-one years
Thirty-ninth annual card in Hubbell's

Baker & Botts listing in Martindale-Hubble Directory, 1927

allowed to release to the public—provides a snapshot of the firm's organization and practice. Prominently displayed was the fact that the firm had been founded more than sixty years before; a list of twenty-seven lawyers indicated that it was large and well established. Although proclaiming its commitment to a "general practice in all courts," the firm nonetheless made clear that it was not interested in all types of work: "Small Collections not desired." Not evident from the listing, but implied by its tone, was the firm's decision to avoid cases involving divorces and other personal matters, which were a staple of traditional partnerships. The entries after "specialize in" suggest the types of law preferred by Baker & Botts, a preference best summarized by the initial entry: "Corporation Law in all its phases."

What this meant in practice was captured in the extensive list of "representative clients" of the firm. The entries for few other Texas firms included such a detailed roster of clients, but Baker & Botts's leadership in its region was embodied in the blue-chip client list it had developed over decades of hard work. Enumerated among those for whom the firm was general counsel were the major local utilities, banks, lumber companies, and oil companies, as well as two national businesses, the Southern Pacific and Stone & Webster. Over 50 percent of firm income derived from railroad, utility, and oil clients.[2] There were as well many more national corporations for whom Baker & Botts worked on individual cases as these arose. These clients, ranging from Aetna Life Insurance Company to Westinghouse Electric & Manufacturing Co., served as a strong argument that Baker & Botts was the law firm of choice for leading northeastern companies seeking legal counsel in the Gulf Coast area. Reinforcing the firm's claim to be the leading corporate law firm in Texas was the final line of the listing: "Compilers of Texas Laws for Hubbell's for thirty-one years."

Implied but not stated in the list of clients was the fact that Baker & Botts remained extensively involved in litigation in the 1920s. By that time, a growing portion of its practice was "office law" of a sort common on Wall Street. The preparation of legal documents required for a variety of business activities, from lending agreements for banks to leasing agreements for oil companies, involved highly specialized work that demanded meticulous attention to detail but seldom required appearances before juries.

Although this office practice was growing, Baker & Botts con-

112

Part II

A Regional

Firm in a

Maturing

Region,

1915–1929

tinued to be heavily engaged in litigation. Most of the lawyers spent some portion of their time in trial work. The firm's work for the Southern Pacific had always included a large number of damage suits, which required the lawyers to hone their courtroom skills. Similar skills were utilized in much of the work for the local street railway company and especially in the services provided after the 1910s for numerous insurance companies. Baker & Botts represented many large insurance enterprises, some in general insurance business and others in the more specialized field of maritime insurance.

The most significant of these clients was Travelers Insurance Company. By the 1920s Travelers had become an important part of Baker & Botts's practice. Not only did the company's business generate steady and profitable legal work, but it also provided an excellent training ground for litigators. The insurance docket gave young lawyers the opportunity to prepare and argue cases before juries. This work could be time consuming and tedious, but it was also quite useful in developing trial skills. At this time the step from a routine damage suit to more complicated business litigation was not so very long, and many of the same courtroom attributes led to success whether the case in question involved five hundred dollars or fifty thousand dollars. Several generations of Baker & Botts trial lawyers received their "postgraduate" training in litigation on the cases of Travelers and other insurance companies, and this shared experience helped build two key attributes of a successful litigator: combativeness and experience in dealing with juries.

As it grew larger and more diversified, Baker & Botts began to organize its internal affairs more systematically, using methods similar to those adopted in this era by other leading corporate law practices throughout the nation. The firm's tone, its internal organization, and its methods for recruiting new lawyers and clients marked it as different from most other law firms in the region. Sustained growth exerted the primary pressure for change. The number of lawyers employed by the firm went from two in 1866, to four in 1900, to twenty-seven in 1923, to thirty in 1933 (table 2). Gross revenues paralleled this expansion, surging from $48,000 to $464,000 in the first twenty years of the century and then remaining in the range of $700,000 to $900,000 per year from the mid-1920s until the late 1930s (table 3). Such growth stretched the loose, informal bonds of the traditional partnership past their breaking point, forcing the partners to forge more

TABLE 2
NUMBER OF LAWYERS AND EMPLOYEES
January 1 Each Year

Year	No. of Lawyers	No. of Stenog- raphers	Others	Total
1918	16	12	7	35
1923	27	17	12	56
1928	25	18	14	57
1933	30	18	14	62
1934	30	18	14	62
1935	29	19	14	62
1936	34	20	14	68
1937	35	21	19	75
1938	39	25	21	85
1939	42	26	22	90

Source: Ralph Feagin notebook, BBHC.

formal, systematic bonds. As in many other business and professional concerns in this era, traditional, highly personal methods of organization gave way to large-scale, hierarchical systems capable of coordinating the activities of more individuals engaged in increasingly specialized pursuits.

One important focus of change was the office of the managing partner. In the 1910s and 1920s the firm's first managing partner, Edwin B. Parker, sought to create an organization that would function more smoothly than the loosely coordinated, individualistic partnership. At times Parker borrowed ideas and procedures directly from his counterparts at other firms, but in general, the process of adaptation was home grown; Parker, the primary builder of Baker & Botts's new organizational structure, was personally and temperamentally the "organization man."

Indeed, in appearance and manner Parker probably "blended in" more comfortably in New York and Washington, D.C., than in turn-of-the-century, frontier Houston. Given to dressing in a cape and spats, carrying a cane, and sporting a continental-style beard, he was a fine specimen of late Victorian manhood. Besides his varied legal career representing oil, utility, railroad,

114

Part II
A Regional
Firm in a
Maturing
Region,
1915–1929

and banking clients, he held a variety of highly visible positions in business and government. At various times he served as the president of Houston Lighting & Power, general counsel for Texaco, and a vice-president of two major Houston banks. As a priorities commissioner on the War Industries Board, Parker had played an important role in guiding the nation's industries through mobilization. After the war, he served as head of the U.S. Liquidation Commission and as umpire for the U.S.-German Mixed Claims Commission. If Captain Baker was the symbol of the firm's presence in Houston, surely Parker was the symbol of its growing presence on the national scene.

With his unshakable faith in hard work, self-improvement, and organization, Parker spearheaded a movement that brought far-reaching changes in the structure of the firm while he maintained a tight grip on the process of change. By all accounts, Parker relished this work, bringing to it a zeal for order and standardization that at times troubled those under his authority. He had volunteered for the job, and his partners had readily agreed on both the need for management and on his acceptability as managing partner. From 1912 until his departure from the firm in 1926, Parker used every tool at his disposal to fashion an organization capable of retaining the high standards established by the firm's founders while also allowing Baker & Botts to grow larger and its lawyers more specialized. He sought to embody in rules and procedures the tone and the standards of a new sort of professionalism, one consistent with both traditional values and the new demands being placed on ever larger, more specialized law firms.

Not surprisingly, Parker from time to time attracted the ire of his partners. He was relentlessly officious and at times pompous. In a steady stream of instructions to his partners, he took to an extreme the stilted style of speaking and writing characteristic of the 1920s. It was not enough that he goaded his partners in an extended memorandum to follow correct bureaucratic procedures in keeping detailed work records, he was also compelled to note in passing the joys of the "delightful summer weather" in Houston in late July. He concluded by informing his colleagues that he had set aside the hour from 5:30 to 6:30 each afternoon to confer with "any member of the organization" who needed to talk with him. As this memo made its rounds of the senior partners, one added a note: "You know I am something of a philosopher and have learned to take things as they come but this whole circular has overcome me with an intense weariness. It will no doubt be a source of amusement to you."[3]

Yet despite the sniping, the partners accepted the fact that Baker & Botts needed a capable, experienced manager to steer it through the transition from a small, personal partnership to a large, modern legal organization. The gentlemanly Captain Baker often tempered Parker's directives by temporarily cushioning individuals from their impact. But Baker understood that Parker's innovations were the wave of the future. Tenfold growth made a more systematic approach to management necessary. Parker also had the active support of most of the partners who entered the firm after 1900. These men had been trained in law schools; they regularly worked inside large corporations; they were closely tied through professional and correspondent relationships to the changing world of corporate law. Several of them, notably Walter Walne and Ralph Feagin, joined Parker in aggressively advocating far-reaching changes in the firm's organization.

Because of the basic nature and traditions of a legal partnership, Parker had to persuade his colleagues of the need for change and then point the direction in which they should move. Only when—and if—the majority of the partners decided to follow would organizational change be absorbed into the daily life of the firm and reflected in the crucial issues of firm finances and the recruitment of new lawyers and new clients.

Parker fired his opening volley in the battle for greater coordination in 1912, when he put together the firm's first formal plan of organization. According to his plan, the managing partner's role was "to see that neither any individual nor the Organization as a whole is to any extent going around in a circle."[4] He set forth the primary duties of each person employed by Baker & Botts, from Captain Baker to the most recently hired secretary. This first plan merely outlined the existing divisions of labor within the firm, noting, for example, which lawyers were primarily responsible for which specific clients and categories of clients.

Having put everyone in his or her proper place, Parker then moved to improve communications among the different parts of the organization. One traditional avenue was well trod by Parker, who poured forth a torrent of memoranda "To All in the Office." Ad hoc communications were insufficient for his purposes, however, and in 1920 he established the *Office Review,* an

116

Part II

A Regional
Firm in a
Maturing
Region,
1915–1929

internal newsletter published every two weeks. The pages of the *Office Review* contained material of general interest to members of the firm about the activities of their colleagues. It also served as an office bulletin board, with notices of meetings and changes in office procedures. A regularly published index enabled Baker & Botts attorneys to recover previously published information about a client quickly. Similarly indexed data on correspondent firms allowed the attorneys to maintain up-to-date working ties with law firms in other parts of the nation. The names of large law firms regularly changed as name partners were added or dropped, and the *Review* gave Baker & Botts a means of keeping up with those developments.

Now, too, the firm began to hold regular meetings, at first monthly, then bimonthly, and then monthly. The manifest goal was to encourage communication; the latent objective was probably to build a unified firm culture. While they lasted, these meetings were intriguing affairs, part proving ground for young lawyers, part forum for exchanging information about trends in the legal profession, and part occasion for defining the values and attitudes of the firm. Held at The Oaks, the home of Edwin Parker and subsequently of Captain Baker, these gatherings served both social and legal functions. They forced all members of the growing organization to meet regularly outside the office while also offering a specified time for serious, systematic discussions of legal developments.

The heart of these meetings over the next twenty years was the review of noteworthy judicial decisions.[5] Each lawyer making a presentation was advised "to state *concisely* and clearly the substance of both the facts involved and the rule or rules of law announced." The leading specialists in the firm generally reviewed important cases in their area of expertise. Thus in the early meetings, Hiram Garwood reviewed noteworthy decisions of the U.S. Supreme Court; Clarence Wharton, decisions affecting public utilities; Jules Tallichet, tax-related decisions. In addition, the managing partner assigned to younger lawyers the task of studying the advance sheets of the *Southwestern Reporter,* identifying each Texas case, and preparing to "present in chronological order all noteworthy decisions."[6] These summaries no doubt were of practical value, although those who were specializing in relatively narrow fields must have grown impatient with discussions of other areas of the law. But the meetings actually advanced a broad, underlying message: we are all a part of a unified practice of law, and all parts of this practice are of value to all lawyers in the firm. Parker sent this message to the various members of the firm in a variety of ways. He found the regular meeting "particularly helpful to the younger members of the organization" as a "potent force in instilling THE FIRM spirit in the organization as a whole."[7]

Parker's preachments hammered home the fact that the role of the individual lawyer within the firm was changing. No longer was the individual practitioner the focus of attention; rather, the firm was becoming the primary center of activity. Parker was particularly emphatic on the implications of this change: "We must keep constantly in mind that our *unit* is THE FIRM, not the individual member thereof. In shaping our course of conduct we must consider first, last and always, not our own pleasure, convenience or interest, but what will most promote the interest of and strengthen the firm from both a professional and pecuniary standpoint."[8] He repeated this idea regularly: "Bear in mind that we are all working not as individuals, but as a firm. The individual must be subordinated to the firm."[9]

Symbolic of this sentiment was a procedure instituted in the first official plan of organization in 1912. After that time all letters were submitted to Parker and his assistant for examination before being signed with the firm name, instead of the name of the lawyer who prepared them. Thus, the lawyers had to be willing to give up a portion of their traditional independence, to "subordinate" their personal success to that of the firm.

The trade-off was straightforward. In return for the loss of autonomy, individuals gained the benefits of affiliation with an institution that enjoyed ongoing client relationships and a standing within the legal profession that no single lawyer could attain. Parker and his colleagues stressed this point in their presentations to the younger lawyers. As Hiram Garwood explained in 1913: "When the present of a life or a business grows logically out of its past and is logically prepared for its future, it rises above the dignity of an episode and becomes an institution." Garwood had a lofty view of Baker & Botts in 1913, which at that time remained a small collection of lawyers practicing in Houston, Texas: "I have always thought of it [Baker & Botts], not as a mere temporary association of individuals, however pleasant or profitable, but as a permanent institution, just as Harvard and the Bank of England is an institution, with a strength, a life and individuality made up from, yet greater than, all or any of its

118

Part II
A Regional
Firm in a
Maturing
Region,
1915–1929

TABLE 3
ANNUAL EARNINGS

Year	Gross Income of Firm
1895	$ 32,000
1900	48,000
1905	112,000
Average, 1910–1920	250,000
Average, 1921–1930	625,000
1930	724,000
1931	575,000
1932	550,000
1933	525,000
1934	600,000
1935	800,000
1936	750,000
1937	883,000
1938	757,000
1939 (est.)	600,000
Average, 1930–1939	676,000

Source: Ralph Feagin notebook, BBHC.
Note: Income is rounded to nearest thousand.

members."[10] Parker reiterated this message, pointing out that the firm was "a permanent, self perpetuating INSTITUTION . . . composed of strong active units."[11]

To strengthen the institution, Parker regularly chided his colleagues to follow office procedures that many of the older lawyers viewed as unnecessarily bureaucratic. He stressed the necessity of professional letter writing and strict adherence to routine office procedures and included rules requiring lawyers to keep written records of all billable hours, to sign in and out of the office, and to observe proper telephone etiquette. All of these procedures were meant to protect and strengthen Baker & Botts's hard-won reputation as the leading representative for modern corporations in Houston. The resulting image of efficiency and professional competence must surely have made the firm seem even more familiar and trustworthy to its primary clients.

New procedures of governance emerged as the firm grew. On the vital issue of the division of profits, fundamental changes took place in the period from 1912, the date of the writing of the first detailed partnership agreement, to 1941, the date of the deaths of two longtime partners (Baker and Wharton). Although most of the partners helped shape this transition, Ralph Feagin played a pivotal role during much of the pre–World War II era.[12] Feagin's love of statistics and passion for detail made him a logical candidate for monitoring the firm's finances. Originally brought into the firm by Edwin Parker, Feagin remained a protégé of Parker until the latter's withdrawal from Baker & Botts. Later, as managing partner, Feagin continued to administer many of the procedures established by his mentor. With the aid of an assistant managing partner and a nonlawyer financial officer, Feagin directed the adjustments made in the financial aspects of the partnership agreements. As the detail man who managed the firm's financial performance as well as the distribution of financial rewards, Feagin shaped firm policy on this vital issue for more than a quarter of a century.

To appreciate the magnitude of the changes, one need only compare the financial affairs of Baker & Botts at the turn of the century with those of the firm on the eve of World War II. In 1904 the firm's financial affairs were neatly summarized in the following entry from the partnership agreement notebook:

1904

Net earnings divided:
J. A. B.—14/20
E. B. P.—6/20

H. M. G. was paid a straight salary of $5,000. J. A. and C. R. W. each received a salary of $2,400.

J. A. B. and E. B. P. were paid equally six per cent interest on the aggregate fixed value of the library ($12,165.56), this interest being treated as an expense of doing business.

Thus, at this early date, Captain Baker (J. A. B.) enjoyed a 70 percent interest in the firm's net earnings and Parker (E. B. P.) was the only other partner receiving a percentage. The apprentice lawyers were not yet full partners, and they received straight salaries based on their experience and skills. Finally, the library was the joint property of the two senior partners, not the collective property of the firm. As these arrangements indicated,

120

Part II
A Regional
Firm in a
Maturing
Region,
1915–1929

the partnership was the sum of the activities of the individual partners.

The firm's growth during the next four decades forced a change in its financial affairs (table 3). Because there was an ever-growing pie to divide, the process of change was not especially painful. But clearly it was necessary. The division of net earnings became ever more complex, and in 1936 the partnership agreement was revised. The obligation of individual members of the firm to purchase the stock of any member who died or withdrew was altered so that the obligation fell to the firm, not to individual partners. This marked a significant departure, since the firm could now acquire shares to be held and distributed when needed to accommodate new members. In 1912 the members of the firm had done much the same thing in purchasing Baker's and Parker's interest in the library, making it the property of the firm.

The important transitions the firm was going through sometimes generated tensions that threatened to split it apart, not the least because money and pride were often involved. The issue of branching could, for instance, be highly divisive. The movement of a client or the pursuit of a client's interest in new areas of practice at times presented opportunities for branching that were hard to ignore. Yet faraway branches conflicted with the firm's oft-repeated claim that it was a Houston institution above all else, an idea that was part of the self-identity that held the firm together. In its early history, Baker & Botts had two experiences with branching, one modestly successful, if only because it was limited, the other larger and more significant, but almost the cause of a split in the partnership.

Baker & Botts's first branch (opened in 1920) conducted operations in Galveston. The completion of the Houston ship channel presented new opportunities in admiralty insurance. The successful settlement of claims arising from the operations of ships moving between Houston and other ports required many of the same skills developed by Baker & Botts in its general insurance practice, and the firm forcefully entered this new area after World War I. Since the admiralty court for the region was in the old port city of Galveston, some forty miles southeast of Houston, Baker & Botts initially entered a joint venture with a prominent Galveston lawyer, Judge H. C. Hughes. Under the direction of Walter Walne in Houston, Hughes cooperated with Baker & Botts in developing a lucrative admiralty practice. This arrangement was not quite the equivalent of a modern-day branch office, since Hughes was not admitted as a partner. Instead, the firm agreed to split fees with its Galveston representative and to cooperate in building up a reliable client base. Frequent trips by Hughes and several Baker & Botts partners to leading admiralty law and insurance companies in New York City helped establish needed contacts in this field; at the same time, much new business flowed from the tanker operations of oil businesses represented by the firm. The resulting work remained an important part of the firm's practice into the post–World War II era, and the Galveston branch did not create any difficult problems, in part because the admiralty work was not voluminous.

More troublesome was the Kansas City branch. Noted at the bottom of the 1927 legal directory (fig. 1) is the listing "Kansas City Office," with a list of several lumber companies. This short description of the firm's first true branch office is accurate but incomplete. Missing is any sign of the intense controversy that surrounded the office from its creation in 1920 through its disaffiliation in 1936. Among the partners in Houston, there were hot debates over the propriety of developing a permanent presence in Kansas City to serve clients with only weak ties to the Gulf Coast. While forcing the members to take a hard look at the costs and benefits of expansion beyond Houston, the controversy also forced the firm to alter traditional assumptions about the role of the individual lawyer within a modern, large-scale legal organization.

Long Bell Lumber Company was the client that led Baker & Botts to Kansas City. From its headquarters there, Long-Bell acquired, processed, and shipped lumber made from southern pine. Baker & Botts first represented the company early in the twentieth century and became its general counsel in the 1910s. At first, Edwin Parker and Hiram Garwood served Long-Bell from Houston, with frequent trips to Kansas City. Both turned down requests by R. A. Long, the company's chairman from 1921 to 1934, to create a permanent office in Kansas City.[15] Jesse Andrews took responsibility for this client when Parker went off to Washington during World War I. He began spending long periods in Kansas City in 1918, before moving there in 1920. Long-Bell generated sufficient work to occupy Andrews full time, and he became a close legal and business adviser to R. A. Long. Aside from the normal work of representing a large corporation, Andrews supervised the activities of a network of lawyers spread

122

Part II
A Regional
Firm in a
Maturing
Region,
1915–1929

throughout the pine belt to handle the lumber company's local affairs.[14] This work was in keeping with Baker & Botts's Houston practice, since the firm represented numerous Texas lumber companies and since the pine forests that supplied Long-Bell were located in part in Texas.

The work of Andrews's Kansas City office grew steadily in volume and diversity. In the early 1920s Long-Bell established a substantial operation in Longview, Washington, a city that the company created as its base of operations in the Northwest. For a time Baker & Botts employed a full-time lawyer in Longview, and Andrews broached the possibility of establishing a permanent branch office in Washington state.[15] At the same time, several other lumber company clients began to provide even more work for Andrews and the new lawyers he hired to assist him in Kansas City.

Although most of the Houston partners urged Andrews not to build a general practice in Kansas City, he gradually accumulated other clients. Most spectacular was the new work involving the construction of the Bagnell Dam, a thirty-five million dollar project that created what was then the largest artificial lake in the world, the Lake of the Ozarks in south-central Missouri. Built from 1929 to 1931, the Bagnell Dam generated a number of controversial suits between the dam's owner, Union Electric Light and Power Company of Saint Louis, and a variety of people with interests in the area flooded by the dam. This work was consistent with Baker & Botts's long history of service to utilities, and Walter Walne spent considerable time away from the Houston office with Andrews on the Bagnell Dam cases.[16] Long-Bell Lumber Company remained the primary client of the Kansas City office, but Andrews oversaw a gradual diversification at what was referred to in Kansas City newspapers as Baker, Botts, Parker & Garwood of Kansas City.

Both the personnel and the revenues of the Kansas City office expanded. In 1923 the office employed four lawyers and a law clerk, along with three stenographers; by the early 1930s there were eight lawyers and eight stenographers. Gross income rose from about $75,000 in the early 1920s to as much as $198,000 in 1935, when Long-Bell fell into bankruptcy and had to be reorganized. This meant that the Kansas City branch was approximately 25 to 30 percent as large as its eighty-year-old progenitor in Houston.[17] Yet those in Houston who favored the dissolution of the branch concluded that it was not self-sufficient, that its operations actually decreased the value of their partnership shares. They feared that, despite its strong growth record, it would become an increasingly heavy drain on the overall profitability of the firm.[18]

Other issues had also arisen. In the early 1920s, as Andrews began to hire new lawyers to assist him in Kansas City, he pushed hard and often for them to be admitted as fully participating partners in the Houston firm. His Texas colleagues had no interest in following this course, despite their acknowledgment of the high quality and productivity of the lawyers being hired. Indeed, one reaction (in sharp contradiction to the traditional values of Baker & Botts) was to argue that Andrews could get by with hiring less-expensive lawyers if he would only stick to routine lumber cases and forget about diversifying his practice.[19]

In an effort to solve these problems, Andrews looked for examples of how other major law firms handled the financial issues raised by branch offices, but apparently he found no useful model in an era when branching was rare. He then sought to use comparisons with other firms to justify higher pay for several of his Kansas City associates. In 1923 the closely related questions of participation and compensation were put aside through a compromise that promised members of the Kansas City office both a minimum and a maximum total annual compensation; this package included a guaranteed base salary supplemented by participation in profits from the Kansas City office, but not from the firm as a whole.[20]

This compromise reflected the basic ambivalence of the Houston office toward Andrews's outpost. The partners never seriously considered Kansas City an integral part of the firm. There was no clearer symbol of this than their unwillingness to admit several excellent lawyers employed by Andrews into full participation as partners in Baker & Botts. The Kansas City office would be tolerated for as long as Andrews insisted on remaining there, but it would never be made a fully integrated branch office.

Given this attitude, it was hardly surprising that Baker & Botts made no systematic efforts to coordinate the work of the two offices. The longest step toward consolidation came in December 1923, when all of the lawyers from the Kansas City office attended the firm's annual meeting in Houston and presented reports on their work. Yet instead of goodwill within the firm, this meeting generated a new wave of intense debate about the future of the branch operation. In the mid-1920s, Andrews con-

124

Part II

A Regional
Firm in a
Maturing
Region,
1915–1929

tinued to report regularly on activities in Kansas City in the *Office Review*. As he sought to build support for the full integration of what he considered Baker & Botts–Kansas City, however, his partners on the Gulf Coast grew increasingly insistent that he give up what they considered his personal adventure in Kansas City and return to Houston.

These debates raised fundamental issues about the firm's values as well as about the practical problems of maintaining a branch office. Clarence Wharton and Walter Walne led the continuing effort to dissolve the Kansas City operation, labeling it "illogical and unusual."[21] Indeed, *illogical* was the word most used by the partners to describe the office. Most members of the firm voiced the strong sentiment that the only natural ties between Baker & Botts and Long-Bell had been based on the company's commitment to the southern pine belt; with the movement of the lumber business to the Northwest, this historical tie seemed to be dissolving. The proper response was to complete work for Long-Bell in the South and then close the Kansas City office. It was unwise to follow the company to Washington state, where its business had no logical economic connection to Houston. In the view of all of the partners except Jesse Andrews, a large, ongoing commitment of personnel and resources to either Kansas City or Longview, Washington, was at cross-purposes with one of the core values of the firm—the commitment to Houston. As Parker forcefully argued: "The firm will never get very far in building up a general practice outside of Houston that does not naturally tie in with and function with the Houston office."[22]

One complicating factor in this debate was Parker's move in the 1920s to New York City to serve as general counsel for Texaco and his subsequent service in Washington, D.C., as umpire of the Mixed Claims Commission for the United States and Germany. Parker, of course, defended his position in New York as different from that of Andrews in Kansas City. Texaco had general offices and a long history in Houston, argued Parker, and its legal matters were predominantly related to Texas. In addition, Parker cited the enduring connections of Baker & Botts to New York City interests. Yet despite the magnitude of the firm's business activities in New York City, Parker and his partners had never established a permanent office there. Moreover, several partners were so concerned about the possibility of dissipating their firm's strength in Houston that they pushed hard for Parker's return, even though they knew their pressure might force their managing partner to withdraw from Baker & Botts. Clarence Wharton summarized the feelings of many of the partners: "From the standpoint of the firm, I feel that it is a great mistake that you [Parker] and Mr. Andrews are away from Houston. . . . Houston and Texas are growing very rapidly. Our business is growing, and it would be a great contribution to its continued growth if you and Jesse Andrews were continually here in touch with the situation as the rest of us are."[23] Parker ultimately chose to remain in the East to finish his government work on war claims.

Parker's withdrawal in 1926 was a strong testament to the depths of the firm's commitment to Houston. This commitment was powerful enough to force the withdrawal of the man who had become far and away the most visible representative of the firm in both New York and Washington. In the face of such sentiment, the Kansas City branch was doomed. As early as 1925 several major partners were arguing for an ultimatum to Andrews: return to Houston or withdraw from the firm. Although Captain Baker for a time deflected such sentiment, the pressure on Andrews intensified. He refused to bend, but the issue would not go away. It dragged on until, finally, in 1935 the Houston partners issued their ultimatum: return to Houston by 1 January 1936, or withdraw from the firm. After much delay, Andrews moved back to Houston, severing the tie between the Kansas City office and Baker & Botts. Several of the lawyers originally hired by Andrews stayed in the midwestern office and continued to serve many of the same clients under the new firm name of Lombardi & Robertson.[24] But Baker & Botts's first extensive experience with branching had ended.

Looking back on this episode from the perspective of the 1970s and 1980s, one is tempted to conclude that the firm was simply ahead of its time, that it mistakenly gave up a successful branch office because it could not see beyond the traditional concept of a law practice. Such a reading of the past, however, does not do justice to the impact of inherited values on decision making or to the Houston firm's array of opportunities. Baker & Botts's identity as a Houston institution was important. Its success had been built on a blue-chip client base active in its region, and the activities of Andrews in Kansas City—and to some extent those of Parker in New York City—did little to strengthen this client base. When Andrews moved to Kansas City, he withdrew from the board of directors of a major Houston bank, a

126

Part II
A Regional
Firm in a
Maturing
Region,
1915–1929

choice that symbolized opportunities lost on the Gulf Coast. Houston was booming in the 1920s, and the absence of two senior partners left the firm short-handed, particularly in the crucial areas of leadership and business development. With the steady expansion of the Houston economy, the spectacular growth of the region's oil industry, and the absorption of traditional local utility clients into national systems, there was more than enough work from Houston-based clients to occupy all of the energies of the firm. Branching under these conditions weakened rather than strengthened Baker & Botts.

To take advantage of Houston's growth, Baker & Botts had to add legal talent fast enough to keep up with the demand. This imperative not only pulled senior partner Andrews back to the city, it also made the recruitment and retention of good, young lawyers of paramount importance to the firm's long-term health. Before about 1910 recruitment had posed few problems. Acquaintances, family members, and experienced practitioners who came to the attention of existing partners rounded out the firm. As the number of slots to be filled grew, however, Baker & Botts began to look for a more systematic way to recruit and train lawyers.

The approach to recruitment being adopted by several Wall Street firms (notably the firm that became Cravath, Swaine & Moore) made sense as well for Baker & Botts. The key assumption was that young lawyers as they graduated from law school were the most logical targets for recruitment. By selecting top graduates from high-quality law schools, the firm could be assured of having good raw material from which to mold new partners. In an eight- to twelve-year apprenticeship under the guidance of the partners, these lawyers could be imbued with the values and the work ethic of the firm. During this "postgraduate" training, the young aspirants worked as salaried associates with no permanent claim to the benefits shared by the partners. At the end of the apprenticeship, an associate usually would either move up to full participation as a partner or be asked to leave. This system had great advantages for the partners, since it enabled the firm to hire increasing numbers of hardworking, relatively low paid young lawyers to help handle a growing work load. Baker & Botts was the first firm within the region to adopt this new approach to the recruitment of potential partners.

Implicit in the associate system was a strong impulse toward meritocracy. In making the decisions to hire new lawyers and then to retain or terminate them, a small organization such as a law firm would pay a high price for considering factors other than demonstrated ability. Traditional firms might have been justified in hiring relatives of partners or of major clients; modern firms courted decline by doing so. Corporate clients demanded competence, not social connections, from their local counsel. As Baker & Botts strove to meet the needs of these companies, it gravitated away from ascriptive patterns of hiring toward personnel policies based on merit.

By the 1920s Baker & Botts had become a curious hybrid, part meritocracy and part family firm. In some cases, such as that of the first "family" hire—Captain Baker—the two parts overlapped quite nicely. But as family and friends of family proliferated within the firm, tensions arose on this most delicate of issues. Captain Baker was joined in 1919 by his son, James A. Baker, Jr. Hiram Garwood had two sons, Calvin and St. John, who practiced briefly with Baker & Botts. Colonel Botts's son, Thomas Hutcheson Botts, came to the firm in 1905 and remained until his death in 1922. The extended family ties went further. W. Alvis Parish was a nephew of Captain Baker. For a brief period, Captain Baker's son-in-law, Murray B. Jones, practiced at Baker & Botts, but his divorce from Baker's daughter removed him from both the family and the firm. Close ties through birth and marriage were certainly not uncommon in professional organizations, nor did they necessarily conflict with the firm's commitment to excellence; indeed, many family members enjoyed long and successful careers as lawyers. Yet the partners remained concerned about the long-term implications of continuing to employ relatives.

Walter Walne (1879–1947) took up this issue and guided the firm toward meritocracy. The son of a Baptist minister, Walne graduated from Baylor University before attending the University of Texas Law School. After his second year, financial hardship forced him to withdraw without finishing his degree, but he nonetheless passed the Texas bar exam and began the practice of law in Dallas. After seven years spent largely trying cases for utility companies, he attracted the attention of Edwin Parker, who convinced him to come to Baker & Botts. Walne later recalled that Parker recruited him primarily by revealing to him how much more money he could make at the Houston firm.

128

Part II
A Regional
Firm in a
Maturing
Region,
1915–1929

When he entered Baker & Botts in 1912, his work was supervised by the partners, who at times went so far as to sit behind him in the courtroom, "coaching, prompting."

After becoming a partner in 1917, he took on much of the responsibility for hiring new lawyers. Through the 1920s and 1930s, Walne exercised primary responsibility for bringing new talent into the organization. Perhaps because of his own experience, he became a strong advocate of performance in law school as the main criterion for selecting new lawyers. Ironically, the last person to become a partner at Baker & Botts without a law degree demanded not just a degree, but a degree with honors: "We began after I came to the firm to seek out the honor students of the University of Texas and other nearby law schools. We seek men of the highest intellectual attainments. Since law is an intellectual business, we want to find men of high quality." Walne himself seemed to enjoy the irony. At the close of his career, he said: "You see, today (1946), with my qualifications, they wouldn't take me into the firm. . . . but times have changed." [25] He helped change them at Baker & Botts.

While seeking lawyers of high quality, Walne looked beyond the familiar areas surrounding Houston. In the firm's first long step away from its "in-bred" hiring traditions, Walne made a momentous recruiting trip in 1929 to the Dallas–Fort Worth area. Baker & Botts badly needed new lawyers, and Walne induced Frank Coates, Gaius Gannon, Tom Martin Davis, and Tom Scurry to join the firm. This impressive collection of new legal talent strengthened the organization while marking a sharp departure from the personnel policies of its past.

Walne also pushed the firm toward an antinepotism rule, which he strongly felt was the logical method for putting to rest once and for all any questions about the firm's commitment to hiring and promoting the best available lawyers. After much general discussion, the antinepotism debate finally came to a head in the early 1930s, when the hiring of two partners' nephews had several prominent partners at each other's throats. The spectacle of two senior partners forcing their colleagues to choose sides on the controversial issue of which of the two nephews to hire proved quite disturbing to Walne and others. This was particularly true because the firm had previously announced that it probably would hire no new lawyers that year. The controversy was resolved in a way that few supported initially, when both nephews were hired. But it was now clear to partners in the firm that a growing organization committed to professional excellence simply could not afford to spend its time, energies, and, ultimately, its scarce job slots hiring close relatives. The imposition of a ban on the hiring of relatives in the late 1930s cleared the air, allowing the partners to make the hard subjective judgments required by personnel decisions free of the questions raised by kinship ties.

The Houston firm made this move simultaneously with several leading Wall Street firms, but the evidence suggests that Baker & Botts based its choice on the difficulties encountered within its own organization, not on the fact that other leaders in its profession had defined the "proper" approach to hiring. The antinepotism rule announced to all that achievement, not personal ties, would be the measure of success at Baker & Botts. In taking this step well before other emerging large law firms in Houston, Baker & Botts further strengthened its claim to leadership in the region.

In moving away from the family style of partnership, Baker & Botts stopped short of adopting an entirely merit-based system. In the 1920s most large law firms on Wall Street as well as Main Street were run almost entirely by white, Anglo-Saxon, Protestant males, and Baker & Botts followed suit. Thus the hiring system at the Houston firm and its rivals for the most part excluded Jewish lawyers, who were being trained in growing numbers at leading law schools by the 1920s; offered limited opportunities to women, who were beginning to make inroads in the legal profession; and took no notice whatsoever of black or Hispanic lawyers, who were very few in number, particularly in the South. Baker & Botts did hire several prominent Catholics but the firm remained overwhelmingly WASPish in this period. This was the norm among prominent law firms of the era, but it nonetheless undermined the much-proclaimed commitment of Baker & Botts to hiring the best available lawyers. In the 1920s and 1930s this was particularly evident in the case of Jewish lawyers, who were regularly represented among the honor graduates of the region's leading law schools, but not among the ranks of the only regional firm strongly committed to merit in hiring.

The firm's personnel policies toward women were especially interesting and show just what merit meant in the early twentieth century. Women had begun to graduate from the University of Texas Law School in 1914, and Baker & Botts hired two of the twenty-two female graduates who trickled out of the school in

130

Part II

A Regional
Firm in a
Maturing
Region,
1915–1929

the next decade. Yet in this early era, these women were never considered to be "real" lawyers with any chance to move up and become partners. Instead, they were hired as librarians and seen as temporary employees. The first female attorney at Baker & Botts was Doris Connerly, who had been elected vice-president of her law school class at the University of Texas in 1919. She joined the firm in the early 1920s. A second female graduate of the University of Texas Law School replaced her in 1925. This tradition continued into the 1940s. In fairness to Baker & Botts, highly qualified female lawyers were not available in great numbers in these years; the University of Texas Law School graduated no more than four women in any single year from 1914 to 1938.[26] But none—including several honors graduates—were considered by the firm for full participation and given the opportunity to become partners.

In pursuit of this qualified, 1920s version of a meritocracy, Baker & Botts began to rely very heavily on promising students at the University of Texas Law School. From its creation in 1883 until well into the twentieth century, the University of Texas Law School was the primary training ground for most of the state's lawyers who had any formal legal education. In the areas of corporation law and oil and gas law, the University of Texas offered courses useful to big-city Texas firms such as Baker & Botts. Of importance also was the social networking that was a significant part of the experience of studying law in Austin.

Of the twenty-nine partners trained at law school who entered the firm from its creation until 1940, twenty-five attended the University of Texas Law School. The firm's first law school graduate, Edwin Parker, took his law degree at Texas in 1889— only six years after the founding of the law school—and for the next half century, Baker & Botts went back to Austin again and again. As the preeminent corporate law firm in Texas, Baker & Botts apparently encountered little difficulty recruiting the highest-ranking students, who wanted to practice law with a large, modern, corporate firm. Indeed, a job offer from Baker & Botts in the 1920s and 1930s was often viewed by students and faculty at the University of Texas as a mark of accomplishment reserved for high-ranking students fortunate enough to graduate in a year when the Houston firm was hiring.[27] In this era, Baker & Botts faced little competition in recruiting, and it consistently enjoyed first choice of the top law students at the University of Texas.

In this regard, Baker & Botts was still a distinctly regional firm. The largest firms in New York City as well as other eastern cities tended to recruit from Harvard and other Ivy League law schools. Before World War II, Baker & Botts hired and retained as partners only four lawyers with Ivy League training, two from Harvard and two from Yale. Even these four were Texans who had gone East for their educations. The firm's continuing commitment to its traditional strength as a Houston firm was embodied in its hiring practices and its success as a "Texas" institution staffed by Texans.

The relationship between the aspiring corporate law firm in Houston and the aspiring law school in Austin remained close in the period before World War II. Edwin Parker and other alumni partners at Baker & Botts retained strong personal ties to their former law professors; through these personal friendships flowed, among other things, frank evaluations of prospective recruits. Such ties proved particularly significant to the firm during the deanship of Ira Hildebrand (1925–1940), who had practiced railroad law briefly before becoming a law professor and whose teaching and research focused on corporation laws in Texas.[28] Dean Hildebrand was a special friend of Baker & Botts, which he strongly recommended to a generation of outstanding students. He stayed in close contact with former students and staunch alumni such as Ralph Feagin, Walter Walne, and James Shepherd, Jr., all of whom became prominent partners in the firm.

The benefits to the law school of its connections to Baker & Botts and other large firms were numerous. These big-city firms provided a job market for those graduates of the school who hoped to build a career in corporate practice. Included among this group in the 1920s were several sons of law professors, and their employment at Baker & Botts further strengthened the personal links between the firm and the law school. Approximately fifty University of Texas law graduates found permanent or temporary employment at Baker & Botts before 1940; both the number of recruits and the type of work available to them through the Houston firm gave Baker & Botts a special standing with the leadership of the law school.

Baker & Botts also joined other law firms and individual lawyers in contributing much-needed financial support to the school. Thus when the University of Texas Law School decided to launch a law review in the early 1920s, Baker & Botts as a firm and numerous of its individual partners subscribed to the stock offering

132

Part II

A Regional
Firm in a
Maturing
Region,
1915–1929

that provided the funds needed to start the *Texas Law Review.*[29] In the mid-1920s, the leadership of the school turned to Hiram Garwood—a prominent Baker & Botts partner—for assistance in encouraging the support of the state bar for the school's efforts to raise funds needed for improvements. The letter to Garwood summarizes the dilemma of a state school with high aspirations: "We have an averagely good school, but it is maintained under handicaps which it should not have to endure."[30] Money was needed for the library, scholarships, and new classrooms and offices, and leading lawyers such as Garwood spearheaded the private efforts to raise funds to augment the state's contributions. At the urging of Dean Hildebrand, for example, Ralph Feagin and Walter Walne personally contributed an annual prize for the best student comment published in the law review, and this prize was taken up in the 1930s by Baker & Botts as a firm. Though relatively small sums of money were involved, such contributions nonetheless were important to the law school as it sought to add the trappings common at more established schools.[31]

For the school and for Baker & Botts, success meant, in part, fuller integration into the national legal profession and a growing reputation as the regional leader in its field. Leadership within Texas in the emerging fields of railroad and corporation law made Baker & Botts a force for change within a region in which most lawyers continued to conduct their practices along familiar nineteenth-century patterns. As a model of a quite different approach to the practice of law—an approach that gradually came to characterize the organization and tone of most large law firms—Baker & Botts served as a symbol of a dawning age in large firm practice in Texas. In the years that followed, the firm would move beyond this position. The tumultuous events of the Great Depression and the myriad of reforms of the New Deal would propel Baker & Botts into the ranks of major national law firms.

**PART III
A NATIONAL FIRM IN A MAJOR CITY,
1930–Present**

The Transformation
of the Legal Framework

B Y THE EARLY 1930s the foundations of both modern Houston and the Baker & Botts law firm had been set. The vigorous growth of the preceding decade had brought new people, new industries, and new capital to the city. Along the recently opened ship channel, Humble Oil & Refining led the way in building giant oil refineries that became symbols of industrialization on the once-rural Gulf Coast. Traditional businesses such as cotton and lumber continued to grow side by side with the industrial complex spawned by oil refining and the production of oil tools and supplies. Power lines, rail lines, and new roads stretched out from downtown Houston to the surrounding countryside, tying more people and more resources into the emerging urban-industrial economy. Complex financial and technical ties continued to grow between the region and the large, nationally active companies that dominated the railroad, oil, and utility industries. The law firm, too, emerged as a smooth-functioning legal organization with clients and professional contacts throughout the regional and national economy.

The legal system did not keep pace with the economic integration of the region into the national nexus of development, however. An increasingly national economy was more and more at odds with a state-based legal and regulatory system. The work of Baker & Botts and similar firms in other regions had helped carve out legal space for large corporations in states with restrictive corporate laws. As the process unfolded, these same states often created new regulatory institutions—such as the Texas Railroad Commission—in an effort to control the economic and social impact of industrialization. In Texas, nineteenth-century corporate laws were initially too restrictive to allow for the full economic benefits of large-scale economic organization;

136

Part III
A National
Firm in a
Major City,
1930–Present

but, paradoxically, the state subsequently proved too weak to regulate effectively many of the social effects of sustained industrialization. With new laws too weak to regulate layered on top of old ones too strict to promote full economic development, Texas faced a dilemma common to many "outlying" states. The central problem was the inability of state laws to deal effectively with nationally active economic organizations. Ultimately, the solution adopted would be a national legal and regulatory system. There had been clear movement in this direction since the late nineteenth century; effective control over railroad regulation had, for instance, moved from the states to the federal government's Interstate Commerce Commission. But by the early thirties, legal change was still lagging well behind the realities of an emerging national economy.

With the Great Depression and the New Deal reforms that followed, the pace of legal change accelerated. In Texas, as throughout the nation, the 1930s prompted a profound reassessment of the role of government in the economy. From the debates of the decade came basic reforms in American political economy. Broad new powers for the federal government tumbled out of the political turmoil of the New Deal. These powers reached into many diverse areas of economic life, but taken together they shared a common historical purpose: they quickened the movement toward the creation of a national legal and regulatory framework to handle the issues raised by a corporate economy whose activities spanned state boundaries. This "federalization" of the law hastened the fuller integration of Texas into the mainstream of American economic life. At the same time, it opened new possibilities for aggressive local entrepreneurs, including the lawyers at Baker & Botts.

Until this era of change, state law had formed the major corpus with which Baker & Botts's lawyers worked. Federal law intruded at certain points, as we have seen, but it was the variations in laws from state to state that sustained and defined the limits of the practices of regional firms such as Baker & Botts. Only the Wall Street law firms practiced at a truly national level, since so much of what would now be called corporation law was actually the law of the states of New York, New Jersey, and Delaware. The policy reforms of the 1930s transformed this legal setting. The new prominence of the federal government and its administrative agencies forced a greater uniformity among the laws of different states. In the 1930s the American Bar Association also worked to make the codes of different states uniform, an effort that would come to fruition in the 1950s. Meanwhile, acceptance in most of the country's major law schools of the Langdell case method, which stressed universally applicable legal principles, further contributed to nationalization.[1]

The New Deal was a major force behind these changes. This complex phenomenon had far-reaching and often contradictory effects on Texas.[2] Among the many reforms of the era, several had particular importance for the practice of Baker & Botts. The creation of the Securities and Exchange Commission (SEC) brought national regulation of financial practices; no longer would Wall Street insiders be the primary rule makers for corporate financing. Baker & Botts now had the opportunity to compete more equally with Wall Street firms on legal matters that had always been central to the practice of corporate law: arranging to float securities and conducting reorganizations. The SEC also was given authority to oversee the granddaddy of legally required reorganizations, the massive redesign of the nation's utility systems under the Public Utility Holding Company Act of 1935. Several other new or revamped regulatory agencies also directly affected the firm's practice. New powers for the ICC brought changes in the railroad work of Baker & Botts. The firm also faced important changes in its oil-related work—under new powers exercised by the Texas Railroad Commission—and in its gas-related services, which came under the sway of the Federal Power Commission.

Looking back with the benefit of fifty years of historical hindsight, John T. McCullough—a longtime Baker & Botts managing partner—captured a sense of the tensions of the 1930s as well as an understanding of the long-term impact of the era's legal reforms when he spoke to the firm in 1979: "There is no doubt in my mind that the greatest changes in the firm's practice and business over the years since I came to work in 1929 resulted from the 'New Deal' legislation which I have mentioned. Of course lawyers were as vociferous as their clients in complaining about the New Deal legislation, but in retrospect one may wonder how lawyers would have survived without the legislation."[3]

As McCullough noted, amid the charged legal and political passions of the 1930s, Baker & Botts kept busy defending its clients. EBASCO and other valued clients were under siege, and Baker & Botts focused its efforts on their defense. Such battles often left members of the firm with a deep antipathy toward the

137

Chapter 7
The Trans-
formation
of the Legal
Framework

138

Part III
A National
Firm in a
Major City,
1930–Present

New Deal. This was particularly true of the long war over the passage and enforcement of the Public Utility Holding Company Act of 1935, which exposed the firm to the strong distrust of big business that colored several major New Deal reforms and much New Deal rhetoric. Nonetheless, despite the rhetoric, many of the reforms of the 1930s were in the firm's long-term interests, as McCullough acknowledged in 1979. And, it turned out, some were even in the short-term interest of the firm's clients.

The New Deal reforms had two faces, one surprisingly probusiness, the other decidedly antimonopoly. Characteristic of the probusiness side of the New Deal were the laws aimed at the nation's railroads. Railroads were still important to Texas and to Baker & Botts's practice. In 1933 Congress passed a new railway act that was the culmination of all the firm had been working for in railroading for twenty years. In 1914 Baker & Botts had been involved in the important *Shreveport* case, in which the Supreme Court had ruled that when federal and state regulation were in conflict, federal power was supreme.[4] This ruling enabled the lawyers to finesse certain restrictive policies of the Texas Railroad Commission.[5] In the period just after World War I, the lawyers and their old partner Robert Lovett had supported a new federal law designed to further the process of supplanting state with federal authority. The Transportation Act of 1920 served this purpose and enabled Baker & Botts partner Jules Tallichet in 1926 to draw up the papers combining all the SP's Texas roads into one subsidiary, the T&NO.[6] The Emergency Railroad Transportation Act of 1933 permitted Baker & Botts to complete the process by merging the T&NO into the Southern Pacific Company.[7] The new federal legislation authorized the consolidation without an evaluation of property, in effect eliminating the old state restrictions on railroad capital. The merger of the T&NO into the SP brought the end of an era in Baker & Botts's long service as the Texas representative to a national corporation operating in a state still hostile to railroad combines.

Other reform legislation followed this same probusiness pattern. Under the comprehensive National Recovery Act, Baker & Botts was able to offer its oil clients a means of avoiding conflict with the Texas antitrust laws. When the state attorney general took the Texas oil companies to court for adhering to the American Petroleum Institute's code of practice, Clarence Wharton countered by arguing successfully that this code conformed to the spirit of federal legislation designed to regulate competition in the industry.[8]

139

Chapter 7

The Trans-
formation
of the Legal
Framework

Some parts of the New Deal aimed to spur growth by lending a hand to private enterprises. The Reconstruction Finance Corporation (RFC), for example, was authorized to make loans to failing firms in an effort to shore up what were deemed vital industries. Run by Jesse Jones, a Houston builder and banker long acquainted with Baker & Botts, the RFC lent some two billion dollars for this purpose. Capitalizing on the opportunity, Baker & Botts helped to secure through Jones funds for Sugarland Industries, an important Houston-based client.[9] With this money, the lawyers reorganized the faltering enterprise, enabling it to acquire a number of new ventures and consolidate its holdings.

The flip side of the New Deal, called by some its antibusiness side, proved more difficult for the lawyers to manage, since the new federal regulatory policies curtailed the powers heretofore exercised by many of the firm's corporate clients. Nowhere was this aspect of the New Deal more threatening to contemporary business than in labor-management relations. The Wagner Act of 1935 transformed the collective bargaining process by creating a new federal agency, the National Labor Relations Board (NLRB), with powers to define unfair bargaining tactics and conduct representation elections designed to permit workers to unionize if they wished. In essence, this new law took labor-management disputes out of the courts and the streets—where managers had historically enjoyed distinct advantages—and placed them before federal government mediators—where industrial unions proved successful in the late 1930s. Baker & Botts joined this battle early on, even before the passage of the Wagner Act, through its representation of the Southern Pacific.

Even before the New Deal, federal regulations in railroading in the 1920s began to encourage unionization. These laws, notably the Railway Labor Act of 1926, helped pave the way for the Wagner Act. In the South, where unions previously had made little headway, the new laws seemed particularly threatening to managers of large industrial work forces. The decision of its long-standing client, the SP, to challenge the Railway Labor Act thrust the firm into one of the most important cases testing the new federal policies toward labor. The railroad's main Texas subsidiary had tried to stave off the formation of a worker's union after the act was passed in 1926. But under the terms of

140

Part III

A National

Firm in a

Major City,

1930–Present

the act (and under the terms of the later Wagner Act as well), pressure tactics designed to prevent employees from organizing were illegal. The Brotherhood of Railway Clerks had taken the railroad to court, arguing unfair coercion. Baker & Botts attorneys Wharton and Tallichet took up the defense of their client, but in a hotly debated case before the firm's old friend, Judge J. C. Hutcheson, they lost to the union.[10] The railroad appealed and the case made it to the Supreme Court, which on 30 May 1930 affirmed the lower court's decision.[11] This ruling not only permitted the unionization of the Texas railroads, but served as a key precedent for the Supreme Court's later affirmation of the more wide-ranging Wagner Act.[12]

Failing to halt the advance of legislation supporting unionization, Baker & Botts had no choice but to sharpen its labor law expertise. With hundreds of suits appearing before the new labor dispute bodies—the Railroad Adjustment Board and the National Labor Relations Board—the firm's clients needed representation. The T&NO asked that one Baker & Botts attorney devote full time to the over three hundred pending railroad labor cases. Though the firm was not prepared to make this commitment, Tom Martin Davis went to Chicago to work with SP management preparing rules for resolving disputes before the federal body. Gaius Gannon, meanwhile, familiarized himself with matters of railroad labor law and for a time devoted his attention to National Railroad Adjustment Board cases and union grievances.[13] Although most of these cases were handled by the SP's in-house counsel, the firm continued to review briefs and make contributions.

Neither Baker & Botts nor the talented lawyers representing other corporate clients could dramatically change the drift of labor policy. What they could do was negotiate the best possible compromises for their clients. They helped ease their clients toward a new accommodation with labor and with federal authority. As in its other areas of practice, moreover, Baker & Botts combined legal expertise with community leadership. Davis and other members of the firm organized a citizens' committee for industrial peace, modeled on similar organizations elsewhere. Supported by local business executives and employers, these bodies tried to regain some of the ground lost to unions.[14] The labor organizations still received recognition from the federal government and penetrated some areas in the South and Southwest. But by the late 1940s, it was apparent that the final result was a compromise that did less to redistribute power between workers and management than most business leaders had feared in the mid-thirties.[15]

For Baker & Botts, the new laws affecting utility holding companies were even more significant than this historic change in labor relations. Sponsored by Sam Rayburn, the longtime Texas representative, the Public Utility Holding Company Act of 1935 was aimed directly at large utility combines such as EBASCO and Stone & Webster, which the firm had long represented. In the eyes of critics, these corporations were nothing more than greedy monopolies, extracting a tribute from consumers in the form of service fees that drained local treasuries to feed corporate coffers. What purpose did the organizations serve, people asked, except to drive up rates and enrich New York and Chicago at the expense of Texas and other states? Rayburn, the son of East Texas farmers, listened closely to these complaints. On the floor of the U.S. House of Representatives, he decried the utility holding companies as "master" of the American people, a "soulless, impersonal, intangible, immortal and well-nigh all-powerful" master. He chastised the combines as a "cancerous growth on the body politic," and he sought legislation that would take "power, authority, and management" from far-flung holding companies and "give it back to the communities of this country where it belongs."[16]

The Wheeler-Rayburn Bill cut right to the heart of utility holding companies. The measure stated that any combine that could not demonstrate its necessity and utility by doing something more than exercising financial control of a large number of operating companies should be broken up. The holding company's shares in local operations would be dispersed and sold publicly to individual investors. This "death sentence" provision gave teeth to the law and proved to be its most controversial feature. If carried through, the death sentence would decentralize the nation's power industry, replacing national with regional organizations.

The plan posed a threat to three decades of legal work by utility specialists at Baker & Botts. As they had argued before city councils and the Texas legislature, the holding companies provided financial stability, technical expertise, and a uniform system of management to small, sometimes financially weak, operating units. The attorneys, who had grown expert at defending their clients against a wary public and aggressive regulators,

141

Chapter 7
The Trans-
formation
of the Legal
Framework

142

Part III
A National
Firm in a
Major City,
1930–Present

had forged strong ties to these power giants. Ralph Feagin had moved from Baker & Botts in Houston to New York to serve as an EBASCO vice-president. When the Public Utility Holding Company Act was first proposed in Congress, partner Frank Coates shuttled between Houston and New York to confer with the head counsels of EBASCO and Stone & Webster.[17] As the companies marshaled their forces for defense, Baker & Botts was positioned to play a major role in the effort.

In November of 1934, the firm entered the debates surrounding the proposed legislation. EBASCO employed Baker & Botts to make a special study of the history and development of the holding company form and its regulation.[18] For four months Feagin and fellow partner John Bullington spent full time in New York, poring over statistics, laws, and reports. Their purpose was to defend their client against the charge that it served no economic purpose in the power industry and to provide guidelines for the areas in which some federal regulation might be useful. Like most large corporations at this time, EBASCO was wary of federal intervention but happy to use it, if possible, as a counterpoise to more parochial state and local regulations.

Baker & Botts completed the study just as Rayburn introduced his bill. The firm's work became a major source of information for the holding companies. It was also widely read and used by a variety of large corporations outside of the power industry, which feared that future federal laws of similar intent might be aimed their way.[19] The resulting publicity strengthened Baker & Botts's ties to the national policy arena and gave it a more significant role in the ensuing debates over the utility bill.

As the bill wound its way through Congress, the firm assumed full responsibility for EBASCO's presentation before Rayburn's Foreign and Interstate Commerce Committee.[20] In their brief to the committee, Bullington and Feagin argued that the proposed legislation would destroy a valuable service relationship between the parent holding companies and their many operating units. In addition, Feagin testified on behalf of the natural gas industry, in which some of the electric utility holding companies also had an interest.[21] According to Feagin, the holding companies realized that some federal regulation was inevitable, and they "offered to cooperate with Congress in the drafting of legislation which would adequately serve the public interest."[22] In 1935, however, Congress was in no mood to compromise. The financial collapse of some of the largest utility combines had angered voters and stiffened congressional support for new regulations. Congress passed the Public Utility Holding Act of 1935 and Roosevelt signed the bill into law, death sentence and all.

Baker & Botts attorneys condemned the new law as "extremely drastic, thoroughly unworkable, and doubtless unconstitutional."[23] Other holding company representatives went even further. A. J. Duncan, president of Texas Electric Service, lambasted the measure. "It would," he predicted, "destroy the investments of literally thousands of people who have attempted to provide for old age by investing in the securities of [the] companies; it would . . . largely destroy the fundamental principles of states' rights."[24]

In fact, none of these dire predictions came to pass. The growth that marked the Texas economy over the years, plus the tutelage of large corporate organizations such as EBASCO, had erased many of the differences in values and business structures that had once separated hinterland states such as Texas from the center of the American economy. As a result, EBASCO, Stone & Webster, and other holding companies could be dismantled without adversely affecting the power industry or interfering with the flow of capital to Texas utilities. The breakup disgorged a number of sound operating companies, which proved capable of managing their finances effectively and capturing economies of scale in power generation and transmission. They became safe and conservative investments for small stockholders. The resulting regional power systems were big enough and strong enough to perform their own engineering services and raise their own capital without the support of an overarching parent company.[25]

While the law firm ardently opposed this innovation in America's political economy, it quickly adapted to and took advantage of the resulting wave of corporate reorganizations. In the immediate aftermath of the new utility law, the lawyers prepared their clients for the breakup. Gathering its forces, EBASCO called its numerous operating company executives and attorneys to New York for a strategy session. Alvis Parish from Baker & Botts attended as the titular head of HL&P and the chief utilities lawyer at the firm.[26] Baker & Botts was then able to participate in a major industrial reorganization. As with many of the New Deal's measures, this expansion of federal power accelerated the maturation of the firm, drawing it further into the national economy.

The breakup of EBASCO brought Baker & Botts for the first

143

Chapter 7
The Trans-
formation
of the Legal
Framework

144

Part III
A National
Firm in a
Major City,
1930–Present

time onto the national financial scene as a major figure rather than a secondary actor. The firm was able to draw on this experience in the postwar era, as HL&P emerged as a leading regional power company. Restructuring under the holding company act redistributed HL&P common stock to the public in exchange for the preferred shares of National Power and Light Company (the EBASCO subholding company that owned HL&P). Under the auspices of the Securities and Exchange Commission, the exchange began in 1941. It proceeded slowly, however, due to the wartime strain on financial markets. Baker & Botts attorneys Feagin and Gannon spent most of the year in Washington, D.C., and New York, where they were able to complete only 21 percent of the transaction. Further progress was inhibited by the war and the refusal of the Securities and Exchange Commission to allow the companies to use normal investment banking channels to underwrite the exchange of stock.[27]

At this point Baker & Botts attorneys were able to play an important and creative role. Appealing to the SEC to relax its ban on investment houses, they put together a banking consortium including Smith, Barney; Lazard Frères; and others to complete the transaction. This effort boosted the stock exchanged to 52 percent, as buyers throughout the nation took the securities of the newly independent HL&P. The remaining 48 percent of the stock was disposed of through competitive bidding handled by these same New York investment bankers, supported by some sixty-nine smaller dealers scattered throughout the country. By 14 May 1943 HL&P was fully disassociated from EBASCO.[28] When the dealing was done, the Houston company's stock was widely distributed across the nation. A few large institutional investors such as Fidelity Trust Company of Philadelphia owned between 3 and 4 percent of the stock, but two-thirds of the new owners were small investors, holding one to fifty shares. Over 20 percent of the stock was owned by Texans. If the final results did not match Rayburn's vision of community ownership, they nonetheless demonstrated that large, independent regional power companies such as HL&P could thrive.

The Public Utility Holding Company Act of 1935 provided Baker & Botts with other opportunities to participate in corporate reorganizations. The firm helped to reorganize and refinance another EBASCO subsidiary, United Gas. Under the terms of the new law, United Gas Public Service Company, the owner of the United Gas properties, was a holding company that would receive a death sentence. But Baker & Botts, working with Simpson, Thacher & Bartlett of New York, conceived of a plan for restructuring the company to eliminate one degree of organization. A new subsidiary, Union Producing Company, took all the gas production properties, while United Gas Pipeline Company took charge of transmission and pipeline facilities. These two new organizations were still controlled by the United Gas Company, which continued to be part of the EBASCO system. But the functional division rendered them nonutility companies, eliminating one level of the holding company structure—United Gas Public Service. The newly formed United Gas Company served both as the umbrella organization for all of the gas properties and as the operating unit in charge of one function of the firm, gas distribution.[29]

Later, United Gas was completely separated from EBASCO, as HL&P had been. In 1944 Baker & Botts took charge of United Gas's first public offering of bonds, valued at about $100 million. At the behest of the SEC, the company raised this capital in order to settle its original indebtedness to EBASCO and put more distance between itself and the giant holding company.[30] Ralph Feagin, by this time back at Baker & Botts, handled the negotiations between United Gas, Electric Bond and Share, and the SEC.[31] The combination of financial, corporate, and regulatory work paid Baker & Botts fees amounting to $160,000, which was 15 percent of the firm's total income for the year. This healthy figure symbolized the firm's steady progress toward a new status as a major national law firm.

Continued SEC pressure led to further reorganization in 1949, when Electric Power and Light (the EBASCO subholding company that owned United) began distributing common shares of the gas company publicly.[32] As a result, United Gas became a publicly held corporation listed on the New York Stock Exchange, and EBASCO was reduced to a minority owner of 4 percent of its stock. Like HL&P, United emerged as a separate, integrated system. With gas becoming a vital source of energy throughout the nation, United proved capable of financing its own expansion.

In an important sense, the New Deal measures opened up opportunities not previously available to Texas institutions. The restructuring of EBASCO's Texas properties permitted Houston's financial institutions to play a greater role in the utility industry. Guardian Trust of Houston served along with Bankers' Trust of New York as the transfer agents for the HL&P deal, while Hous-

145

Chapter 7
The Trans-
formation
of the Legal
Framework

146

Part III
A National
Firm in a
Major City,
1930–Present

ton Land and Trust and Continental Trust of New York acted as registrars. In accord with the new local orientation of HL&P, Baker & Botts decided to use a local organization as trustee for the securities—Captain Baker's South Texas Commercial National Bank.[33]

Despite its intense early opposition to the Public Utilities Holding Company Act of 1935, Baker & Botts was thus one of the beneficiaries of change in the utility industry. From the breakup of the national holding companies, the firm gained valuable national exposure in finance, law, and policymaking. Its work on United Gas foreshadowed its move into mergers and acquisitions in the postwar era. Its participation in congressional debates over the Wheeler-Rayburn bill, its work for EBASCO's defense, and its involvement in the restructuring of HL&P brought Baker & Botts a variety of important contacts. The list of participants involved in the reorganizations included some eighty organizations. Among them were Wall Street stalwarts like Chase National Bank, Chemical Bank, and the investment houses of Dillon, Read & Company, Dean Witter, Brown Brothers–Harriman & Company, and Goldman, Sachs & Company. In addition, a significant part of the HL&P stock was taken by large institutional investors, such as Aetna, Equitable, Travelers, and other insurance companies. These institutions would play a major role in the postwar financing of HL&P. By contrast, when the Houston power company had been an EBASCO subsidiary, it had relied on Halsey, Stuart as its underwriter, and Baker & Botts had maintained close ties only with this house.

In the restructuring, Baker & Botts also gained substantial experience in dealing with federal agencies. The SEC oversaw and approved the refinancing, giving Baker & Botts its first opportunity to deal with this regulatory agency. The firm was also called on by another EBASCO subsidiary, American Power and Light, to prepare a report to the SEC on the fair value of its properties.[34] In preparation of this report the lawyers made contact with numerous regional operating companies, which, like HL&P, were being spun off from the holding company.

In the long run, Baker & Botts seems to have gained more than it lost from the breakup of the holding companies. It no longer served the giant EBASCO system, and another of its major clients, Stone & Webster, was also forced to abandon its Texas utility properties.[35] But the firm was able to become lead counsel for the now-independent HL&P and to establish close relations with United Gas Pipeline.[36] In the booming postwar economy, both HL&P and United Gas greatly expanded their operations and consumed staggering amounts of capital, all of which demanded constant legal service from Baker & Botts.

147

Chapter 7
The Trans-
formation
of the Legal
Framework

New regulations in the oil and gas industries in the 1930s also tied Baker & Botts more securely into national affairs. In both industries the federal government assumed significant new powers. In the case of oil the outcome broke sharply with the classic pattern of the federal government's taking new powers that overrode state laws. Instead, the federal government asserted authority over the shipment of oil across state lines in order to sanction a newly constructed regulatory system built around the Texas Railroad Commission and similar agencies in the other major oil-producing states. Thus, the states acquired effective controls, backed by federal laws. The system that emerged proved beneficial to most sectors of the Texas petroleum industry, including the large, nationally active oil companies represented by Baker & Botts.

Congress created the new regulatory structure in response to a glut of crude oil in the United States and throughout the world. Extremely low prices threatened chaos in an industry historically plagued by boom-and-bust cycles. The discovery of the giant East Texas oil field in 1930 brought producers throughout the nation to their knees.[37] Millions of barrels of oil from the largest field discovered in the United States up to that time overwhelmed an oil market already struggling to absorb substantial excess capacity. Texas, which had become the largest oil-producing state in the 1920s, now became the focal point of intense debates on the regulation of the nation's oil supply. Suddenly, a longtime acquaintance of Baker & Botts, the Texas Railroad Commission, found itself in the midst of a crisis for which it was ill-prepared.[38]

The crisis arose in part because most oil producers and many influential congressional representatives of the southwestern producing states had strongly opposed the creation of a federal agency with the power to regulate production. Yet these normally vocal advocates of "free enterprise" also had finally acknowledged that private efforts to curtail production had failed miserably. A consensus gradually emerged within the industry that some form of control was necessary and that state control would be preferable. Public officials and the representatives of the several interested parties hammered out a compromise that left the power to regulate at the state level. Aided by demand

148

Part III
A National
Firm in a
Major City,
1930–Present

forecasts from the U.S. Bureau of Mines, state commissions in Texas and other southwestern states were thus able to limit production by prorationing. This involved assigning an "allowable" production to each producing well in the state each month. The federal role was to prohibit the interstate shipment of oil produced in violation of these state regulations. As the state commissions gradually established their legal authority and their ability to achieve results, they became an accepted part of the political economy of oil.[39]

The new prorationing system did not enjoy unanimous support. Indeed, many of the small independent oil producers initially viewed it as a thinly disguised ploy by big companies (such as Texaco) and their lawyers (such as Baker & Botts) to squeeze the independents out of the industry. During the controversy over the legality of prorationing, such criticisms found voice in a variety of forums, including paid advertisements in Texas newspapers: "Has the time arrived when the 'big boys' of the oil industry can tell the people of Texas who may produce oil, when they may produce oil and what oil prices should be? We say NO."[40] Unfortunately for the purchasers of the advertisement, the courts and the state legislature said "yes," giving the Texas Railroad Commission ample authority to regulate the production of independents and "big boys" alike.

The new regulatory setting prompted Baker & Botts to take on an important new category of oil-related work: hearings and cases on prorationing decisions made by the Texas Railroad Commission. Many smaller producers in the state did not survive the imposition of these regulations, which of necessity slowed the production of oil and forced some small interests to wait longer than they could afford to in marketing their reserves. But the large vertically integrated companies long represented by Baker & Botts generally survived and prospered under the new regulations. Baker & Botts pursued the legal interests of these clients as the new regulatory regime was taking shape. No single group and certainly no single law firm was able to dominate the new system, but Baker & Botts represented the interests of the one group, the large oil companies, that proved quite successful over the long haul. Given the vital role the Texas Railroad Commission now played, Baker & Botts assigned a senior partner, Walter Walne, "to specialize in oil proration matters and work and litigation incident thereto, including regular attendance at the im-

149
Chapter 7
The Trans-
formation
of the Legal
Framework

portant general proration hearings conducted by the Railroad Commission."[41] His efforts were supported by those of numerous young oil and gas specialists in the 1940s and 1950s, all of whom were intently concerned with the decisions of the commission. Together they helped to forge successful outcomes for the firm's large, corporate clients.

The regulation of natural gas took a markedly different form. The waste of natural gas had evoked widespread concern in the years before the 1930s, as large quantities of the valuable resource were simply flared in oil fields not connected to pipeline systems capable of transporting it to markets. As concern over gas conservation and fears about the economic consequences of a glut mounted in the 1930s, many in the industry and in society as a whole looked to the federal government for answers. The solution that emerged was, however, neither as coherent nor as durable as the one put forward for oil.[42]

This outcome reflected the particular characteristics of the gas industry. Only recently had gas production and marketing begun to move beyond local or regional distribution systems. New technologies for transporting natural gas efficiently were becoming available, but pipelines capable of moving gas from the major producing fields in the Southwest to the largest markets in the Northeast were not yet in place. Indeed, many prolific natural gas fields in West Texas and the Texas Panhandle were not even thoroughly integrated into the regional gathering systems. In addition to such supply-side considerations, the demand for natural gas differed from the demand for oil in ways that ultimately shaped the regulation of this dynamic industry. In the 1930s numerous municipalities were deciding or had recently decided to grant franchises for the supply of natural gas to their cities. These municipal customers sought guarantees that natural gas would remain available at reasonable prices and they voiced effective political demands for regulatory guarantees on this vital issue.[43]

As a result, the gas regulatory system in the 1930s was a curious hybrid of federal and state policies. To regulate the production and ultimately the price of natural gas sold in interstate markets, Congress in 1938 gave the Federal Power Commission (FPC) new and potentially far-reaching powers.[44] Yet neither Congress nor the American legal system tackled the tricky question of what to do about natural gas in intrastate markets. The

150

Part III
A National
Firm in a
Major City,
1930–Present

distinction between interstate and intrastate commerce was not crucial in oil, where the coordinated policies of numerous state regulatory commissions added up to a coordinated policy on interstate oil. Had natural gas fields been discovered throughout the nation, the FPC could perhaps have effectively "federalized" the issue of natural gas regulation. Such was not the case, however. The state of Texas alone continued to produce between 35 percent and 50 percent of all gas in the country.[45] Indeed, for several years in the mid-1950s, a reconstituted Republic of Texas would have been the leading gas-producing nation in the world. Far from simply a Texas brag, this fact is of fundamental importance in understanding the tensions that characterized the legal struggles over the regulation of natural gas.

Baker & Botts led the charge in many of these battles; not surprisingly, its primary clients were the large companies that had invested heavily to construct the major pipeline systems connecting natural gas fields to markets. These corporations generally owned substantial reserves in the fields served by their pipelines. Their idea of "orderly development" at times differed sharply from that of the smaller producers, who often had no way to move their gas to markets without access to the major pipelines. These differences found their way into court in the 1930s and 1940s. There, the task of defining a set of generally accepted rules was complicated by the lack of coordination between federal and state policies and by the extraordinary dynamism of an industry that refused to stop growing while regulators finished their work.

Within Texas prorationing of natural gas did not evolve as early or as systematically as prorationing of oil. Instead, the gas industry in the 1930s was shaped by the forces of free competition, constrained by the demands for conservation, by the limited access some producers had to transportation, and by the reality of federal price regulations lurking just over the state line. As competing interests pushed for different solutions to the problems that arose, Baker & Botts handled a number of significant cases stemming from the conflicts.

Perhaps the firm's most important and most highly publicized natural gas regulation case in the 1930s was *Texoma Natural Gas Company* v. *Railroad Commission of Texas.*[46] This was one of several suits brought by major pipeline companies against members of the Texas Railroad Commission, the attorney general of Texas, and the governor. At issue were the powers of the

Railroad Commission under the so-called Common Purchaser Law, a law passed in 1931 that required pipelines to prorate their purchases from producing leases in a field (including their own leases) on an equitable basis. If applied to the natural gas industry, this law seemed to give the Railroad Commission authority to create a prorationing system enforced by the activities of the pipeline companies. Each pipeline would have to take only a measured quantity of gas from each producer, even if it meant forcing a pipeline owner to give preference to other producers over his or her own output. The pipeline companies resisted strongly, calling on the legal firepower of a formidable team of the leading oil and gas law firms in Houston, Fort Worth, and Amarillo, as well as lawyers from Oklahoma and New York.

151

Chapter 7

The Trans-

formation

of the Legal

Framework

The *Texoma* case brought this issue to a head by challenging the Railroad Commission's orders in a major gas field serviced by several large pipelines in the Texas Panhandle. Baker & Botts was brought into the case by Texaco, which owned a portion of the Texoma Natural Gas Company. Other major pipelines active in the Panhandle joined in filing similar suits, and their teams of counsel included two other growing Houston-based law firms, Vinson & Elkins and Andrews & Kurth.[47] At a conference in Kansas City in November 1931, the three Houston-based firms constituted a board of strategy to direct the course of the prospective litigation for all the companies (which represented together about $250 million in capital). Their plan was to show that the Texas Railroad Commission was attempting to exercise powers beyond its regulatory mandate to prevent the waste of natural gas. More specifically, they argued that the commission's orders in the Panhandle natural gas fields sought to force producers with access to markets through their own pipelines to share these markets with other well owners who had not contributed to the development of the pipelines. Their argument that the Texas Railroad Commission was, in effect, confiscating the property of the pipeline owners without due process of law carried the day. Victory in the courts invalidated these commission orders. While the decision left unanswered the question of what should or could be done to regulate the production of natural gas, it prevented the commission from achieving a solution that impinged unduly on the pipeline operations of these major firms.[48]

The court threw the burden of choice back to the Texas legislature. In the absence of a clear mandate from the legislature to undertake systematic prorationing of natural gas, the com-

152

Part III
A National
Firm in a
Major City,
1930–Present

mission accepted a variety of accommodations between pipeline owners and producers in different fields through the state.
A patchwork system of informal production controls and negotiated access to pipelines emerged, and the commission and the
courts for the most part left these solutions unchallenged. Prorationing of gas production by the Texas Railroad Commission
gradually evolved, but the Federal Power Commission exerted a
shaping influence on the industry by regulating (after 1954) the
price of gas sold in interstate commerce. Not until the onset of
the energy crises of the 1970s would the contradictions between
federal price controls and a market-oriented intrastate system
provoke another round of legislation and litigation.[49]

Overall, the changes of the 1930s were an important part of
the process that brought Texas and one of its leading law firms
more securely into the national economy. The Holding Company
Act and federal and state energy policies reworked the political
economy of Texas, putting to rest many of the nagging conflicts
and unresolved issues of the preceding decades regarding regulation. Under these new laws, Texas companies such as HL&P
emerged as independent national concerns and Texas political
institutions, the Railroad Commission especially, played nationally significant roles. New federal rail policies finally loosened
the grip of state government on the transportation industry while
federal law and uniform state codes furthered the nationalization
of the law. These developments preempted important aspects of
traditional anti–big business policies in Texas law, something
that Baker & Botts had been trying to do for years. This helped to
close the gaps that separated business in the state from business
elsewhere.

Not even the antimonopoly side of New Deal policy departed
radically from this basic trend. It brought about convergence by
using federal power to disperse private concentrations of capital.
By forcing large-scale power firms to justify their existence on
economic and technological grounds, the Public Utility Holding
Company Act put an end to a pillar of the old colonial economy
and allowed strong Texas companies to emerge in the power
and gas industries. The labor acts eased the way to unionization among Texas workers who had been unable to organize in
the face of employer opposition reinforced by industrial under-
development. While the New Deal did not replace large private
corporations with smaller, locally controlled organizations, as
some more radical critics of American business had hoped it

would, it did use concerted public power to foster a homogeneity between places, to redistribute resources among regions, and to close the gaps between the advanced and the less-advanced sectors of the national economy.[50]

Some of the new policies probably went too far in trying to protect small local firms. In the depths of the depression, Texas, along with other states, passed a Chain Store Act designed to penalize large merchandisers who operated multiple-unit enterprises.[51] Congress later passed a similar national provision, sponsored by Wright Patman of Texas, to protect the small retailer. Baker & Botts lawyers bemoaned this trend in legislation and characterized it as populist, confiscatory, and irrational. It was, however, simply the other side of the New Deal compromise, protecting small business even as other policies encouraged corporate growth. While the Texas legislature was passing its anti–chain store act, the state's attorney general was permitting Baker & Botts to bring about consolidations in the meatpacking industry.[52] There was still room for dispute as to when consolidation and when antitrust was the right policy, but overall, the New Deal compromise made it easier for skeptics to accept big business.

With the postwar expansion of such companies as HL&P and United Gas, and the general prosperity of Texas's oil and gas industries, the arguments of Baker & Botts against aspects of the new political economy rang hollow. This raises an important question. Had the firm acted, as its critics charged, as a defender of special interests against the public good? Perhaps because they had so long devoted their energies to fighting uneconomic state regulation for their clients, and perhaps because much of the rhetoric that accompanied the new legislation was inflammatory, the lawyers initially misjudged the long-term import of the New Deal. The experiences of Baker & Botts in the New Deal era suggest some of the problems inherent in our adversarial legal system. Law firms are expected to represent their clients faithfully; yet lawyers and law firms can have a substantial impact on public policy. In Baker & Botts's case, so long as economic development required the presence of strong national corporations, the firm, which tended to represent such interests, could generally be expected to act in ways that furthered development. When the situation changed, however, Baker & Botts could not change in the short run, tied as it was to its existing client base and type of practice. Critics of law firms' role in

153

*Chapter 7
The Trans-
formation
of the Legal
Framework*

154

Part III
A National
Firm in a
Major City,
1930–Present

policymaking have pointed to this very situation as the reason public policy so often reflects the interests of private groups. With so many interests commanding so much specialized legal expertise, they argue, major policy decisions turn into distorted, costly compromises.

Difficult as policymaking is in our legal system, the experience of Baker & Botts also shows how law firms could help improve policies. Strong antimonopoly forces within the Roosevelt administration, for example, had sought to take the breakup of the power giants further and replace all large companies with locally owned and controlled competitors under the supervision of state and municipal authorities. The Public Works Administration (PWA), a relief agency under the direction of Harold Ickes, had begun to use its funds to support these endeavors. Such efforts raised the old issue of local control once again. The devotees of localism were opposed by others in the Roosevelt administration, as well as the power companies and their lawyers. The result was a "power fight" between federal planners, large power concerns, and state and local governments.[53] Located in an area with strong sympathies for local control but serving a large power concern, Baker & Botts was positioned in the center of this three-way split. Representing its utility clients, the firm opposed plans to build competing, small-scale power-generating stations to relieve towns and cities of dependence on large companies. The large companies, HL&P included, argued that such a course was irrational and counterproductive, for small municipal systems could not achieve the economies of scale that the larger systems did. PWA director Ickes, however, persisted, receiving much support from other like-minded New Dealers, as well as state and local governments in areas such as Texas. It fell to the lawyers of the government and of the large companies to work out a solution to this dispute.

Baker & Botts was involved in five such cases, taking the PWA and its director for federal court to block use of federal funds to build competing power systems.[54] Neither this effort nor appeals to local business interests wholly succeeded in stopping the construction of competing facilities because the Supreme Court in 1938 declared that the use of PWA funds in this manner was constitutional.[55] Through the persistence of their law firms, however, the large power companies were able to slow down and restrict the degree of localism in the industry. Given the limitations on small firms in such a capital-intensive industry, these efforts were probably to the good. Thus while the large corporations through their lawyers were looking after their own interests, the final results were not necessarily bad for society as a whole.

Whatever the outcome in particular cases, neither Baker & Botts nor its clients had much choice but to accept the new direction in which public policy had turned. Self-interest dictated that the firm adapt its practice. By diminishing the differences between the laws governing business in Texas and those in the rest of the nation, the federal government undermined the value of Baker & Botts's traditional expertise as the local "Texas" representative of outside corporations. The same New Deal regulations also established the preconditions for the firm to move from its previous status as a regional firm to a new position as a national one. This transition was not inevitable, nor was it easy. But as the firm evolved along with the region, it soon entered a new era of prosperity that eased the process of change. In the postwar boom, Baker & Botts would adapt its historical strengths to the demands of an emerging national market for legal services.

155

Chapter 7
The Trans-
formation
of the Legal
Framework

The Coming of Age of the Firm and Its City

IN THE POSTWAR BOOM YEARS, Houston came of age as a major urban center. The city's population and its industrial base expanded steadily and at times spectacularly, presenting Baker & Botts with excellent opportunities for growth and diversification. During and after the war, an increasingly wide array of industries prospered on the coastal plain surrounding Houston. Oil- and gas-related development led the way. The expansion of oil production, transportation, and refining, petrochemicals, natural gas production and transmission, and the complex services used by the energy industries offered Houston law firms tremendous opportunities for involvement with corporations of national and international stature. Capital from the East, followed by people, poured into the city, and many needed the services of knowledgeable legal counsel. Houston was now the home of several prominent national corporations, which occupied multiple floors of the city's growing downtown office space. Capital inflow and indigenous corporate growth fueled the expansion of the region's basic infrastructure—its highways and electric power capacity. By the mid-1950s, Houston was an attractive spot for investment of all sorts. Its expanding market spawned hundreds of new retailers and service sector firms each year. These businesses, too, had need of legal services.[1]

As Houston's economy matured, Baker & Botts's practice became more varied. No longer did simple labels such as "the railroad firm" or "utility specialist" or even "oil and gas specialist" aptly describe the firm's practice. The partners still had the blue-chip client list developed before World War II, but now it was greatly expanded by the addition of such important new clients as Tenneco and Pennzoil in oil and gas, and Gerald D. Hines Interests in real estate. To such clients, Baker & Botts could offer a tradition of excellence in business-related litigation as well as in the "office work" needed by corporations. On issues of corporate organization and finance the firm had an excellent track record. The strong connections Baker & Botts had to sources of capital in the East also shaped much of its postwar practice, since the extraordinary growth of the city after 1945 generated a demand for investments far beyond the capacities of regional financial institutions. Great sums of money were needed to build the city's skyline, construct the pipelines that took its oil and gas to outside markets, expand its utilities, and provide the various goods and services needed by a modern metropolis. Baker & Botts frequently stood in the center of the vital stream of investment that flowed into the booming region after World War II.

157

Chapter 8
The Coming
of Age
of the Firm
and Its City

This process can be seen clearly in the firm's relationship with one of its most significant and oldest clients, Houston Lighting & Power. The ties between the two organizations went back to their earliest days. After HL&P was spun off from EBASCO, Baker & Botts continued to represent the now-independent utility company. HL&P had the franchise to supply the booming city of Houston with electric power, and after 1945 HL&P had to strain to keep pace with the city's expansion. Baker & Botts at times strained to keep pace with the legal work generated by HL&P's operations. Alvis Parish was the lead attorney in this endeavor, following in the footsteps of such former partners as Edwin Parker and Ralph Feagin. He further followed tradition by serving as a director of the power company, and in 1953 he withdrew from Baker & Botts to become president of HL&P. Under Parish's direction, the company continued its climb up the ranks of the nation's largest utilities, and in the course of that expansion generated a sizable business for Baker & Botts.

Much of the work was routine and repetitious. Rights-of-way had to be acquired; rates had to be determined; damage suits had to be defended. As HL&P spread over a larger geographical area, it needed funds to pay for the growing physical plant. Baker & Botts took care of the considerable legal work required to raise money for HL&P under the SEC's rules. In the 1950s and 1960s the company regularly sold millions of dollars in bonds, and Baker & Botts gradually became so experienced at managing these efforts that even bond issues involving hundreds of millions of dollars became more or less ordinary business.

As the utility's in-house legal department gradually took over more of the routine business, Baker & Botts's efforts were in-

158

Part III
A National
Firm in a
Major City,
1930–Present

creasingly concentrated in several new and controversial areas of law. Beginning in the late 1960s, a wave of environmental legislation at both the state and the federal levels placed significant new regulatory constraints on HL&P's operations, and a generation of new environmental law specialists within Baker & Botts joined hands with the firm's experienced trial lawyers to help resolve the legal issues raised by the application of these laws to the affairs of the utility, as well as those of major manufacturers. In addition, important New Deal legislation like the Wagner Act affected labor relations at a host of companies, while controversial matters such as the possibility of a state income tax worried many local concerns. These matters could not be handled easily by in-house legal departments. Longtime clients such as HL&P expanded operations and had a growing need for both the day-to-day skills of in-house lawyers and the specialized knowledge and experience of large outside law firms.

Houston's large corporate law firms were among the leaders in the effort to roll back or contain government regulation in these and other areas. All of them, Baker & Botts included, maintained active lobbying staffs in Austin to help defeat repeated attempts to pass a state income tax, which business feared would be used to tax corporate profits as well, and to assure that Texas had weak environmental laws. Emphasizing the need for a "good business climate" to keep people and capital pouring into the city in the postwar years, they effectively expounded the same themes that had been so useful in blunting municipal utility regulation a generation earlier. To a large extent, the lawyers and their clients were also aided by the ideology of smaller local business leaders, who combined a hatred of communism with a strong antilabor bias (in the form of right-to-work laws) and a determined resistance to any change in race relations. These even more conservative forces at times went far beyond the more tempered goals of Houston's elite big business leaders and their well-educated lawyers.[2] But the net result of this chorus of sometimes conflicting voices was a strong commitment in Houston, through the 1960s, to laws favorable to unfettered business growth. In representing its corporate clients, Baker & Botts constituted one of the many voices.

Not all of Baker & Botts's longtime clients found this era a happy one. Some went through turbulent changes in the new Houston economy. South Texas Commercial National Bank, for example, encountered difficult legal constraints in its efforts to expand after World War II. The Baker family and Baker & Botts maintained their strong ties to the bank in this era, as James Baker, Jr., followed in the footsteps of his father, Captain Baker, in managing the bank's legal affairs and in serving as both a director and an officer. Other Baker & Botts partners, notably H. Malcolm Lovett and Dillon Anderson, also joined the bank's board. Together they helped guide the bank through a difficult period.

159

Chapter 8
The Coming
of Age
of the Firm
and Its City

South Texas Bank, which had been hard hit by the Great Depression, staggered into the postwar era in need of growth. Even the largest Texas banks were far too small to meet the growing demands for loans and other banking services made by the big corporations active in the state. In this sense, the state's financial institutions were not keeping pace with the remainder of the economy. Legal barriers to growth stymied these banks as they sought additional capital and higher lending limits.

Of particular importance was the state's unit banking law, a constitutional stipulation that limited banks to one place of business. This nineteenth-century law had been designed to keep banks small, under local control, and thus less capable of abuses. As the state's economy expanded and industrialized, however, this law became a substantial barrier to the rise of a banking system capable of financing development. Large companies simply turned elsewhere for funds while the leading banks in Texas lagged further and further behind the needs of the state economy. South Texas, with the help of Baker & Botts, tried to grow by way of mergers.

The first such combination took place in 1953, when South Texas consolidated with the Union National Bank, a small organization housed just across the street. Baker & Botts steered the two banks through a variety of regulatory challenges from state and federal authorities with the power to approve bank mergers. This consolidation raised few questions in the eyes of regulators, but one seemingly trivial dispute threatened the banks' plans until Baker & Botts came up with a creative solution that avoided a direct challenge to the unit banking law.

The management of South Texas had begun construction of a modern office building before the merger proposal, and the new building promised sufficient space to house the combined operations of the two institutions. Yet the new home for Texas National Bank (TNB)—the name chosen for the merged entity—would not be completed for several years after the merger. In

160

Part III
A National
Firm in a
Major City,
1930–Present

the meantime, management hoped to continue to operate TNB from their two buildings. Despite the fact that these buildings were across the street from each other, this arrangement would nonetheless be illegal under the prevailing interpretation of the unit banking law.

In preparing an opinion on this issue, Baker & Botts's lawyers found a compromise that allowed the merger to proceed. Several years earlier, the Texas attorney general had allowed another Texas bank to open a drive-in window in a garage across the street from its main building with only a message tube linking the two locations; the tube made them legally acceptable as a unit bank. This opinion opened the door for a strange, yet effective, answer to the problems of TNB and its potential "branch" across the street. The construction of a pneumatic tube between the two buildings convinced regulators to allow the bank to operate temporarily out of two buildings.

Less successful were Baker & Botts's efforts to merge TNB with Houston's second-largest bank, the National Bank of Commerce (NBC). Dillon Anderson helped negotiate a merger for TNB that appeared to hold out excellent prospects for the bank in its union with the larger NBC, which had long been identified in Houston as "Jesse Jones's bank." Yet what began as a friendly merger turned into a bitter battle in which many top officials of TNB left the new organization. This outcome temporarily left Baker & Botts as one of the only major corporate law firms in Houston not closely tied with one of the city's major banks. Only with the passing of time did the firm gradually reestablish ties with Texas Commerce Bank, which was the name ultimately taken by the bank created in the TNB-NBC merger.[5]

Another client long served by Baker & Botts, Rice University, much more successfully adapted to changing conditions after World War II. After Captain Baker's death in 1941, other Baker & Botts attorneys, including H. Malcolm Lovett, the son of the first president of Rice, remained deeply involved in both governance and fund raising at the school. In the 1960s, they helped the school make some fundamental choices about its future. While Rice had taken long strides toward building a national reputation, there were several barriers to a move up the ranks of the nation's leading universities. As stipulated in its original indenture, Rice was "free" (that is, tuition-free) and for "whites only." When its leaders decided that their institution needed to alter both of the restrictions, they turned to Baker & Botts for legal guidance. Tuition would assist Rice in paying for the costly equipment and personnel needed to become a top-flight school; integration was essential if Rice was to change its image as a discriminatory southern university.

161

Chapter 8
The Coming
of Age
of the Firm
and Its City

Wishing to test the legal waters, in 1963 the Rice trustees petitioned in district court for the authority to remove the bothersome restrictions from William Marsh Rice's indenture. Thus began a much-publicized case that thrust both the university and Baker & Botts into the spotlight of public scrutiny. Several angry Rice alumni decided to intervene to the suit to block these changes. They argued vehemently that the trustees should not be allowed to "break the Rice will." As the controversial trial got under way, Baker & Botts attorneys countered with a dramatic rendering of the choice facing Rice. Would it remain a parochial southern college, or would it become a first-class university? In microcosm, this was the pivotal issue facing Houston and all of its leading institutions in the early 1960s. If they aspired to national prominence, it was past time to move out of the shadows of a segregated past and a local orientation.

With an eye toward the wave of changes sweeping through the South in the early 1900s, the attorneys identified the winning ground for their client. They argued that the trustees were bound by the primary goal of the indenture when and if changing conditions placed it in conflict with any of the secondary stipulations of the document. The overriding purpose of William Marsh Rice, they asserted, was the creation in Houston of a university "of the first class." In the 1890s this goal had not been incompatible with the idea of a free, segregated institution of higher learning. Now the trustees' primary responsibility was to adapt the stated intent of the founder to the new realities faced by the university. The court agreed, concluding that "free" and "for whites only" would have to give way to the indenture's overriding goal, the creation of a university of the first class. After a series of highly publicized appeals, this view prevailed, and Rice began admitting black students and charging tuition in 1965.[4]

As a force in city building, Baker & Botts's success in the postwar period was more mixed than during the heyday of Captain Baker. The loss of South Texas Bank certainly hurt the firm at a time when its competitors had all established close ties to major local banks. Vinson & Elkins was growing rapidly under the direction of Judge James Elkins, who pushed forward both his law firm and his bank, First City. This crosstown rival was building

162

Part III
A National
Firm in a
Major City,
1930–Present

up an impressive list of clients among independent oil producers, whose fabulous fortunes and colorful personalities made
them almost larger-than-life local figures and extremely powerful within the confines of the region. If there was a center of political and civic power in postwar Houston, it most certainly was
to be found in the "8-F crowd," which met regularly at that suite
in the downtown Lamar Hotel. Prominent members of this influential group included Judge Elkins, builder Jesse Jones, up-and-
coming construction magnates Herman and George Brown, and
insurance man Gus Wortham. No Baker & Botts partner figured
prominently in the affairs of this powerful circle of influence,
which enjoyed a position in the affairs of the city similar to that
once held by members of Baker & Botts.[5]

Yet in another sense, the nature of power in the city had
changed. No single elite, not even the 8-F crowd, could really
control a population of nearly a million people. Houston's business community was made up of international oil conglomerates
and wildcat drillers, real estate moguls, and nationwide retail
stores. It was an increasingly complex economy attuned to the
winds of international change as well as the price of suburban
housing. In this world, expertise and cosmopolitan connections
as much as a wad of money and an outsized personality determined who had power. As the law firm that had long played on
its eastern connections and high standards of professionalism,
Baker & Botts had some assets at its disposal not available to its
more locally centered competitors. It successfully parlayed them
into strong working relationships with clients seeking to move
aggressively into the national economy.

A number of these clients carried the firm much further into
high-level corporate and financial matters on the national scene.
Nowhere was the firm's postwar maturity more evident than in
its representation of Tenneco,[6] a Houston-based company that
surged to the forefront of the natural gas transmission industry
in the 1940s and 1950s. Baker & Botts performed for Tenneco
most of the roles it had previously undertaken for businesses entering the region. It took care of local suits while furnishing general legal and business advice to management. But in addition,
Baker & Botts served as the general counsel for the corporation.
In that capacity, the partners took the lead throughout Tenneco's
extensive pipeline system in coordinating the work of local attorneys, managing the filing of numerous securities issues before the SEC, and participating in the resolution of a variety of

regulatory matters before the Federal Power Commission and state utility commissions. In many ways, representation of Tenneco marked Baker & Botts's coming of age as a nationally active law firm.

163

Chapter 8
The Coming
of Age
of the Firm
and Its City

Tenneco and other leading natural gas firms—notably Texas Eastern Corporation and Transcontinental Gas (Transco)—were on the cutting edge of Houston's postwar boom. By World War II the city had built the foundation for sustained economic growth around a core of oil- and gas-related industries. In the decades after the war, a modern metropolis arose on this foundation. The gas industry was not the only engine of growth; oil, petrochemicals, medical sciences, and by the 1960s the space industry all contributed heartily to Houston's ascent into the ranks of the nation's largest cities.[7] But gas was a relatively new industry whose dramatic expansion was particularly important to modern Houston. The major natural gas fields in the nation were concentrated in Texas, Louisiana, and Oklahoma. Most of the leading cross-country shippers of this fuel established corporate headquarters in Houston. As a clean, inexpensive fuel for local industries, natural gas also provided a part of the competitive advantage that helped attract new business to the Gulf Coast area.

Through its work for Tenneco, Baker & Botts was able to stay near the center of this expanding industry. The firm's initial contacts with Tenneco came through Stone & Webster, which had acquired a controlling interest in Tenneco in 1945. When Tenneco set out to expand its operations, it hired Baker & Botts without a retainer to assist in preparing an amendment to its original mortgage and a plan for recapitalization. H. Malcolm Lovett, who had joined Baker & Botts in 1924 after graduating from the Harvard Law School, directed much of the Tenneco legal business. His introduction to the company had involved a routine matter of no special import at the time, but over subsequent decades the company's affairs came to absorb much of his time.[8] He also became a close associate of Tenneco's dynamic president, Gardiner Symonds, and served on the company's board from 1959 to 1972, after which he remained an emeritus member.

Tenneco could make good use of Baker & Botts's extensive experience in the oil and gas field and in railroad work. The former was crucial in the meticulous preparation of gas purchase contracts, a routine matter of vital significance to a gas transportation company. The latter helped the law firm in coordinating the activities of the numerous local attorneys on whom Tenneco

164

Part III
A National
Firm in a
Major City,
1930–Present

relied to look after its legal affairs in the communities along its pipelines. Baker & Botts managed the affairs of this network of lawyers. In search of good local counsel, the firm made use of the extensive legal correspondent records it had maintained for its internal use since the 1920s. While this endeavor in part replicated its previous work for the SP, the Houston partners no longer stood midway between the corporate attorneys and the network; now Baker & Botts was the corporate counsel supervising a system stretching across half the nation.[9]

Baker & Botts was also called on to assist in another critically important task—the preparation of Tenneco's bid for the Big Inch and Little Big Inch pipelines. These two lines were built with government funds and private expertise and management during World War II to assure the flow of essential crude oil and refined petroleum products from the southwestern producing and refining regions to the East Coast. They were the first pipelines directly connecting the nation's major producing regions with the large eastern markets, and the government's decision about how and when to convert them to peacetime use was the source of much concern in the oil and gas industries.

Both Baker & Botts and Tenneco were already quite familiar with the pipelines. Brady Cole had served as associate general counsel for the War Emergency Pipelines (WEP) during the early phases of their construction in 1942. He was brought into the project originally through Burt Hull, Texaco's pipeline specialist, who was chosen to manage the construction of the WEP.[10] Tenneco's involvement came after the war. Severe shortages of natural gas in the Appalachian region in 1946 persuaded the Department of Interior to lease the Inch lines temporarily to Tenneco, which was to use them to ship natural gas to help relieve the fuel shortage in West Virginia. Under this agreement, Tenneco operated the Inch lines from December 1946 through April 1947, and this experience whetted the company's appetite for the acquisition.[11]

As the government launched the bidding process, Baker & Botts helped Tenneco create a 100 percent–owned subsidiary, called Eastern, to handle this business and assisted CEO Gardiner Symonds in formulating strategy. This work included planning Tenneco's bid and formulating a variety of contingency plans.[12] As it turned out, Tenneco's bid proved too low; in a competition with momentous implications for the evolution of the cross-country natural gas industry, the Inch lines went to the newly organized Texas Eastern Corporation, which had strong personal and working ties to Vinson & Elkins, one of the emerging Houston-based rivals of Baker & Botts. Tenneco and its lead law firm looked for possible ways to disqualify Texas Eastern's winning offer. These efforts also failed, so Tenneco and Baker & Botts turned quickly to their contingency plans.

165

Chapter 8

The Coming

of Age

of the Firm

and Its City

While bitterly disappointed, Tenneco soon moved to extend its existing pipeline system into the major eastern markets. As the firm aggressively constructed new lines, Baker & Botts supervised the demanding legal work involved in securing rights-of-way and in defending various local cases that arose as a result of this expansion. Under the terms of the Natural Gas Act of 1938, gas transportation companies could exercise the power of eminent domain to acquire rights-of-way necessary for pipeline construction. But state-by-state implementing legislation had to be passed to define the terms on which this power could be used, so Baker & Botts and the local attorneys under its supervision had considerable work to do in resolving the questions raised by Tenneco's expanding pipeline system.

Tenneco president Gardiner Symonds chose the Boston area as Tenneco's first goal among the urban markets of the Northeast, and as his firm pushed hard to complete the construction of its new pipeline into New England, the Baker & Botts lawyers found themselves in an ironic position. The law firm had long ago learned to live with the recurring criticism that it was the representative of Yankees exploiting the South. Now it was perceived by New Englanders as "these Texas boys in their cowboy boots and their big hats going up there with a machete in each hand and chopping down hedges and clearing the rights of way."[13] The firm was seen once more as the representative of "foreign" interests who threatened local interests. As had been the case before, it was an agent of industrial change, this time in an industrialized region not completely prepared to embrace a new mode of "progress."

Sustained expansion required additional infusions of capital, and Baker & Botts's lead role in this work represented a clear advance in the firm's evolution. Financing for large national corporations had generally been done by Wall Street firms. This had simply been an accepted part of the "natural order" of the legal profession in an era when most large corporations had headquarters in New York and when the laws governing such financial transactions remained largely the laws of New York state.

166

Part III

A National

Firm in a

Major City,

1930–Present

Tenneco was based in Houston, however, not New York. More significantly, the rules governing corporate finance had been "federalized" by the creation of the Securities and Exchange Commission. As a result, the Houston law firm mounted Tenneco's forays into Wall Street, relying on its previous experience for United Gas and HL&P and working closely with Cahill Gordon & Reindel, Tenneco's New York counsel. By one estimate, "New York's money men anted up no less than $1.3 billion over the years (before 1957) for Symonds' projects. All but an inconsequential part of this amount [was] raised by financings in which this Firm [Baker & Botts] acted as counsel for Tennessee Gas." [14]

The representation of Tenneco also carried the firm into new sorts of work before federal regulatory commissions. The Federal Power Commission exercised broad powers over the interstate gas business. Any company engaged in interstate shipments needed a clear understanding of the regulatory rules of the FPC and a smooth working relationship with the commission's staff. Baker & Botts was at first not well situated to provide effective representation in Washington, so Tenneco continued to maintain a close relationship with a Washington-based firm throughout these years. But Baker & Botts became more familiar with the world of Washington law practice and with the special demands of work before the FPC and other federal regulatory commissions. [15]

As Tenneco began to diversify, Baker & Botts had excellent opportunities to develop its expertise in matters of corporate mergers and reorganizations. Tenneco built one of the first and the most successful conglomerates, and Baker & Botts handled much of the legal work required to acquire, finance, and integrate new acquisitions into that corporation's existing business. Members of the law firm provided advice to top management on legal and business strategy; Baker & Botts partners retained a place on Tenneco's board of directors. As the first nationally active Houston-based corporation for which Baker & Botts served as general attorney, Tenneco remained a symbol of the law firm's growing maturity. As Tenneco moved steadily up the ranks of the nation's largest corporations, Baker & Botts enjoyed access to high-level work and a more visible standing within the legal profession.

This work for Tenneco helped prepare the firm for its new role in the oil industry. In the 1950s innovations in oil financing fed a wave of consolidations that resulted in the absorption of

the assets of several Houston-based oil concerns by major, nationally active petroleum corporations. Baker & Botts, which
served as counsel for the acquiring companies, encountered new
and exciting legal issues at the cutting edge of corporate law.

167
Chapter 8
The Coming
of Age
of the Firm
and Its City

Only after World War II did the nation's major financial institutions venture into the business of oil financing. The regulatory
system now ensured price stability and greater predictability in
the recovery of reserves. The Texas Railroad Commission and
other regulators succeeded in limiting the production of oil to
the maximum recoverable rate under the direction of profes-
sionally trained petroleum engineers. This revolutionary change
encouraged banks and other financial institutions to lend money
to oil producers, using as collateral oil reserves in the ground.
Baker & Botts quickly became a prominent member of a relatively small group of law firms and banks deeply involved in oil
lending.

One particular kind of transaction, the so-called ABC deal,
proved particularly significant for the oil industry as a whole and
for the emerging modern corporate practice of Baker & Botts.
First introduced in the 1930s, these complicated transactions became standard fare in financing the growth of oil production in
the 1950s and 1960s. In essence, such agreements were a means
for converting future production from proven reserves into investment dollars in a way that took fullest advantage of existing
tax laws, especially the oil depletion allowance. The depletion
allowance permitted a producer to exempt from federal income
tax 27.5 percent of the gross wellhead value of oil or gas production up to a limit of 50 percent of the net income from that
property.[16]

The inner workings of the ABC transaction suggest the cre-
ativity with which this generation of tax and oil and gas lawyers
attacked the problem of providing their clients with the capital
they needed to expand their operations. Baker & Botts partner
James L. Shepherd, Jr., was nationally recognized as a leader in
this field, which remained little understood or even noted by any
but a small group of specialists. Indeed, oil and gas specialists
within Baker & Botts felt the need from time to time to walk their
colleagues at the firm through these transactions step by step to
explain just how they worked. As the *Office Review* explained in
1951: "This type of financing involving the creation of a production payment which constitutes the security to be mortgaged
to the Banks is nothing new. However, it is perhaps unusual

168

Part III
A National
Firm in a
Major City,
1930–Present

enough to justify a review of the 'package' of documents by any lawyer who happens to represent an enterprising oil operator."[17] The entry then summarized how a particular oil operator, "B," negotiated a $2.4 million purchase of gas-producing properties. "A," the seller of the properties, received a $2.4 million cash payment from "C," a "straw-man" corporation set up specifically for the transaction. The cash used by "C" for the purchase came from two sources: a $300,000 payment from "B" (the real buyer) and a $2.1 million bank loan from the South Texas National Bank, which was represented in this transaction by Baker & Botts. The bank's loan bore interest at the rate of 4 1/2 percent per annum on the unliquidated principal balance of the loan and was secured by a mortgage from "C" covering a "production payment"—the right of "C" to receive the proceeds from the sale of 90 percent of the gas produced from the properties until "C" realized the primary sum of $2.1 million plus an amount equivalent to interest at the rate of 5 percent per annum on the unliquidated balance of that primary sum. Simultaneous with the sale of the properties by "A" to "C," "C" conveyed the properties to "B," with "C" reserving the production payment and mortgaging it to the bank.

What was the point of all of this shifting of resources? "B" was able to buy the properties with a relatively small cash outlay while saving a considerable amount in taxes over a straight purchase agreement.[18] The proceeds realized by "C" from the production payment were the taxable income of "C," not "B," and "C" could offset this income by $2.1 million of cost depletion and the amount of interest paid on the bank loan. The bank received a good rate of interest on a very secure loan; the front corporation paid off the bank loan as it matured and netted an amount equal to one-half of one percent per annum on the unliquidated balance of the primary sum of the production payment. All parties to the transaction thus benefited.

Although critics decried the ABC transactions as a subsidy through the tax code to oil and gas producers, the complicated system built by legal and financial experts served a useful societal purpose by channeling investment funds into domestic production at a time when imported oil was making inroads on American markets. Working within the flexible boundaries of existing tax laws, oil and gas lawyers fashioned these creative transactions while pursuing the financial interests of their clients. In this sense, the ABC transaction serves as a useful symbol of the historical role of corporate lawyers in exploring the flexibility inherent in much American public policy toward business. When lawmakers came under pressure to examine the favorable tax treatment of the oil and gas industries, these laws were changed in the late 1960s in ways that spelled the end of ABC transaction as a common financing tool in these industries.

169

Chapter 8
The Coming
of Age
of the Firm
and Its City

ABC transactions became a staple of Baker & Botts's oil practice in the postwar era, but the firm quickly moved beyond such basic loans to more creative uses of ABC financing. Beginning in 1955 the firm took part in a series of transactions involving the liquidation of several Houston-based oil companies through the sale of their assets to major oil corporations. Sinclair Oil Company and Atlantic Refining Company, two longtime clients, were the acquiring companies in these expensive and highly publicized transactions which were paid for in part by loans secured by ABC production payments. The newly developed skills of Baker & Botts in the area of production payments facilitated corporate consolidation, a traditional area of strength at the firm since the early days of railroad work. In the process, the firm assisted several of its long-standing clients in the oil industry to grow by way of acquisition to compete on more equal terms with the largest companies in their industry.

The first such transaction involved the purchase of a well-established Houston company, American Republics Corporation, by a longtime client of Baker & Botts, Sinclair Oil. This large and complex transaction involved more than a dozen Baker & Botts attorneys. As the primary representative of Sinclair in Texas, the law firm "had the major responsibility in this matter for the title work and approval of the documents, as well as corporate proceedings, as valid and sufficient." [19] As representative for the acquiring firm, Baker & Botts took much of the responsibility for coordinating the work of all of the different teams of southwestern lawyers involved. Numerous prominent eastern firms participated, including Milbank, Tweed, representing the Chase National Bank; Simpson Thacher & Bartlett, another leading Wall Street firm; and the Philadelphia firm of Ballard, Spahr, Andrews & Ingersoll. Sinclair made use of the firm of Dunnington, Bartholow & Miller, while the investment bank of Lehman Brothers served as broker for the deal. Baker & Botts thus found itself in a nexus of legal and financial talent drawn from an array of the leading law firms and banks in the nation. The fact that Shepherd and his colleagues at Baker & Botts played a central

170

Part III
A National
Firm in a
Major City,
1930–Present

role in this transaction points up the firm's status as one of the accepted leaders in the nation in oil and gas law.

The tone and tempo of these new efforts were different from those of much of the earlier corporate work done at Baker & Botts. The large sums of money and the diversity of the properties involved added a sense of urgency to the proceedings. The work on the entire Sinclair transaction took only about four months to complete, and during that relatively brief period, Baker & Botts and the other law firms involved pushed very hard to finish a quite complicated task. To record required legal documents in a timely fashion, Baker & Botts coordinated the dispatch of copies via five airplanes and two cars from Houston on one pivotal Saturday in March of 1955. After stops in sixty-three counties in Texas, fourteen parishes in Louisiana, and a handful of counties in Arkansas, Alabama, and New Mexico, the groundwork had been laid to complete the deal in New York. Shepherd reported with awe to his partners that the cost of the printing bills alone for this work "will run in excess of $250,000."

Others took note. The *Wall Street Journal* reported that the $75 million production payment was the "largest production payment ever carved out in connection with the purchase of an oil property."[20] This type of publicity had far-reaching ramifications in the oil industry as well as in the investment community, since the successful use of an innovative legal/financial arrangement convinced others to consider this option for their own transactions. A wave of ABC-financed consolidations followed in the wake of the Sinclair deal, and Baker & Botts remained quite active in this area in the late 1950s and early 1960s. The clients involved were varied; the sums of money ranged between fifty million dollars and two hundred million dollars; the primary actors continued to include major money center banks, notably Chase Manhattan, and leading Wall Street law firms, notably Milbank, Tweed. Baker & Botts now had the expertise and experience needed to make even the most complicated of these transactions readily available as a strategic option for companies interested in acquiring or selling valuable oil properties.

The ABC transactions demonstrated that Baker & Botts was capable of applying a broad array of special skills to its clients' diverse legal needs. The clients, too, became more diversified. One in particular, Gerald D. Hines, took Baker & Botts into whole new areas such as real estate law. In the decades after World War II, Hines moved from building warehouses in Houston to a position as one of the leading investment building firms in the nation.[21] During most of these years, Baker & Botts represented Gerald Hines and his organization, Gerald D. Hines Interests (GDHI), as its real estate business surged forward in Houston and in other cities. More than any other developer, Hines built modern Houston; his various projects defined much of the city's modern skyline. Baker & Botts could not have chosen a better client as the centerpiece for an expanding real estate practice. In meeting the needs of Hines, the firm developed new skills and refocused old ones on the variety of legal issues that accompanied major construction projects.

171

Chapter 8
The Coming
of Age
of the Firm
and Its City

Hines, who was trained at Purdue University as an engineer, came to Houston in 1948, just when the city's postwar boom was getting under way. Looking for investment opportunities to supplement his full-time job as an industrial engineer for an air conditioning company, he entered the real estate business in 1951 as a renovator of small buildings. From there he moved into the construction of small warehouses. Using the profits and the experience from these early projects, he advanced to larger and larger structures. As his projects grew, so, too, did his financial and legal needs, and early on he turned to Baker & Botts.

To the law firm this relationship presented important opportunities as well as unique problems. As Hines's projects grew more demanding, he organized Gerald D. Hines Interests, a sole proprietorship in 1957. Even after GDHI expanded dramatically, it remained essentially a sole proprietorship, at times using affiliated corporations to accomplish specific purposes. This legal status gave Hines extraordinary flexibility to enter into an array of partnerships and joint ventures, including equity participations with the tenants of his projects. Yet this approach also entailed grave risks, for Hines's personal liability became extremely high and his agreements with partners and tenants extremely complicated. This situation demanded expert legal advice; unlike most major developers, Hines did not build up a large in-house counsel. Instead, he depended on Baker & Botts.

During the 1960s and 1970s several of the firm's partners played significant roles in Hines's business. Ben White had joined the firm immediately after World War II, and his training and experience were valuable in the intricate financings required for Hines's major deals. James Lee, who had moved into the Oil and Gas Department after joining the firm in 1950, had a command of real property law that proved useful in acquiring and leasing

172

Part III
A National
Firm in a
Major City,
1930–Present

properties. These two attorneys became significant members of a growing team of experts gathered by GDHI. They embodied Hines's innovative approaches to development in legally binding documents. In this case, the clarity of their legal documents was in effect part of the sales ability involved in the undertaking. Baker & Botts helped reassure investors and tenants that Hines's creative concepts were legally sound and did not entail unacceptable risks.

Hines's trademark became the high quality of his buildings, particularly their architectural and aesthetic excellence. As a participant in these projects, Baker & Botts reinforced its own historical image as an institution of high quality and standards, and its ties with GDHI proved quite helpful in recruiting young lawyers interested in becoming involved in top-level real estate law. The city of Houston was also a major beneficiary. It was the site of many of Hines's most visible projects, including the Galleria and One Shell Plaza, a fifty-story, locally financed skyscraper to which Baker & Botts moved its offices in 1971. These and similar undertakings made Houston a recognized center of "progressive architecture," enhancing its image as a city of great dynamism and growing maturity.

The success of the Galleria and One Shell Plaza catapulted GDHI to the top ranks of the nation's developers. The years since 1971 have witnessed an extraordinary wave of building by GDHI. Hines's projects have spread to many locations outside of Houston, and Baker & Botts has remained his general counsel on the major ones. These endeavors have kept the firm closely in touch with the evolving field of real estate law, and its renamed and expanded Oil, Gas, and Real Estate Department is a nationally recognized presence in this field. The law firm has benefited from the legal fees (GDHI was one of its largest clients) and from the prestige of representing one of the country's most innovative developers.

Other new clients brought a wide array of equally challenging issues. Those considered significant enough to require specific descriptions under the heading "Group Assignments" in the firm's plan of organization in 1968 include the following: Bank of the Southwest (now Bank One), Eastex Incorporated, HL&P, Pennzoil United, Schlumberger Limited, Southern Pacific, Tenneco, Texas National Bank of Commerce, Travelers Insurance Company, United Gas Distribution System (now Entex), and Zapata Off-Shore Company. This list suggests the growing diversity of Baker & Botts's practice. But perhaps more indicative of the evolution of the legal work of the firm in these years are the specific descriptions of the work of each of these groups. All of the groups include an extensive list of the particular client's varied legal needs and a corresponding list of the specialists within Baker & Botts primarily responsible for meeting each one.

173
Chapter 8
The Coming
of Age
of the Firm
and Its City

One company—Schlumberger—illustrates well how change and growth placed new demands on the law firm. Schlumberger Well Surveying Corporation—as the company was named in its early history—used technological breakthroughs in surveying for oil to become the international leader in this field. In 1937, soon after entering Texas for the first time, this French company turned to Brady Cole to help solve difficult patent infringement cases. From that point forward, Baker & Botts and Texas became increasingly important to Schlumberger. The company gradually expanded both its operations in the oil fields of the southwestern United States and its administrative offices in Houston. The close ties between Schlumberger and Baker & Botts were cemented by service of members of the firm on the company's board, a tradition that began in the 1940s with John Bullington. Attorneys from the firm were also closely involved in the creation and operations of a subsidiary organized to conduct defense-related work. Schlumberger became the sort of internationally known leader in its industry that major corporate law firms built practices around.[22] By the late 1960s the plan for handling Schlumberger's work included specialists in antitrust, corporate, general and special litigation, labor, patents and trademarks, government contracts, Defense Department security clearance problems, stockholder relations, pension and profit sharing, Latin American matters, the Schlumberger Foundation, and taxation.[23]

It should be noted that the firm's list of major corporate clients in 1968 contained a mix of national companies, Houston-based companies with operations throughout the United States, and more strictly local concerns, such as HL&P and Houston banks. This last group, the local companies, remained a vital part of Baker & Botts's practice, and the firm's work for them continued its long tradition of contributing to Houston's steady development as a modern city. Yet by the 1960s many of the local clients traditionally represented by Baker & Botts had matured into institutions of national prominence. Other relatively new "local" clients, notably Gerald D. Hines Interests, also helped

174

Part III
A National
Firm in a
Major City,
1930–Present

pull Baker & Botts into exciting new areas of the law as they expanded both inside and outside the region. As such companies grew with their city, the legal work performed for them by Baker & Botts became more demanding—and more in line with the modern corporate work performed for other clients. In this sense, these local companies and their law firm matured together, propelled by the long era of postwar prosperity that completed the century-long transformation of Houston into a major city.

No single "local client" did more to pull Baker & Botts into innovative corporate work than the Houston-based oil company that became Pennzoil. In its often spectacular expansion, this company relied heavily on the legal advice of Baine Kerr and the Corporate Department of Baker & Botts. In the course of Pennzoil's aggressive growth, the company explored several relatively new strategies, including hostile takeovers and tender offers. As a result, Baker & Botts became one of the first law firms in the nation to deal with the legal ramifications of these business policies.

Pennzoil climbed up the ranks of the major oil companies through a series of often-spectacular acquisitions and divestitures that brought Baker & Botts a cluster of new clients, notably Zapata Petroleum, Zapata Off-Shore, and POGO. The much-publicized thirteen billion dollar court judgment for Pennzoil in its conflict with Texaco over the acquisition of Getty Oil in the early 1980s was the climax of these steps in the company's history. Well before the 1980s Pennzoil's drive to build a major oil company had led Baker & Botts into little-explored areas of the corporate law governing mergers and the restructuring of acquired companies.

Leading the way at Pennzoil was J. Hugh Liedtke, the son of a prominent oil lawyer in Tulsa, Oklahoma. After completing his education at Amherst College, the Harvard Business School, and the University of Texas Law School, Liedtke served in the navy in World War II and then turned to the booming West Texas oil fields in search of opportunity. His lifelong vision was the creation of a major oil company capable of competing against all comers. This was no small task in an industry dominated by giant, vertically integrated international companies, but the Permian Basin in the 1950s was the right place and time to start his quest.

After setting up headquarters in the oil center of Midland, he went in search of capital for exploration. In this crucial task, he joined with a partner, George Bush, the son of Sen. Prescott

Bush of Connecticut. Like Liedtke, Bush had been drawn to Midland by the lure of an open field for new competitors. The two young men pooled resources drawn from investors in Tulsa and Connecticut and obtained leases to drill for oil. Using a name borrowed from the marquee of a local movie house, in 1953 they launched the Zapata Petroleum Corporation, which enjoyed excellent success finding oil in West Texas. In 1954 they organized a second venture, Zapata Off-Shore Company, as a subsidiary to search for oil off the shores of Louisiana and Texas.[24]

Here Baker & Botts entered the picture. When Zapata Off-Shore made its first public offering of stock, the firm served as counsel for the underwriters. As was the case with many independent oil companies active in West Texas and in the Gulf of Mexico, both of the Zapata ventures were drawn to Houston as the most logical source for finance, transportation, and marketing. There Off-Shore came to the attention of Bush's friend from prep school Robert Parish, who was at the time associated with Underwood, Neuhaus & Co., investment bankers. Parish guided the new company to Baker & Botts, where his father, Alvis Parish, was a name partner and a longtime utility specialist. Following the success of Zapata Off-Shore's initial underwriting, Baker & Botts became the principal counsel for the business. In 1959 Zapata Off-Shore—under the direction of George Bush—became an independent company, and Baker & Botts remained both its and Zapata Petroleum's counsel.[25]

Baine Kerr, one of the founders of the Corporate Department at Baker & Botts, played a central role in these developments. An honors graduate from the University of Texas Law School in 1942, he entered Baker & Botts in 1945 after serving in the South Pacific in World War II. His brief apprenticeship under Jesse Andrews included detailed work on the financing of a major department store in Houston. He then worked under Alvis Parish, who by this time was engaged primarily in matters pertaining to the financing of Houston Lighting & Power and United Gas Corporation. Both of these companies returned again and again to the capital markets, and Kerr regularly accompanied Parish on extended trips to New York City for the preparation of the legal documents needed to complete these financial transactions. By the mid-1950s Kerr was well prepared to step forward and handle the legal work of Zapata. By that time he had already developed a substantial reputation as a creative corporate lawyer.

In handling the challenging issues raised by the legal work

175

Chapter 8
The Coming
of Age
of the Firm
and Its City

176

Part III

A National

Firm in a

Major City,

1930–Present

spawned by Liedtke's ambitious expansion, Kerr could call on the support of a growing corps of specialists within the Corporate Department of Baker & Botts. Of special importance was Kerr's longtime colleague John Mackin, who came to the firm in 1941. Mackin and Kerr formed a potent duo. Mackin, who performed much of Tenneco's legal work, was a consummate corporate lawyer whose steady, forceful presence provided an excellent counterpoise to Kerr's more flamboyant personality. Together, the two built the modern corporate practice of Baker & Botts.

The work they performed for Zapata Petroleum was anything but routine. Liedtke wanted to explore every legal avenue to rapid expansion, and his efforts placed Baker & Botts in the middle of several of the earliest merger battles of the postwar era. The typical corporate consolidation of the 1950s had been a negotiated transaction—like the ABC transactions—in which lawyers played the role of facilitators who helped the parties involved strike a mutually desired bargain. The conciliatory tone reflected the mood of the so-called American era of postwar prosperity. What Liedtke heralded was a dawning age of increased competition in which industries grown fat and lazy during several decades of easy prosperity would be forced into drastic transformations. These adjustments would be accompanied by struggles between established organizations and newly aggressive competitors. The tone of this new wave of consolidation would be confrontational; the role of lawyers would be that of gladiators instead of facilitators. Liedtke and others seeking to improve their competitive positions would need corporate counsel capable of mapping new legal strategies to sustain their expansion policies.

The first challenge for Baine Kerr and his colleagues came in the early 1960s, when Zapata Petroleum sought a profitable investment for the funds generated by the spin-off of Zapata Off-Shore. As Liedtke scanned the ranks of potential merger partners, his gaze came to rest on the South Penn Company, which had been active in the Pennsylvania petroleum industry since its incorporation in 1889 as part of John D. Rockefeller's original Standard Oil combine. After the Supreme Court broke up Standard Oil in 1911, South Penn survived as a specialty oil company using Appalachian crude to produce Pennzoil motor oils for sale in national and international markets. South Penn had refused to venture far from this successful formula, and the high quality of its products made it a profitable operation.

Liedtke recognized the value of the Pennzoil brand name and saw an opportunity to increase South Penn's profitability through more aggressive management. South Penn, he knew, was vulnerable to a well-designed takeover bid. Its stock was widely dispersed, with no single stockholder controlling more than about 10 percent. The largest block of stock was owned by J. Paul Getty, the legendary oilman who had created Getty Oil Company while also investing in a variety of petroleum-related concerns. Liedtke had a passing acquaintance with Getty and close ties to several of his top aides. Liedtke reasoned that South Penn's largest stockholder might be persuaded to refrain from attempting to block his plans for a takeover—or even to throw his stock and his influence into the Liedtke camp. But Getty demurred. When Liedtke's investment in the company matched his own, he said, he would be willing to discuss the matter further.

Liedtke accepted that challenge and pushed forward in search of investment capital. To this end, John Mackin of Baker & Botts created the Choctaw Company, a legal entity established to purchase shares in the targeted company in the names of prominent stockholders in Zapata Petroleum. In these calm days before the frenzied merger movement that began in the late 1970s, few SEC regulations constrained takeover activities. There was no warning of the sort required today, so the management of South Penn suddenly found itself confronted by a new and assertive minority interest. Before top managers had much chance to analyze their options, Liedtke had gained a spot on the board of directors. Now he received the support of the Getty-controlled shareholder interest, and in 1962 Hugh Liedtke became CEO of South Penn. He had the springboard he needed to even bigger things.

The first step was a corporate reorganization, handled by Baker & Botts. The boards of Zapata petroleum, South Penn, and another company, Stetco Petroleum Corporation, all sent representatives to a meeting in Chicago in March 1963, to discuss the issues raised by consolidation. Baine Kerr, who outlined the legal questions, then took the lead in creating a unified organization. The result was the creation of a new company, Pennzoil, with administrative headquarters in Pittsburgh and an office for exploration and development in Houston. Baker & Botts became

177

Chapter 8
The Coming
of Age
of the Firm
and Its City

178

Part III

A National
Firm in a
Major City,
1930–Present

the lead law firm for the new company, and Kerr earned a spot on its board.[26]

Under Liedtke's leadership, Pennzoil quickly sought more opportunities to expand. Even before the consolidation was completed, Liedtke acquired Wolf's Head Refining Company, and in 1965 he began discussions with another major Pennsylvania-grade motor oil specialist, Kendall. When this venture ran afoul of the Justice Department, Liedtke did not stop to brood over his misfortune. Instead, he almost immediately embarked on what was to become one of the most controversial takeover battles of the 1960s.

His new target was United Gas, a longtime Baker & Botts client. Pennzoil's management identified United as a likely candidate for a takeover for several reasons. Aside from its profitable pipeline system, United also owned substantial oil- and gas-producing properties on the Gulf Coast, a region in which Pennzoil was especially weak. In addition, United owned a 78 percent interest in Duval Mining, an independent subsidiary that was highly regarded as a producer of sulfur. Although United Gas was a strong company, approximately five times as large as Pennzoil, Liedtke and his strategists concluded that enough stock could be acquired to give Pennzoil a dominant position within United. The fact that United was not a willing partner to a merger was troublesome, but not enough reason in and of itself to convince Liedtke to look elsewhere.

Baker & Botts now faced a ticklish problem. United Gas was a major client and any representation of a company involved in an attempted hostile takeover obviously represented a conflict of interest. Kerr, who had spent part of his apprenticeship at Baker & Botts working with Alvis Parish on United financings, quickly disqualified himself from representing Pennzoil in its battle for United. The Houston firm of Fulbright & Jaworski stepped in to handle the acquisition.

But still, how could David take over Goliath? It was clear that Pennzoil could not succeed by simply approaching its much larger target to negotiate a deal. To avoid warning United management with a direct approach doomed to certain failure, Pennzoil opted to make a cash tender offer for United's stock. Such a tactic had seldom been used in the United States, but one of Pennzoil's directors was from Scotland, and he reported that cash tender offers were quite common in Great Britain. The procedure was deceptively simple. Pennzoil merely announced its intention to buy at a specified price all of the shares of United that it was offered. The trick was to set a price that would attract the shares needed to gain a dominant position within the company—and to raise the money necessary to pay for them.

179
Chapter 8
The Coming
of Age
of the Firm
and Its City

Once the tender offer was announced, United's management moved to defend itself. Turning to the Wall Street law firm of Simpson, Thacher & Bartlett, United sued Pennzoil in New York in an effort to gain an injunction against the tender offer. The acquisition, they argued, would be detrimental to the interest of United's stockholders, since Pennzoil would have to register as a public utility holding company if it succeeded in gaining control. Pennzoil knew that far-reaching adaptations in the operations of the consolidated company would be required under the Public Utility Holding Company Act of 1935, but it countered that such adaptations could be made without harming shareholders of either company. By the time this suit had been resolved in favor of Pennzoil, United stock had come pouring forth in response to the tender offer.[27]

Both companies now had a common interest, the completion of the merger. With Pennzoil in control of United Gas, Baker & Botts no longer had a conflict of interest and could represent them both. Before confronting the difficult legal issues raised by the merger, Baine Kerr and his colleagues at Pennzoil had first to secure the almost forty million dollars needed to purchase the unexpectedly large number of shares tendered by United shareholders. Working under severe time constraints, the principals in Pennzoil-United turned to friends and investors in Houston, in West Texas, and in New York City for the funds needed to close the deal. There were frustrating delays as representatives of investors sought legal and financial safeguards. With the closing set for Pittsburgh, many of the principals remained in New York hammering out the last-minute details needed to satisfy all parties to this many-sided agreement. As the deadline neared, the final indenture and purchase agreement was put together "with paste and staples." The completion of complicated transactions under demanding deadlines was becoming the norm in high-level corporate work, especially that involving mergers and acquisitions. By this time, Baker & Botts knew how to work effectively under these conditions.

Then, suddenly, the pace of the transaction slowed. Since Pennzoil-United would be a public utility holding company under existing law, its attorneys had to complete the merger under the

180

Part III

A National

Firm in a

Major City,

1930–Present

supervision of the SEC (which had authority to enforce the Public Utility Company Act). Despite Baker & Botts's familiarity with the relevant negotiations, the process of gaining SEC approval moved at a snail's pace. The merged company was required to dispose of its retail gas distribution division. This meant spinning off United Gas, Inc., which formally became an independent company in 1970. Renamed Entex, Inc., in 1974, this business continued to serve as a major retailer of natural gas in Houston and in other sections of Texas, Louisiana, and Mississippi. Even after the divestment of Entex, Pennzoil-United's assets of over one billion dollars made it one of the largest corporations headquartered in the Southwest. Baker & Botts, which had helped complete one of the largest consolidations ever accomplished under regulatory proceedings, now served as the general counsel for both Pennzoil-United and Entex. As both an attorney and an officer, Baine Kerr stayed deeply involved in the legal and economic affairs of Pennzoil; John Maginnis, a utility specialist for the law firm, played a similar role at Entex.[28]

Kerr had much to do because Liedtke was still on the move. He kept United's oil and gas reserves on the Gulf Coast and offshore in the Gulf of Mexico, as well as the majority holding in the Duval Corporation. But he decided to sell off the backbone of the old United Gas Corporation—its extensive pipeline system—and this brought forth another round of legal work for Baker & Botts. With the completion of this spin-off, Pennzoil dropped United from its name, and the pipeline system reclaimed a part of its historical name by becoming United Gas Pipeline. Both companies still qualified as large corporations; both had extensive operations in Houston; both also retained Baker & Botts as their lead counsel.

To keep pace with Hugh Liedtke's ambitions, the law firm helped him develop some creative means of financing. This was perhaps most evident in the formation of a separate company, POGO, to engage in the risky business of oil and gas exploration in the Gulf of Mexico. Pennzoil provided its new affiliate with administrative services for a management fee. It also supplemented the funds public investors provided to enable POGO to compete effectively with large international oil companies for offshore leases. Pennzoil backed POGO's venture with a unique guarantee to investors that it would exchange shares of Pennzoil's common stock for outstanding POGO debentures in the event of a default. Reassured, investors poured money into what became a highly successful venture (and another major client of Baker & Botts). This sort of financing required extensive guidance from lawyers who shared Liedtke's faith in Pennzoil and his aggressive approach to expansion. Baker & Botts supplied both by providing this growing company access to a wide range of specialists in corporate, oil and gas, tax, and securities law.[29]

By the early 1970s it was clear that the nature of Baker & Botts's practice had changed substantially. No longer was it a regional firm or a single-interest partnership. Its practice was diversified. It had adapted successfully to the wide variety of legal services demanded by its clients. Through a new generation of partners like Baine Kerr and John Mackin, it had gained a whole array of new clients. The next challenge for the firm was to mold its organization and membership to fit this exciting but demanding work in an increasingly competitive legal market.

181
Chapter 8
The Coming
of Age
of the Firm
and Its City

Organizing for a National Practice

T HE MOVE IN 1971 to new offices in One Shell Plaza was symbolic of broad changes in the organization of Baker & Botts. Since the late 1920s the firm had been housed in the Esperson Buildings, and the contrast between the old quarters and the new was striking. One of the city's first modern skyscrapers, One Shell Plaza was a sleek, boxlike structure dominating the northwest corner of Houston's skyline. It looked down on the shorter, squatter Niels Esperson Building, whose ornate carvings bespoke its origins. More than physical differences in the buildings suggested the significance of Baker & Botts's move. The very names of the two structures highlighted the coming of a new era to the city and the firm.

Born in Denmark, Niels Esperson had come to Houston in 1905 via California, Oklahoma, and Kansas. He made his fortune in oil, rice, and insurance. People such as Esperson, Captain Baker, William Marsh Rice, and Jesse Jones had recognized the opportunities in a small frontier city and devoted their lives to building both it and their personal fortunes. By contrast, One Shell Plaza heralded an era of large corporations, not large personal enterprises, on the Gulf Coast. The building's "name" tenant—Shell, U.S.A.—was an important part of one of the world's largest multinational corporations. The move of this major company's administrative headquarters from New York to Houston in the 1970s was one much-publicized measure of the city's arrival as a major urban center.

The decision to move out of the Esperson Building culminated many other important organizational and managerial changes in the firm. Beginning with Captain Baker's death in 1941, the generation of partners who had built the firm passed away. By 1953 Baker, Clarence Wharton, Edwin Parker, Walter

Walne, Ralph Feagin, and Brady Cole were gone. Other younger partners had also died or moved on during the 1940s and early 1950s. For much of the postwar era, Baker & Botts was a firm in the midst of a long generational transformation. While the founders were no longer present, the group they had trained was running the firm, carrying on the traditions. At the same time, a new group was emerging from a different world that possessed different ideas.

Sustained growth and a maturing practice were also steadily, if at times imperceptibly, pushing the firm toward fundamental changes. For a time in the 1950s and 1960s, the pressures for change were contained by relatively minor adjustments in governance and structure—the organizational equivalent of absorbing new office space down the hall at the Esperson Building. But by the early 1970s the time for minor adjustments had passed. A nationally active law firm growing steadily toward the two-hundred-lawyer mark could no longer be managed in the same manner as the much smaller organization of Edwin Parker's days.

William Harvin, who took over as managing partner in 1972, was committed to basic alterations in the firm's organization. Harvin was the first managing partner drawn from the ranks of those who had entered the firm after World War II. After joining the firm in 1947 and advancing steadily as a trial lawyer, he and others from the postwar generation began to speak with a louder voice in firm governance. Having proven his ability on various governance committees, Harvin entered the managing partner's position with an expressed desire to modify existing management and reward systems so as to increase the standing of lawyers younger than the small group of "seniors" who still dominated the firm's affairs. Harvin and his allies pushed through reforms that altered many phases of firm operations, from recruitment to compensation. As a whole, these changes moved Baker & Botts closer to the national model of large law firm governance that had emerged as firms came to grips with the new realities of increased size, greater specialization, and a more competitive market for new lawyers and clients.[1]

The sustained growth of the firm was clearly one factor driving these adjustments. Between 1948 and 1968 Baker & Botts nearly tripled in size, expanding from 47 to 132 lawyers and, in the process, keeping pace with the leading firms in New York, Chicago, and Washington. As shown in table 4, this rate of growth was not unusual, but the cumulative results of expansion

183

Chapter 9
Organizing
for a
National
Practice

184
Part III
A National
Firm in a
Major City,
1930–Present

TABLE 4
GROWTH OF FIRM

Year	No. of Lawyers	No. of Partners	No. of Associates	Associate/ Partner Ratio	% Increase Lawyers
1866	2	2	0	NA	NA
1878	2	2	0	NA	NA
1888	3	3	0	NA	NA
1898	3	2	1	0.50	NA
1908	7	6	1	0.16	NA
1918	16	12	4	0.33	NA
1928	25	10	15	1.50	56
1938	39	16	23	1.44	56
1948	47	14	33	2.36	20
1958	76	25	51	2.04	62
1968	132	41	91	2.22	74
1978	221	79	142	1.80	67
1988	329	121	208	1.72	49

Source: Baker & Botts personnel records.
NA = Not calculated because numbers too small to be significant.

began to be felt acutely as Baker & Botts surged past the 100-lawyer mark.

Lawyers in the 1950s had no precise answer to the question "How large is too large?" but they did have a vague sense that an organization with one hundred lawyers was on the edge. Yet by the mid-1960s, Baker & Botts and other leading corporate firms had moved past the century mark without experiencing overwhelming problems. Now they could say the enterprise should be "as large as we need to be without sacrificing standards." But as Baker & Botts continued to expand, the task of balancing size and quality became more difficult, the debate over the proper balance more intense.

The debate was not primarily over the financial impact of growth. By all financial measures, the firm and its members were prospering. As the number of lawyers rose, the addition of nonlawyer support personnel and more sophisticated office equipment increased productivity and enabled them to handle more work at greater speed than before. Not all of the costs could be passed on to clients, however, and the ratio of expenses to gross income rose from a prewar average of 34 percent to 43 percent in the postwar years. But all the while profit per lawyer more than kept pace (table 5).

185
Chapter 9
Organizing
for a
National
Practice

More disconcerting than the ledgers was the sense that Baker & Botts was somehow losing the top spot among corporate law practices in Houston. Over the years the firm had certainly been successful in "rainmaking," or bringing in new business. As young Walter Walne had long ago explained, an important attribute for an attorney in this firm was "an ability to draw business."[2] For a time during the postwar boom, however, Baker & Botts became less aggressive in seeking new clients; all the work that the firm could handle seemed to appear at the door without solicitation. Baker & Botts continued to grow at a steady pace, but it was during these years that such rivals as Vinson & Elkins and Fulbright & Jaworski expanded even more rapidly. Baker & Botts was charged by some outside observers with complacency, with exhibiting a sense that its partners somehow felt themselves above the competitive fray. Reflecting on this era, Baine Kerr—whose rainmaking helped flood the Corporate Department with creative new work—recalls that the firm did little to encourage or to reward client development.[3]

Competing firms' aggressive move to center stage in the postwar era made it clear that Baker & Botts could not take for granted its standing as the leader among legal organizations in the region. Its only true rival among Houston's large law partnerships had been Andrews & Kurth. By the 1950s, however, Vinson & Elkins and Fulbright & Jaworski were comparable in size and focus to Baker & Botts.[4] Indeed, when Judge Elkins completed the merger that created First City National Bank in 1956, he controlled the largest bank in Houston. Like Captain Baker earlier, Elkins had established a powerful circle of influence. The bank and the law firm grew together, each reinforcing the other's expansion by serving the financial and legal needs of common clients.[5] Besides its historically strong ties to Houston's independent oil producers, Vinson & Elkins was beginning to represent dynamic Houston enterprises such as Brown & Root and Texas Eastern Corporation. By the early 1970s it was the largest law firm in Houston and the third-largest in the nation.

By that time Fulbright & Jaworski was also larger than Baker & Botts. The visible symbol of its growing reputation was Leon

186
Part III
A National
Firm in a
Major City,
1930–Present

TABLE 5
GROWTH IN PROFITS

Year	Total Income	% Increase	Net Income	No. of Partners	Profit/ Partner	% Change
1895	$ 32,000					
1900	48,000	50	$ 33,000	3	$ 11,000	
1905	112,000	133	83,000	3	27,600	151
1910	181,000	62	124,000	6	20,666	−25
1915	256,000	41	197,000	8	24,625	19
1920	464,000	81	329,000	9	36,555	48
1925	723,000	56	416,000	11	37,818	4
1930	724,000	0	387,000	13	29,769	−21
1935	800,000	11	549,000	17	32,294	9
1940	NA					
1945	NA					
1950	NA					
1955	2,001,000		1,139,000	21	54,238	
1960	3,017,000	51	1,766,000	29	60,896	12
1965	4,255,000	41	2,571,000	38	67,657	11
1970	8,393,000	97	4,655,000	49	95,000	40
1975	20,610,000	146	11,909,000	74	160,932	69
1980	43,571,000	111	25,946,000	96	270,270	68

Source: Baker & Botts financial records.
Note: All figures are rounded.
NA = Figures not available.

Jaworski, whose tenure as president of the American Bar Association and as special prosecutor during the Watergate crisis kept the firm in the national spotlight. Meanwhile, the steadily expanding Andrews & Kurth and Butler & Binion created still more competition. All of these firms—like Baker & Botts—developed national practices.

To weather the initial changes in firm size, orientation, and competitive position, Baker & Botts relied on conservative and steady leadership in the managing partner's office. Alvis Parish had assisted managing partner Ralph Feagin during the trying years of World War II. When Parish briefly assumed the office after Feagin's death in 1946, he continued traditions first learned

187
Chapter 9
Organizing
for a
National
Practice

TABLE 6
AVERAGE CHARGEABLE HOURS

Year	Partners	Associates
1968	1,580	1,952
1969	1,557	1,915
1970	1,548	1,906
1971	1,643	1,974
1972	1,588	2,061
1973	1,752	2,029
1974	1,718	1,930
1975	1,767	1,947
1976	1,776	1,946
1977	1,787	2,052
1978	1,749	2,020
1979	1,755	2,036
1980	1,780	2,077
1981	1,819	2,066
1982	1,804	1,981
1083	1,865	2,053
1984	1,878	2,081
1985	1,830	2,008
1986	1,820	2,005
1987	1,914	1,982

Source: Price Waterhouse & Co. Survey, BBHC.
Note: Records are available detailing hours by lawyer for 1971–1987.

during the 1920s under the tutelage of Edwin Parker and Feagin. His successor was Dillon Anderson, a native of McKinney, Texas, and a graduate of the Yale Law School. Anderson entered the firm in 1929 and was a versatile lawyer and a man of varied talents outside the practice of law. A sought-after public speaker as well as an engaging essayist and novelist, Anderson's experience as an army colonel seemed to make him an excellent choice to lead the firm. He was not, however, particularly interested in the day-to-day tasks of managing and was more than happy to delegate most of these duties to others. His was a gentle and brief reign, which ended with his departure for Washington, D.C., to serve as President Eisenhower's national security adviser.[6]

188

Part III
A National
Firm in a
Major City,
1930–Present

In the absence of an activist managing partner, nonlawyers in the office of the managing partner came to assume considerable sway over the details of running the organization. Financial matters became more and more the domain of, first, Raymond Neilson and then J. H. Freeman, assistants to the managing partner who might best be described as chief financial officers. Freeman's responsibilities in particular expanded steadily as the firm grew in the postwar era. He had joined the enterprise in 1938 to assist Captain Baker with his personal financial matters. From then until his retirement in 1985—with an interval away during World War II—he served as the firm's accountant, controller, managerial consultant, and unofficial "father confessor" for the lawyers. Officially, he held the position of administrative assistant to the managing partner, but he ranged widely and his tasks grew to include regular participation in the assignment of routine work to lawyers and the development and interpretation of statistics used in charting the progress of both the firm as a whole and of individual lawyers. This allowed the managing partner to remain a part-time administrator while continuing to practice law.

Anderson's replacement, John T. McCullough, began a nineteen-year tenure in the office in 1953 that continued very much in the tradition of a part-time managing partner who remained a practicing lawyer. An unassuming, almost self-effacing, man, McCullough could have served as a model for the typical lawyer at Baker & Botts between 1920 and 1960. He was reared in the Central Texas city of Waco, where his father farmed and for a time served as mayor. He received both an undergraduate degree and a law degree with honors from the University of Texas at Austin. After joining Baker & Botts in 1929, McCullough undertook a variety of matters, ranging from oil and gas to banking to utilities work. His selection as managing partner reflected the fact that in the early 1950s, Baker & Botts felt comfortable with a steady hand on the tiller.

Not everyone in the firm agreed that McCullough moved fast or far enough to modernize the governance and the tone of the firm, but all acknowledged that he was a meticulous lawyer and a patient administrator who sought fair compromises on critical issues. McCullough's reign typified the relaxed attitude of the postwar American era, when the nation's institutions—including well-established law firms—could take a business-as-usual approach to management.[7] McCullough's signal achievement was to maintain the unity of the firm during two decades in which Baker & Botts confronted basic changes in its traditional practice. Although he was of the prewar generation, McCullough held the confidence of the younger lawyers, who sought a greater say in the firm's affairs.[8]

189
Chapter 9
Organizing
for a
National
Practice

For assistance in formulating policies on vital issues, McCullough turned to the "seniors," the small group of attorneys who had progressed to full partnership. As late as the 1930s Baker & Botts had been small enough so that the entire partnership could still meet when they needed to resolve any major issues. By the 1950s the firm's growth made consultation among all of the partners unwieldy. They all retained a say in the admission of new partners to membership, but a relatively small number of senior partners, most of whom had joined the firm in the 1920s, generally advised McCullough on critical governance issues. McCullough relied on informal consultation with trusted senior partners and with younger partners with a special interest in such issues as recruitment. Led by such men as Dillon Anderson, the seniors had a vested interest in maintaining the status quo on issues of leadership and the distribution of profits.

As a group these men had worked hard to achieve their high status in the firm, the legal profession, and the city, and they felt entitled to enjoy the fruits of their labors. The leaders of the next generation of lawyers, however, began to feel entitled to more of the profits from their innovative work. They expressed concern that some of the senior partners were taking advantage of the lack of a formal retirement policy to hang onto the rewards of a partnership even though they no longer contributed their fair share to the firm's income. These intergenerational tensions were hardly unique to Baker & Botts, and they intensified through the 1960s. When McCullough and the other seniors seemed unwilling to address these tensions, some members of the younger generation sought a larger role in firm governance.

McCullough ultimately responded to their pressure. First he created a fifteen-member Management Committee consisting of senior partners, department heads, and the managing partner. But this large group proved unwieldy and was abandoned after several meetings. In 1969 he formed a five-person Executive Committee, which proved more successful and became a permanent element in the firm's governance. Included on the initial Executive Committee were two prominent members of the postwar generation, John Mackin from the Corporate Department

190

Part III

A National
Firm in a
Major City,
1930–Present

and William Harvin from the Trial Department. This committee gradually became the focus for debates on firm policy. It brought the postwar generation into the process of governance while strengthening the managing partner by giving his policies a stamp of approval. The Executive Committee brought Baker & Botts into the mainstream of accepted governance practices among large law firms, most of which adopted a formal governance committee of some form in the postwar era.[9]

It was in the course of the changes that William Harvin became a leader of the postwar generation, so much so, in fact, that some members of the senior group were hesitant to advance him to the role of managing partner. But in the end it was hard to oppose Harvin's central idea: those in the forefront of the firm's creative—and lucrative—legal work should also be in the forefront in terms of governance and compensation. Seats on the Executive Committee were one obvious reward. Beyond that, however, lay the much more divisive issues of compensation and retirement.

When he was finally selected as managing partner in 1972, Harvin set out to ensure that rewards were distributed equitably between older members who had already arrived at top positions and those who were working their way up. In doing so, he was responding to the fears of some of the firm's coming generation of high achievers that too many of the senior partners were willing to rest on past performance while claiming the lion's share of the rewards from current operations. Statistics on billable hours and compensation lent credence to these fears.

As managing partner, Harvin improved the system of compensation, creating a better balance between input and rewards.[10] Harvin—supported by John Mackin and George Jewell—introduced two other changes that merit special attention: a revised retirement plan, and the redefinition of the status and compensation of "senior partners." The lack of a retirement plan before the 1960s meant that partners drew full shares of the firm's annual income until they personally decided to retire. Few ever made this decision. The firm's history offered one striking counterexample in Captain Baker, who voluntarily relinquished his interest in the firm in the late 1930s so that deserving younger lawyers could be awarded a full share on making partner. Yet Baker's magnanimous act was hardly the model for an effective retirement program; he was, after all, nearing eighty and had long been a part-time practitioner. More common were senior partners who died with their three-piece suits on, having neither relinquished nor diminished their interest in the firm.

191
Chapter 9
Organizing
for a
National
Practice

The first formal effort to solve this problem was introduced in the early 1960s, and Harvin built on that foundation. The original retirement program required partners to begin a six-year phasing-out of their interest on reaching age sixty-eight. Harvin made the plan more restrictive, with a three-year phaseout beginning at age sixty-five. Even this system was quite expensive, but it went a long way toward the goal of making more room for the growing number of younger partners.

A second part of Harvin's program was the redefinition of the role of senior partner. Until the 1970s all lawyers who became partners and remained with the firm ultimately gained a full share in the income. All longtime partners thus naturally progressed to the status of "senior partner," the phrase used to designate all of those with a full share. Through the 1940s and into the 1950s, this system was not a source of concern. But as the number of members moving toward the status of senior partner grew, several questions arose. Could a large organization continue to justify using such a crude, binary measure—senior partner or "others"—in determining the relative status of partners? With only two graduations on the scale, leaders of the firm faced a difficult dilemma. If senior status were granted routinely, both finances and quality control would suffer; if granted too strictly, a growing number of middle-aged partners might despair of ever jumping this final hurdle.

Harvin's answer was a system of differential pay within the ranks of the seniors, with this term redefined to include all lawyers with 80 percent or more of a full partner's share in the firm. This new system cleared the way for the promotion of some partners who previously might not have advanced to the senior rank. The new policy also had the desirable effect of diluting the power of the small cluster of most senior members. After some controversy, the firm accepted this new arrangement, in part, probably because sustained growth in the 1970s made even 80 percent of a full partner's share more valuable than a 100 percent share in previous decades.

The new leadership also recognized the need for changes at the broad base of the pyramid, where the associates were striving to become partners. Personnel policy at this level focused on recruitment, evaluation, and retention. From the late 1940s through the 1960s, the firm adhered to its traditional policy of

'192

Part III
A National
Firm in a
Major City,
1930–Present

hiring the most highly ranked law school graduates, primarily from the University of Texas.[11] Like its counterparts on Wall Street and elsewhere, Baker & Botts enjoyed the benefits of only limited competition for legal talent. Before the mid-1960s young associates had few options: starting salaries were low, movement between firms rare, and demand for corporate legal services far smaller than today.

As the need for new lawyers intensified, however, and as other firms began to make inroads into the limited pool of honors graduates from the University of Texas, Baker & Botts had to change course. It no longer had the luxury of enjoying first call on the top graduates of the leading law school in its region.[12] Now it began to reach out more aggressively. With a much greater emphasis on organized recruitment, including lavish summer intern programs, the firm began to recruit at a variety of law schools throughout the nation. The market for young lawyers had decisively changed and, in fierce competition with other leading corporate law firms nationwide, the partners sharply increased the salaries for new hires and cut the time from entry into the firm to the partner review.[13]

Until the late 1960s the firm was not able to base decisions such as these on good comparative data. In 1967 Price Waterhouse & Co. began to collect and publish comparative statistics on the operations of the nation's largest law firms, and the earliest reports opened eyes at Baker & Botts. These surveys consistently ranked associates at Baker & Botts first in hours worked; partners also worked more hours than the average among partners in similar firms.[14] The statistics also revealed that the hardworking associates at Baker & Botts received lower compensation than their contemporaries at large law firms in other parts of the nation. At a time when associates at the firm collectively produced three to four times their salaries in billings, such figures were disturbing—both to the firm's leaders and to its associates (table 6).

Baker & Botts moved to improve the lot of its associates. The loss of one particularly promising young lawyer in 1967 had left an unsettled feeling among his peers that the trail to partnership might not be worth the ultimate reward.[15] Changing conditions in the market for young lawyers gradually forced the firm to respond. Starting salaries, which had only grown by 75 percent over the decade 1958–1968, leaped an additional 71 percent in the next five years (table 7). After 1968 the partner-to-associate ration began to drop back to its prewar level, and the number of years spent in associate status fell from over eleven to just over eight (table 8).

193
Chapter 9
Organizing
for a
National
Practice

In the early years of William Harvin's tenure as managing partner, the firm also systematized its approach to recruitment. Statistical studies of patterns in hiring suggested that one figure had remained relatively constant throughout much of the firm's history: the retention of each permanent partner had required the hiring of an average of 2.5 new associates. With this figure as a planning tool, Harvin's goal was to recruit 25 new lawyers per year, a figure that would produce 10 new partners per year in the future. In Harvin's view, these figures embodied a commitment to orderly expansion; these were the maximum figures that he found compatible with the firm's commitment to hire only high-ranking graduates of leading law schools.[16] Although the firm seldom reached this goal in the 1970s, Harvin clearly placed recruitment on a more orderly basis, one consistent with the firm's traditions and historical trends.

These developments as well as the firm's shifting practice gradually made for a greater diversity of lawyers at Baker & Botts. More and more partners came from outside of Texas (tables 9 and 10). The degree of change was less marked in racial, gender, and ethnic categories than in geography, as, in the words of Leon Jaworski, the city's major law firms remained "country clubs—meaning no Jews or blacks. Membership by invitation only."[17] Gradually, some progress was made in the case of women and Jews. Baker & Botts elected its first female partner in 1980; by June 1990 women made up 6 percent of the partnership and 36 percent of the associates. Barriers to Jewish partners fell in the 1970s, somewhat later than was the case at other large law firms. Fulbright & Jaworski hired its first Jewish associate in 1958, while many elite East Coast firms had Jewish partners by the 1960s.[18] Baker & Botts also hired its first black associate, Rufus Cormier, in 1974, and he became a partner in 1980. But in common with other large corporate organizations—in other cities as well as Houston—Baker & Botts enjoyed little further success in recruiting and retaining black lawyers.[19]

The patterns suggest how highly personal the legal partnership still was. Collegiality, its virtues notwithstanding, can have the effect of inculcating in an organization the pursuit of sameness in outlook, background, and values. The emphasis on academic achievement in nationally prominent law schools as the

194
*Part III
A National
Firm in a
Major City,
1930–Present*

TABLE 7
EVOLUTION OF STARTING SALARIES

Year	Annual Salary
1958	$ 4,800
1959	5,100
1960–1963	6,000
1964–1966	7,200
1967	8,400
1968 (1st half)	8,400
1968 (2d half)	10,800
1969	10,800
1970	13,200
1971	13,200
1972	13,200
1973	14,400
1974	15,600
1975	15,600
1976	15,600
1977	18,000
1978	20,000

Source: Baker & Botts financial records.

TABLE 8
YEARS TO PARTNER

Years on Payroll	Mean	Standard Deviation
To 1930	9.60	4.04
1931–1945	11.20	2.05
1945–1960	11.30	1.48
1960–1970	8.17	1.30

Source: Baker & Botts personnel records.

195
Chapter 9
Organizing
for a
National
Practice

TABLE 9
EDUCATIONAL BACKGROUND OF PARTNERS

				Law School			
Year Hired	*University of Texas*	*Ivy League*	*Other*	*Total*	*% UT*	*% Ivy League*	*% Other*
Before 1920							
All lawyers	11	1	0	19	58	5	0
All law school							
graduates	11	1	0	12	92	8	0
1921–1930	8	2	0	10	80	20	0
1931–1950	18	2	0	20	90	10	0
1951–1960	13	2	3	18	72	11	17
1961–1970	22 .	5	5	32	69	16	16
1971–1987	17	17	11	45	38	38	24

Source: Baker & Botts personnel records.
Note: Percentages may not add to 100 because of rounding. Before 1920,
seven new lawyers did not attend law school.

TABLE 10
BIRTHPLACE OF PARTNERS (%)

			Birthplace			
Year Hired	*Houston*	*Texas*	*South*	*West*	*Northeast*	*Other*
Before 1920	16.0	50.0	33.0	0	0	0
1920–1930	0	50.0	30.0	10.0	10.0	0
1931–1950	7.6	52.7	4.3	4.3	4.3	26.8
1951–1960	10.0	35.0	30.0	5.0	20.0	0
1961–1970	14.0	48.0	21.0	14.0	3.4	0
1971–present	13.0	38.0	22.0	15.5	6.6	5.0

Source: Baker & Botts personnel records.

196

Part III
A National
Firm in a
Major City,
1930–Present

primary attribute required of a new recruit further limited the pool of lawyers considered for employment. As a consequence, the firm only slowly changed the traditional pattern of employing almost exclusively white male Texans.

Baker & Botts also began to improve the training and placement of new recruits in the firm's increasingly diverse practice. The organization had used a functional department structure since the 1950s: corporate; trial; oil, gas, and real estate; utility; railroad; and tax. Newly hired lawyers still generally received several years of wide-ranging exposure to the firm's general practice before beginning to specialize within a given department, and their choice of department was shaped by their own wishes as well as the needs of the firm. In essence, the system provided group support for individual specialties. It collected lawyers with similar interests under the direction of a colleague who understood their work and their needs. In the 1970s Harvin worked with the department heads to ensure that the associates received the training they needed and were well situated in their choice of departments.

In general, the firm selected these department heads not from among the established senior partners but from among "comers." As heads of their departments, such lawyers had a strong incentive to think strategically about the place of their specialty within the firm and within the profession. They served as advocates for their departments before the managing partner and the firm as a whole; they also served as conduits of information from the managing partner to the lawyers who made up each group. Department heads monitored the work of their group, trying to assure the most efficient use of existing labor, the addition of new lawyers when required by expanding work loads, and the proper training of new lawyers. Important clients remained primarily the responsibility of the individual lawyers in charge, but department heads were in a good position to channel additional resources toward the work of clients when needed.[20]

Harvin himself had been the first of the postwar generation to become head of the Trial Department. In this capacity he had set about reducing the overwhelming commitment of his department's resources to the trying of relatively routine damage suits. Harvin pushed the firm toward the emerging field of business litigation. Here the skills of the trial lawyer could be put to use in cases involving major clients and significant legal issues—as well as higher fees. Harvin's own experience in representing Braniff in a much-publicized suit to determine liability in a series of crashes of Electra airplanes suggested one model of general business litigation. As the Trial Department moved in this direction, it became increasingly involved in major cases that drew on the talents of several departments.

197

Chapter 9
Organizing
for a
National
Practice

Indeed, as Baker & Botts matured as a nationally active law firm, it handled more and more matters that required a variety of specialists. A major merger, for example, demanded the expert attention of specialists in tax law and antitrust as well as corporate law. The talents of the firm's leading trial lawyers might also be needed if problems arose in completing the transaction. In such instances, departmentalization helped rather than hindered cooperation within the firm, since the department heads were in an excellent position to mobilize legal resources from other departments. The capacity to coordinate the work of a variety of specialists in completing increasingly complex corporate transactions grew in importance as the firm became larger; department headships and the managing partner position were now of crucial significance to the practice.

In addition to this functional mode of organization, Baker & Botts also developed a geographical alignment through branch offices. After World War II the partners had established branches in Mexico City, Washington, D.C., Austin, and Dallas. These offices became outposts of the values and the business of the firm.

From its creation in 1947 to its disaffiliation from Baker & Botts in 1973, the Mexico City office was an important venture into international law. Through this branch office, the firm provided services to many of its clients, including numerous Houston-based companies and a variety of other U.S. businesses that had used the firm in matters of Texas law. This international operation had its roots in a close friendship between Henry Holland, who had worked for the U.S. embassy in Mexico before joining Baker & Botts, and two young Mexican lawyers with postgraduate legal training at the Harvard Law School, Fausto R. Miranda and Eduardo Prieto López. The three young attorneys often discussed the establishment of an international firm, and after 1945, Holland pursued this idea with then–managing partner Dillon Anderson. Miranda's training, his fluent English, and his experience as the head of the Legal Labor Department of American Smelting & Refining Company in Mexico marked him as a potential leader for the Mexico City venture. Anderson ham-

198

Part III

A National

Firm in a

Major City,

1930–Present

mered out an arrangement satisfactory to all parties in 1947 and established the Mexico City firm of Baker & Botts, Miranda & Prieto. The agreement reflected Baker & Botts's previous history with its Kansas City office as well as its reluctance to surrender too much control over this venture into uncharted territory. As had been the case in Kansas City, the partners in Baker & Botts were also partners in Baker, Botts, Miranda & Prieto, but partners in the Mexico City office did not enjoy membership in the home office in Houston.

Baker & Botts, Miranda & Prieto nonetheless enjoyed several benefits from its affiliation with a well-established firm. Client referrals helped, as did assistance early on in creating a highly professional tone that was comforting to American clients accustomed to certain procedures and attitudes in large U.S. firms. Years later, Fausto Miranda noted that "Baker & Botts helped immeasurably in such matters as time reports, accounting procedures and human relations in general and in the management of the law firm in particular."[21]

The branch quickly developed a thriving practice in mining, petroleum, the food industry, and agricultural equipment. Its most significant work came in helping to establish joint ventures between U.S.-based multinationals and interests in Mexico. Nabisco became a partner with Famosa, a Mexican company; Union Carbide Mexicana took in Mexican partners, sold stock to the Mexican public, and ultimately became managed and largely owned by Mexicans; Kimberly-Clark de México took somewhat the same evolutionary path, as did John Deere and Monsanto Association in Industrias Resistol. In all these ventures, the experienced Mexican lawyers assisted the companies in adapting to Mexican law and in satisfying changing legal stipulations governing foreign investments in Mexico. Fausto Miranda, who took the leading role in forging joint ventures, also became increasingly active in Mexican and U.S. business organizations.

Baker, Botts, Miranda & Prieto prospered, expanding to as many as fifty lawyers in the 1960s. Unfortunately, several of the conditions underlying this prosperity were undermined by personal and political changes that gradually altered the relationship of the Mexico City office and Baker & Botts in Houston. The careers of Henry Holland and Dillon Anderson took them away from Baker & Botts's practice, while new Mexican laws made joint ventures more difficult to conduct. At the same time, with

the withdrawal of Fausto Miranda from active, day-to-day participation in the affairs of the Mexico City office, a younger generation of attorneys concluded that their firm had matured to the
point where separation from Baker & Botts would be practical
and potentially profitable. Pressure from the Mexican government, which began to frown on joint professional associations,
reinforced their decision. In 1973 their firm severed its formal
ties with Baker & Botts, though it continued to maintain a close
working relationship.

199

Chapter 9
Organizing
for a
National
Practice

Just as the Mexican branch was going its separate way, Baker
& Botts in 1972 opened a Washington, D.C., office. A few years
later it branched out to Austin, and in 1985, to Dallas. As had
been the case with Mexico, as well as the earlier Kansas City
office, the primary impetus for branching was the desire to
better serve clients whose businesses were national and international. As Houston's economy matured, more of the firm's clients needed such services.

As it had throughout its history, Baker & Botts adapted its practice to the changing realities of the Houston economy. Sometimes
this adaptation came slowly, and the firm showed remarkable
consistency in certain areas. Beginning in the 1930s the firm
earned a preponderance of its income from a few areas of practice: oil and gas, utilities, insurance, banking, and (especially
after 1940) corporate work. From the 1930s through the mid-
1960s, these categories consistently earned Baker & Botts 75
percent of its income or more. After 1965 the categories changed
somewhat, with the elimination of corporate work as a separate
heading and the distribution of fees in this category among the
other industrial groups. Nonetheless, oil and gas, utilities, banks,
and insurance still accounted for almost half of the firm income
and that figure held steady through the mid-1970s.

Within this relatively consistent pattern, however, there were
numerous important developments. Old clients slid off or down
the list. Work in railroads and lumber shrank considerably, following their rapid decline in economic significance to the region. New interests forced their way onto the list of the firm's
top clients. Whereas the Southern Pacific and local banks once
dominated that list, major oil companies, new corporate giants
such as Tenneco, and city builders such as Gerald D. Hines now
made their appearance. Work for insurance companies at Baker
& Botts rose after World War II, when capital from these huge

200

Part III
A National
Firm in a
Major City,
1930–Present

institutional investors poured into the city, and then that work declined somewhat as the pace of development slowed. Certain clients have remained important to the firm, but for new reasons. Baker & Botts's banking and real estate work rose after a period of decline as these areas took off in the booming mid-1970s.

Even more indicative of change than the names of the top clients was the shifting nature of the work. The firm abandoned certain types of work as it became routine. Although routine work may generate substantial income, it is not highly profitable in terms of fees generated per worker-hour or of experience easily transferable to other areas. Baker & Botts was no longer interested in title searches on oil and gas leases or standard drilling agreements. Nor were lending agreements for local banks attractive. These services were increasingly out of step with the type of work needed to recruit and retain good lawyers. To build and protect its standing as a leading national corporate law firm, Baker & Botts focused on more creative—and more profitable—areas such as business litigation and mergers and acquisitions. In this sense, the firm maintained its traditional commitment to orderly growth. By paring down legal work not deemed appropriate for its modern practice, Baker & Botts chose quality of practice and profitability over absolute size.[22]

This general trend is well illustrated in the firm's corporate practice, particularly in the financial area. For a time, the preparation of SEC registrations and other legal documents required by major financings was an important part of the firm's practice. Houston-based clients such as Tenneco, HL&P, and United Gas floated huge bond issues. With its connection to insurance companies, the main financial investors in this type of corporate security, and its long-established relationship with eastern banking houses, Baker & Botts was perfectly positioned to play an intermediary role in arranging this financing.[23]

At first, such financing was quite unusual, particularly for Houston corporations, but later, as these corporations grew to national scale and as the legal forms that secured the money became commonplace, much of this financial work moved in-house. Baker & Botts's work in routine corporate financing dropped considerably, just as its involvement in creative approaches to financing increased. The ABC agreements and the merger and acquisitions business moved the law firm on to the cutting edge once again.

Changes of this sort sometimes generated internal conflict. Whether to decline insurance damage work for major national companies such as Travelers, for example, became in the postwar years a hotly debated issue at the firm. A substantial number of partners in the Trial Department insisted that this work could not be abandoned, for it was excellent training for young litigators. Other partners, however, maintained that such experience, while useful for cultivating basic trial skills, had little relevance to the complexities of modern litigation in patent law, product liability, and antitrust.[24] The debate was largely settled by the late 1960s, after the firm revamped its fee structure. Rising fees combined with increased efforts on the part of the insurance companies to contain costs essentially priced Baker & Botts out of this work.[25]

201
Chapter 9
Organizing
for a
National
Practice

Major corporate clients accelerated the changing pattern of firm work by internalizing routine legal functions. Cost cutting was the key, particularly in industries beset by international competition or new competitive pressures unleashed by deregulation during the 1960s and 1970s. By using in-house attorneys, particularly in some of the more routine areas, corporate legal departments could often save money without sacrificing quality. Pressures from clients have forced Baker & Botts to be more entrepreneurial in work selection.

In making these transitions and in reformulating its own structure and mode of operation, Baker & Botts has been selective. As a well-established firm with excellent access to major corporate clients, the Houston firm has been able to be conservative in this regard. It also has strong traditions and a deep sense of history. If at times attachment to the past has slowed change, history has also proved an asset in an unsettled period. Unlike many large firms, Baker & Botts has never experienced a major rift in the partnership. A sense of shared tradition provided a strong glue to hold the organization together as it was buffeted by the more competitive legal marketplace of the 1960s and 1970s.[26]

In taking on new work and clients, the firm has always been aware of the need to attract top-flight young lawyers while strengthening its status as a leading corporate law firm in the nation. In responding to the imperatives of an increasingly competitive market for legal services, Baker & Botts has developed three key attributes of a modern corporate law firm: a formal ad-

202

Part III

A National

Firm in a

Major City,

1930–Present

ministrative structure that enhances the firm's operating efficiency and its ability to renew itself; strength in cutting-edge legal specialties; and the capacity to mobilize specialists in a variety of fields to meet the complex legal needs of large corporate clients. In this sense, the firm has maintained its oldest traditions while adapting to far-reaching changes in the legal system.

Epilogue

FROM THE PERSPECTIVE of the late twentieth century, one is still struck by the audacity of Hiram Garwood as he surveyed the hardly developed world of Houston in the 1910s and compared Baker & Botts to two other "permanent institutions": Harvard University and the Bank of England. Garwood's comparison was meant to exhort his fellow lawyers to commit their loyalty and energy to building a lasting institution worthy of respect. He noted that the "accumulated knowledge and achievements of its members, past and present, becomes the common capital of all to preserve increase and transmit to those who shall come after us."[1] That statement came three-quarters of a century into the firm's history. Now, almost three-quarters of a century after Garwood's observations, the "common capital" of a long and successful history remains important to Baker & Botts. As sweeping changes take place in both the legal profession and the Texas economy, the firm's history provides a powerful bond that can help hold together a growing organization while suggesting directions for its development.

We have chosen to stop our account of that history in the early 1970s on the grounds that there is far too little perspective on events since that time to allow for historical analysis. Yet we also recognize that the reader deserves a brief account of the basic changes that have taken place in the recent life of the firm. Having come along for the ride since the days of Colonel Botts and Judge Baker, the reader has a right to ask what has happened since "the end of history"—or at least the end of our written history. This epilogue is designed to finish the story by summarizing the trends we think were most important in the 1970s and 1980s.

As our history has shown, Baker & Botts has always been tied

204

*Baker & Botts
in the
Development
of Modern
Houston*

closely to its region, and in the early 1970s the Houston area entered an extended period of flux. Boom was followed by bust in the petroleum industry, the mainstay of the regional economy. In our judgment, the energy crisis of 1973–1974 marks the beginning of a new era in Houston's history, one that future scholars will most likely see as distinct in important ways from the period of sustained growth in the decades after World War II. In the 1970s oil prices soared, creating an unprecedented boom in the Houston economy. Suddenly in the early 1980s, however, the bottom fell out. As a rapid downward spiral in oil prices began, the Houston economy entered the worst downturn in the city's history.

Much of the practice of Baker & Botts since the early 1970s has been shaped—either directly or indirectly—by this pattern of boom and bust in the energy industry. Not all of the firm's major clients were in the oil or gas business, but most were affected by the fluctuations in the prices of these commodities. The energy crisis had a particularly significant impact on the Corporate Department. The late 1970s and early 1980s witnessed a wave of mergers, many of which involved oil companies seeking to diversify or to expand their oil operations through acquisition. Unlike most previous merger movements, this wave included numerous hostile takeovers. Baker & Botts already had some exposure to this sort of work through its representation of Pennzoil, but the scale of such takeovers expanded enormously in the turbulent economy of the 1970s. The intense legal conflicts set off by these hostile takeovers became an important growth area for many leading corporate law firms, including Baker & Botts.

One of the firm's most active clients was T. Boone Pickens, who became in the 1970s and 1980s a national media symbol of the restructuring of the oil industry. Baker & Botts first made contact with Pickens in 1963, and had since then played an important role in his frequent acquisitions. When his maneuvers were resisted, as they frequently were, the law firm played a central role in these "unfriendly takeovers." By the early 1980s Pickens was hunting for bigger game. His company, Mesa Petroleum, was regularly in the headlines of the nation's business news, as this small West Texas concern challenged numerous large oil companies in takeover battles.

Pickens's philosophy was simple: the management of many large oil companies had forgotten the shareholders and the businesses needed to be reorganized and forced to become more efficient. Mesa's purchase of a significant block of stock in a particular company generally marked the onset of a feverish round of negotiations and legal challenges that shook management to the core. Often it forced them to reorganize or seek a more comfortable merger partner. Cities Service, GAO, Gulf Oil, Phillips Petroleum, and Unocal all felt the heat of a hostile takeover bid by Mesa. Although Pickens ultimately acquired none of these companies, each instituted drastic changes to avoid this outcome.

Baker & Botts lawyers represented Mesa in these corporate wars and found themselves in an enterprise at once challenging, creative, and controversial. Takeover struggles spilled over from the stock exchanges into the courts, leading to often-intense work that at times required the talents of dozens of lawyers. The firm's efforts were directed by partner Robert L. Stillwell. Stillwell had entered the Corporate Department when he joined the firm in 1961. There he became an important adviser to Pickens while participating in many of the key legal developments in the takeover field. Stillwell had a wide array of talent on which to draw. Partners such as tax specialist William C. Griffith contributed their specialized skills to matters such as the complex tax issues raised by takeovers.[2]

The oil industry and commentators from the nation's business publications were divided as to the overall costs and benefits of these hostile takeover attempts. They often caused the targeted company to take on extraordinary debt to protect itself. Pickens's critics lambasted him in harsh attacks reminiscent of those a century earlier against Jay Gould, one of the first nationally prominent clients of Gray, Botts & Baker. The firm ardently pursued its responsibility to provide Pickens and Mesa the best possible representation without reference to the intense controversy they were arousing. Nevertheless, Baker & Botts was in a ticklish position. Many of its large clients among the oil companies were real or potential targets of Pickens's takeovers. Indeed, his most ambitious charge was against the giant Gulf Oil Corporation, and he ultimately drove this sometime client of Baker & Botts into the arms of another longtime client, Standard Oil of California (Chevron). At the time of its completion in 1984, Chevron's acquisition of Gulf was the largest merger in American history.

By the 1980s mergers and acquisitions work gave Baker & Botts a leading role in one of the most bizarre and highly pub-

206

Baker & Botts
in the
Development
of Modern
Houston

licized cases in recent American history, the struggle between Pennzoil and Texaco over Getty Oil. The damage suit generated by this takeover battle pitted one of the firm's most significant clients of the post–World War II era, Pennzoil, against a company, Texaco, that had been among its most valued clients in a previous era. The legal warfare over Getty Oil lasted four years (1984–1988). At its conclusion, managing partner E. William Barnett said: "In our long history, no other matter has ever so gripped the attention of the entire Firm." He might have added the attention of much of the legal profession, the business community, and the public at large, because the trial in this case produced "by many times, the largest civil judgment and the largest civil payment in history."[3]

The essentials of the case can be summarized easily. Hugh Liedtke at Pennzoil seized the opportunity presented by tensions between the owners of Getty Oil to come to an agreement with the company's board to acquire a substantial portion of that firm's stock. This company's excellent domestic oil reserves promised to push Pennzoil one more big step toward the achievement of its strategic objective of joining the ranks of the nation's largest oil companies. But just as Pennzoil felt that an agreement had been reached, Texaco entered the bidding and succeeded in acquiring Getty. Pennzoil responded with a suit claiming that Texaco was guilty of "tortious interference," meaning that it had offered indemnities and exerted other pressures to induce Getty to renege on its deal with Pennzoil. Texaco argued in response that Pennzoil had never completed an agreement and that the suit was simply an effort by the company to win in court what it had lost in the marketplace.

In an extended trial before a jury in Texas, Baker & Botts lawyers—led by John Jeffers and G. Irvin Terrell—teamed with Houston lawyer Joseph Jamail, the so-called King of Torts, to plead Pennzoil's case. Corporate partner Moulton Goodrum, who was the firm's principal contact with Pennzoil, was also an important member of this team. With the Baker & Botts lawyers preparing the strategy and Jamail handling the presentation in court, they were able to convince the jury that Texaco *had* been guilty of tortious interference and assigned a stunning $10.5 billion price tag to the damages that Pennzoil should receive. After a series of appeals exhausted Texaco's legal options without overturning the judgment, the company sought refuge in the bankruptcy laws before finally agreeing in 1988 to a negotiated cash settlement of $3 billion.

This case highlighted several aspects of the evolution of Baker & Botts. With literally billions of dollars on the table, the firm was given a crucial role in preparing and trying the case. It had expertise and resources for business litigation that complemented the efforts of Jamail (a close friend of Hugh Liedtke), whose background was largely in personal injury litigation. Jeffers, Terrell, and the numerous other Baker & Botts lawyers who worked on this case brought to their work both a wide-ranging expertise in corporate law and the skills needed to present the case to the jury.

One of the ironies of the case was that Pennzoil (a Houston-based company) convincingly presented itself to the jury as an aspiring Texas company that had been damaged by an eastern giant, Texaco (actually a homegrown Texas firm). Baker & Botts had come full circle. Early in the twentieth century, the firm had become the general attorney in Texas for the Texas Company when New York investors had purchased control of the business from Joseph Cullinan and Gulf Coast interests. In the oil industry, at least, Houston itself had also come full circle. Local companies such as Pennzoil, Exxon, U.S.A., Shell, U.S.A., and even Texaco, U.S.A., were all running national and even international operations from headquarters in Houston.

In this regard, Baker & Botts's growing representation in the 1970s of Exxon, U.S.A., one of the largest firms in the world, was of particular moment.[4] Initially, the partners handled a series of cases relating to the fair market value of natural gas and to Exxon's related obligations to royalty owners. Other cases followed. In a series of major antitrust suits, Baker & Botts successfully represented Exxon and several other oil concerns as plaintiffs against Brown & Root and Halliburton for alleged price fixing and job allocation on offshore drilling projects. The firm also took the lead for Exxon in a series of major cases over the evaluation of natural gas reserves. These involved enormous sums of money and important legal principles, and Exxon's choice of Baker & Botts as its counsel symbolized the firm's new reputation as one of the country's leading corporate law firms.

Oil-related work also drew the firm more deeply into an international practice. Of particular importance here was work for Roy Huffington, a Houston-based oil producer with a deep and

208

*Baker & Botts
in the
Development
of Modern
Houston*

long-standing involvement in Indonesia. Under the guidance of partner Ross Staine and other lawyers, the firm has developed skills in handling the complex legal issues raised by the development and production of large natural gas reserves, the conversion of that gas to liquefied form (LNG), and its shipment and sale to other countries. The representation of Huffington has also opened opportunities for the firm to work with the government of one of the major oil-producing nations, Indonesia, and to have substantial dealings with the governments of other leading countries in the Far East.

Another new line of work has been provided by a very old client, Houston Lighting & Power. In the 1970s and 1980s the firm handled a series of suits spawned by the South Texas Project. The massive project consisted of two large nuclear plants being built for a consortium of utilities, including HL&P as operator, in Bay City, Texas, southwest of Houston. Planning for the South Texas Project (STP) began in the early 1970s in response to the fears of natural gas and oil shortages. Baker & Botts lawyers were on the scene from the beginning, attending planning meetings and preparing the contracts that would govern ownership and operation of the project. The venture finally came to fruition when HL&P and the City Public Service Board of San Antonio signed joint ownership agreements in July 1973. The City of Austin, an original member of the early planning group, joined the project later that year. Amid calls for alternative energy sources in the early 1970s, the initial permit process moved relatively smoothly, and by 1976 construction of the nuclear facilities was set to begin.

At that point, however, one of the co-owners of the nuclear plant, Central Power & Light Company, announced its intention to join other companies in forming a large, integrated interstate network. This decision would have forced HL&P into interstate operations as well, an outcome the utility wanted to avoid. HL&P sought relief in a four-year battle fought on multiple fronts, including state and federal court, the Federal Energy Regulatory Commission, the U.S. Securities and Exchange Commission, the U.S. Nuclear Regulatory Commission, and the Public Utility Commission of Texas. Baker & Botts lawyers represented HL&P in each of the forums and played a vital role in structuring a unique and successful settlement.

In the meantime, STP itself became quite controversial. In the wake of the accident at the Three Mile Island plant in 1979, the nuclear power industry came under much closer regulatory scrutiny. STP had to answer allegations of construction errors and questions put by quality assurance inspectors. These charges resulted in one of the most extended hearings ever held before the Nuclear Regulatory Commission, and Baker & Botts participated in the hearings together with lawyers specializing in nuclear licensing.

As a result of those allegations the owners in 1981 made a dramatic decision to replace Brown & Root, Inc., the firm that had been managing the design and construction of STP since 1973. In December they filed suit against Brown & Root and its parent, Halliburton Company, and set into motion a massive piece of litigation that tested the resources of Baker & Botts like no case before or since. Baker & Botts took on the role of lead counsel for the owners and had six partners and numerous associates committed to the case. Heading the team was Finis E. Cowan, who had returned to the firm after serving a brief stint as a federal district judge. The STP litigation became his entire occupation. Brown & Root was ably defended by Vinson & Elkins, which mounted a "scorched earth" defensive battle that raged for four years. At the peak of the action in 1984, each side had committed forty to fifty lawyers and six to eight law firms to the struggle. In 1985 this litigation finally produced a settlement for the owners of $750 million, thought to be the largest cash settlement in any construction-related litigation.

But STP-related litigation did not end there. In 1989 Baker & Botts took the lead in defending HL&P against charges of fraud in its role as project manager of the STP. The City of Austin, one of the four original co-owners of the project, brought suit against HL&P, seeking damages on the grounds that HL&P had withheld information from the City of Austin. In July of 1989 a Dallas jury found that HL&P had not disclosed all of the information that it should have disclosed, but that no damages resulted from this failure. While trying this case in Dallas, Baker & Botts also took an important role in hearings before the Public Utility Commission (PUC) in Austin to investigate the prudence of all aspects of the construction of STP. Under existing rate-making procedures, the determination of "imprudence" in management is grounds for the disallowance of expenditures from a project's rate base. In a prolonged bargaining process with the PUC, Baker & Botts assisted its client in limiting the amount of expenditures judged to be imprudent. In this hearing, as throughout much of the

210

Baker & Botts
in the
Development
of Modern
Houston

firm's involvement in the litigation spawned by the South Texas Project, Baker & Botts has remained deeply involved in resolving critical issues regarding the power supply of a broad section of East and Central Texas; these cases manifestly have far-reaching ramifications for the nuclear power industry as a whole.

Similar and equally significant questions have arisen of late about Texas's financial institutions, and here too Baker & Botts is working at the forefront of a national issue. After a decade of unprecedented expansion, the state's financial institutions were ill-prepared for the rapid and unanticipated fall in oil prices in the early 1980s. Large outstanding loans to oil, gas, and service companies and to real estate developers proved disastrous for the banks and savings and loan industry. The litigation and regulatory work spawned by the reorganization of many of the hard-pressed financial institutions in Texas pulled Baker & Botts into a variety of matters involving both banks and savings and loans. These legal issues threaten to remain quite important well into the 1990s.

In all of this work, for old clients and new, there runs a thread of creative tension as competition increases in the national legal profession. Questions have been raised about the "institutional loyalty" of major clients. For most of the history of modern corporate law firms, strong ongoing ties to blue-chip clients have been the backbone of a successful practice. But in recent decades some observers have speculated that "transactional" relationships are replacing "institutional" ones in the field of corporate law. According to this view, competitive pressures have forced corporations to seek lower legal fees and the best possible specialized services. They thus drift away from the sort of permanent commitment to a single firm that has marked much of the historical relationship between Baker & Botts and such clients as the Southern Pacific, HL&P, Tenneco, and Gerald D. Hines Interests.

The experience of Baker & Botts in the 1980s suggests that major clients are indeed "shopping" more for specialized legal services. But this trend has had largely positive results for the firm. As even our brief overview of recent clients and cases should make clear, Baker & Botts has continued to represent most of its long-standing clients in important cases. It has also used the opportunities opened by competition to establish new client relationships with such companies as Exxon, NCNB-Texas, Electronic Data Systems (EDS), and Citibank. From the perspective of Baker & Botts, the current pattern of client relationships seems to fall somewhere between traditional institutional ties and purely transactional ones, with longtime clients retaining a measure of loyalty on many matters while also seeking the best possible legal specialists in matters of special importance or extreme financial exposure.

These important changes in client relationships actually seem to have been part of the broader transformation of the market for legal services examined in the previous chapter. As competition in a national market mounted, several much-publicized "megafirms" surged up the list of the nation's largest law firms through aggressive recruitment and branching. Baker & Botts—like most other well-established firms—responded slowly. But as the most aggressive of the new giants moved toward the one thousand–lawyer mark and as they established branch offices in more and more cities, organizations like Baker & Botts had to face some hard choices. How could a history of excellence based on more than a century of success be adapted to the new conditions? What would the winning competitive strategy be?

Serious thought about these issues began at Baker & Botts when William Harvin became managing partner in 1972. His primary thrust, as we have seen, was to shake the firm out of old habits and structures. Building on these changes, his successor, E. William Barnett, has sought to formulate a new strategy, provide the organization with the personnel it needs to implement that plan, and then build a consensus on the policies needed to effect the new program. Barnett entered Baker & Botts in 1958 after graduating from the University of Texas Law School. He has spent much of his career at the firm as an antitrust specialist, which has given him a wide exposure to lawyers and law firms throughout the nation. His work as the head of the Antitrust Division of the American Bar Association further broadened his contacts throughout the legal profession. Armed with a good perspective on the changes taking place in the profession and experience on the firm's Recruitment Committee, Barnett was ready to take over in 1984, when Harvin decided to step down as the managing partner.

As summarized by Barnett, one of the central tenets of the firm's strategy is "controlled expansion." Baker & Botts has chosen not to read too much into the listing of law firms by size in such national magazines as the *American Lawyer*. In these listings Baker & Botts has moved down from as high as the tenth

212

*Baker & Botts
in the
Development
of Modern
Houston*

largest firm in the nation (early 1970s) to the thirty-first largest, with 358 lawyers, in 1989.[5] Yet over the same period, the firm has enjoyed impressive growth in absolute terms.

The most pressing imperative has been to enhance financial performance. In the late 1970s and early 1980s the firm faced a disturbing downturn in the ratio of associates to partners, one that had far-reaching financial ramifications. This ratio fell from about 1.5 to 1 in 1979 to about 1 to 1 in 1984, as new hiring failed to keep pace with promotion to partner. Indeed, in that one five-year period, the number of partners increased from 85 to 117 while the number of associates fell from 130 to 114.

Since associates have been critically important in supplying the economic leverage on which the profits of Baker & Botts— and other modern law firms—depend, this trend was a serious threat. Barnett quickly addressed the problem by adopting a more aggressive hiring program for associates and by encouraging the retirement or withdrawal of unproductive partners. In practice, this has meant more aggressive recruitment from good law schools throughout the nation and a willingness to make selective lateral hires from other firms. As a result, the ratio of associates to partners has climbed beyond previous levels. But unlike many other firms, Baker & Botts has not greatly exceeded its historical ratio.[6] While this choice has slowed the rate of growth, the firm's management has been willing to pay the price in an effort to keep from diluting the overall quality of its personnel or services. Controlled expansion, in this case, embodies more systematic planning to enhance the firm's profitability.

A commitment to controlled expansion has also raised basic questions about the role of the branch offices. For more than a century, Baker & Botts proclaimed its identity as a Houston institution. But can a nationally competitive law firm afford to remain confined largely to one city, particularly when that city is not New York? Houston was an excellent home base for an aspiring law firm during most of the twentieth century; its image as a city on the move and sustained economic expansion assured Baker & Botts ample opportunities for growth. But Houston's problems in oil, real estate, and banking in the 1980s raised doubts about the future and drew the firm toward new places.

The firm first took a hard look at its existing branches in Austin and Washington. The creation of the office in Austin in 1983 was a formal acknowledgment of the ties between Baker & Botts and the Central Texas city that is home to state government. Indeed, government is the chief industry in Austin and the chief service of this branch's legal work. The office there is small, growing from one lawyer at its creation to twenty-one in 1990. Its primary strengths are in litigation, finance and banking, agency practice, legislation, and real estate. Among the numerous political matters handled by this office, one issue loomed above all others in the 1980s. As Texas grappled with the erosion of its energy-dominated tax base, the state explored new avenues for raising revenue. Since changes in tax policies were bound to have a significant impact on Baker & Botts's clients, this issue alone assured the need for a strong presence in Austin.

The firm's Washington office handles similar issues, but in the nation's capital, Baker & Botts has faced much more intense competition than in Austin. Baker & Botts entered Washington on the strength of its oil and gas clients, who needed a knowledgeable law firm in hearings before the Federal Power Commission (subsequently renamed the Federal Energy Regulatory Commission). The office was originally headed by Gordon Gooch, who joined the firm after a stint as general counsel for the FPC. Gooch was succeeded by Perry Barber, who came to the Washington office in 1984 after seven years as general counsel and a director for Pennzoil Company. Under Barber's leadership, the office began to grow more rapidly and to move toward a more diversified practice.[7] Most recently it has come under the direction of O. Don Chapoton, who has been adding strength in corporate, tax, and real estate work to supplement energy related matters. By 1990 Baker & Botts–Washington included thirty-nine lawyers. That number placed it well down the list among Washington branch offices, but it has excellent prospects for growth as it diversifies in the booming capital district–northern Virginia region.

Among the branches in recent years the most rapid strides have been made in Dallas. Managing partner Barnett was determined to build a Dallas office that would give Baker & Botts a leading presence there. Historically, the two cities were viewed as competing centers of urban-industrial growth, but as the Texas economy matured, the economies of the two cities became increasingly complementary. Many Houston-based oil companies operated in and around Dallas. Large corporations migrating to Texas after World War II usually went first to these highly populated metropolitan areas. When the major Texas

214

*Baker & Botts
in the
Development
of Modern
Houston*

banks created statewide bank holding companies in the 1970s, most banks sought a presence in both Houston and Dallas. Improved transportation and communication brought the two cities ever closer.

From the early planning for the Dallas office, the goal was to establish "a leading presence" as quickly as possible. The city did not have large, well-established corporate law firms of the sort that were now common in Houston. Baker & Botts wanted as soon as possible to develop a branch of the size needed to provide the complete package of legal services required by the largest corporate clients in the city. Barnett proposed that the firm achieve that goal by merging with another large firm, but a significant number of the partners had difficulties with that radical proposal. Like the firm's earlier experiences with Kansas City, the proposed merger involved the tricky question of dilution of the value of partners' shares. Instead, they opted for growth along traditional lines.

Baker & Botts's commitment to building a strong presence in Dallas was nevertheless deep enough to persuade a number of the partners from the Houston office to transfer to Dallas. This group included senior members R. C. Johnson and Ronald L. Palmer. Quietly, they pushed the Dallas office ahead; it grew from eight lawyers at its creation in 1985 to sixty-nine by June of 1990. They also attracted a high quality of clients to the office. Despite being a relatively new kid on the block, Baker & Botts has represented EDS (one of the city's leading corporations) and NCNB-Texas, the North Carolina–based holding company that acquired the largest bank holding company in Texas. The Dallas office has rapidly become an important profit center, as well as a source of opportunities for associates to advance their careers.

In branching, as in personnel policies, Baker & Botts has chosen a strategy of conservative adaptation, one that seeks to protect its traditional position of strength while extending its practice into new areas. In essence, this represents a "southwestern strategy," with the firm attempting to grow steadily into one of the leading nationally active law firms based primarily in the Southwest. Such a choice is quite in keeping with the firm's historical development. The "common capital" holding Baker & Botts together in the late twentieth century is composed of many of the same ingredients as that which has held the firm together throughout its history: major clients with legal matters on the cutting edge of the practice of corporate law; an ongoing effort to hire the very best young lawyers; and a sense of commitment to Houston and the Southwest as the firm's primary base of operations. In each of these critical areas, Baker & Botts has made more than a rhetorical commitment to excellence; it has compiled a 150-year history that abundantly supports that claim. As much as the conscious choices of its current and future leaders, the firm's history will shape its development in the coming years.

Appendix

BAKER AND BOTTS PARTNER ADMISSIONS, 1840–1990

1840	Peter W. Gray	1945	Joseph C. Hutcheson III
1865	Walter Browne Botts	1948	John T. Maginnis
1872	Judge James A. Baker		Denman Moody
1887	Capt. James A. Baker	1949	William R. Brown
1892	Robert S. Lovett		Garret R. Tucker
1900	Edwin B. Parker	1950	Hugh M. Patterson
1904	Hiram M. Garwood		Henry Holland
1906	Jesse Andrews		Thomas M. Phillips
	Clarence R. Wharton	1953	B. John Mackin
1909	Clarence L. Carter		John F. Heard
1915	Jules H. Tallichet	1955	James K. Nance
	Thomas H. Botts		Robert Jewett
1917	Walter H. Walne		A. B. White
1921	Ralph B. Feagin		Baine P. Kerr
	Palmer Hutcheson	1956	William C. Harvin
1923	W. Alvis Parish	1958	C. Brien Dillon
1927	James A. Baker, Jr.		William R. Choate
1929	James L. Shepherd, Jr.	1960	Frank G. Harmon
	Gaius G. Gannon		John S. Sellingsloh
	Francis G. Coates		George H. Jewell, Jr.
	Homer L. Bruce		Frank B. Pugsley
1933	Tom Scurry	1961	Frank M. Wozencraft
1935	Brady Cole	1962	James G. Ulmer
	John P. Bullington		Ross Staine
1938	H. Malcolm Lovett	1963	John B. Abercrombie
1940	Tom M. Davis		James P. Lee
	William M. Ryan		Ralph S. Carrigan
	Dillon Anderson		Richard B. Miller
1944	John T. McCullough	1964	Wiley Anderson, Jr.

Thomas E. Berry
Alvin M. Owsley, Jr.
Ewell E. Murphy, Jr.
1966 Charles G. Thrash, Jr.
J. Thomas Eubank
Finis E. Cowan
1967 R. D. Richards
1969 Reagan Burch, Jr.
E. W. Barnett
B. D. McKinney
Moulton Goodrum
1970 Sam G. Croom, Jr.
Walter G. Workman
Robert J. Piro
Richard B. Dewey
Robert L. Stillwell
William C. Griffith
1971 Robert J. Malinak
John C. Held
James C. Johnson
James D. Randall
O. Don Chapoton
1972 R. Gordon Gooch
Perry O. Barber
William G. Woodford
Richard C. Johnson
1973 Daryl Bristow
Harold L. Metts
Joseph D. Cheavens
John M. Huggins
Thad T. Hutcheson, Jr.
1974 Steven A. Wakefield
Michael S. Moehlman
F. Walter Conrad, Jr.
Larry F. York
1975 Stanley C. Beyer
Larry B. Feldcamp
Mont P. Hoyt
Frank R. Hubert
John L. Jeffers
Philip J. John
Ronald L. Palmer
Jeron L. Stevens
L. Proctor Thomas

Wade H. Whilden
Mark G. Winslow
1976 Roy L. Nolen
James M. Turley
Richard R. Brann
William R. Burke
James L. Leader
John P. Mathis
1977 D. Thomas Moody
J. Patrick Garrett
L. Chapman Smith
John P. Cogan
James R. Doty
1978 Robert A. Webb
Theodore F. Weiss
Bruce F. Kiely
1979 I. Jay Golub
David Alan Burns
David P. Cotellesse
Fred H. Dunlop
Hugh Rice Kelly
Benjamin G. Wells
William C. Slusser
1980 Stephen M. Hackerman
R. Joel Swanson
G. Irvin Terrell
Joseph A. Cialone
John B. Connally
Michael L. Graham
John E. Neslage
J. Gregory Copeland
Rufus W. Oliver
Charles M. Darling
Richard L. Josephson
1981 Justin M. Cambell
Alan Shore Gover
Ross Harrison
Michael Paul Graham
Diana E. Marshall
Carol C. Clark
Rufus Cormier
1982 Louis L. Bagwell
Stacy Eastland
Roderick Goyne

217
Appendix.
Baker & Botts
Partner
Admissions,
1840–1990

218

Baker & Botts
in the
Development
of Modern
Houston

Randy Hopkins
James R. Raborn
Alan D. Rosenthal
Walter J. Smith
James A. Taylor
Stephen G. Tipps
Charles Michael Watson

1983   James E. Maloney
Stephen A. Massad
Randy J. McClanahan
Scott Rozzell
Charles Szalkowski
Randolph Q. McManus

1984   George F. Goolsby
James A. Hime
Gray Jennings
Allister M. Waldrop, Jr.
Karen L. Wolf
Robert P. Wright
J. Patrick Berry

1985   J. Michael Baldwin
W. John Glancy
Lee L. Kaplan
Marley Lott
J. Patrick Berry
Thomas J. Eastment
B. Donovan Picard
Robert W. Jordan

1986   James C. Treadway, Jr.
Tony P. Rosenstein
Lee H. Rosenthal
Kerry C. L. North
Richard C. Breeden
Steven R. Hunsicker
Keith P. Ellison

1987   Neil Kenton Alexander
Linda Broocks

Joe S. Poff
Andrew M. Baker
Larry D. Carlson
Kirk K. Van Tine
Rod Phlelan
Phillip N. Smith, Jr.
William F. Stutts

1988   Ronald W. Kesterson
Gregory V. Nelson
Robert W. Strauser
Bryant C. Boren, Jr.
Jack L. Kinzie
George C. Lamb III

1989   Thomas H. Adolph
Pamela B. Ewen
Jay T. Kolb
David E. Warden
Robert W. Kantner
Robb L. Voyles
Stephen L. Teichler
Ronald K. Henry

1990   Claudia Frost
Michael S. Goldberg
J. David Kirkland, Jr.
Holly A. Nielsen
David R. Poage
Stuart F. Schaffer
Louise A. Shearer
George T. Shipley
Robert M. Weylandt
Paul Yetter
Patrick Zummo
Earl B. Austin
Jonathan W. Dunlay
David N. Powers
Hugh Tucker
Jerry W. Mills

Notes

ABBREVIATIONS USED

BBHC	Baker & Botts Historical Collection
CCMB	Houston City Council Minute Books
Fed.	*Federal Reporter*
GSUM	Gulf States Utilities Company minutes
HMRC	Houston Metropolitan Research Center
RUW	Rice University Woodson Center
SP	Southern Pacific Railroad; Southern Pacific files, BBHC
SW	*Southwestern Reporter*
TXRRC	Railroad Commission of Texas
U.S.	*United States Reports*
UPN	Union Pacific Railroad Company Collection, Nebraska State Museum and Archives, Lincoln

INTRODUCTION

1. Among the most useful studies of law in American history are Lawrence Friedman, *A History of American Law* (New York: Simon and Schuster, 1973); and Kermit Hall, *The Magic Mirror: Law in American History* (New York: Oxford University Press, 1989). These studies emphasize doctrinal issues, however, and pay little attention to lawyers or law firms.

2. The historical literature is scant. See, for example, James Willard Hurst, *The Growth of American Law: The Law Makers* (Boston: Little, Brown & Company, 1950), 305–322; Wayne K. Hobson, "Symbol of the New Profession: Emergence of the Large Law Firm, 1870–1915," in *The New High Priests: Lawyers in Post–Civil War America,* ed. Gerald Gawalt (Westport, Conn.: Greenwood Press, 1984). Also Thomas Paul Pinansky, "The Emergence of Law Firms in the American Legal Profession," *UALR Law Journal* 9 (1986–1987): 593–640. For a treatment of contemporary corporate law firms, see Robert L. Nelson, *Part-*

ners with Power: The Social Transformation of the Large Law Firm (Berkeley: University of California Press, 1989).

3. Three published versions of this type of firm history are Fredrick M. Eaton, *Shearman and Sterling, 1873–1973* (N. p.: Shearman and Sterling, 1973); Robert T. Swaine, *The Cravath Firm and Its Predecessors,* 2 vols. (New York: Ad Press, 1946 and 1948); and Robert M. Lunny, *Kelley Drye & Warren: An Informal History, 1836–1984* (New York: Kelley Drye & Warren, 1985).

4. Erwin Smigel, *The Wall Street Lawyer: Professional Organization Man?* (New York: Free Press of Glencoe, 1964).

5. Paul Hoffman, *Lions in the Street: An Inside History of the Great Wall Street Law Firms* (New York: Saturday Review Press, 1973). See also Mark Stevens, *Power of Attorney: The Rise of the Giant Law Firms* (New York: McGraw-Hill, 1987). For an "unauthorized" history of an individual law firm, see Nancy Lisagor and Frank Lipsius, *A Law unto Itself: The Untold Story of the Law Firm of Sullivan & Cromwell* (New York: Morrow, 1988).

1. BREAKING WITH TRADITION

1. Quoted in Marion Merseburger, "A Political History of Houston, Texas, during the Reconstruction Period as Recorded by the Press: 1868–1873," M.A. thesis, Rice Institute, 1950, 211.

2. James Willard Hurst, *The Growth of American Law: The Law Makers* (Boston: Little, Brown, 1950), 305–308.

3. Committee on History and Tradition of the State Bar of Texas, *Centennial History of the Texas Bar, 1882–1982* (Burnet, Tex.: Earin Press, 1981).

4. Harold Platt, *City Building in the New South* (Philadelphia: Temple University Press, 1983), 78–84. Platt discusses railroads and the development of Houston in the mid-nineteenth century.

5. See Baker & Botts historical collection (hereafter BBHC), client files, Southern Pacific, "Firm Representation of the 'Southern Pacific' Lines." By 1870 the partners were earning a healthy income as general counsel for what was emerging as the most important line in the area, the Houston & Texas Central Railway.

6. Alfred D. Chandler, Jr., *The Visible Hand: The Managerial Revolution in American Business* (Cambridge, Mass.: Harvard University Press, 1977), 79–187.

7. For background on southern railroads, see John Stover, *The Railroads of the South, 1865–1900: A Study of Finance and Control* (Chapel Hill: University of North Carolina Press, 1955).

8. Harry N. Scheiber, "Federalism, the Southern Regional Economy, and Public Policy since 1865," in *Ambivalent Legacy: A Legal History of the South,* ed. David J. Bodenhamer and James W.

Ely, Jr. (Jackson: University Press of Mississippi, 1984), 69–105, discusses the attitudes toward railroad receiverships in the South.

9. John Spratt, *The Road to Spindletop: Economic Change in Texas, 1875–1901* (Austin: University of Texas Press, 1970, 1983), 207.

10. On conflict between southern states and northern corporations, see Kenneth Lipartito, *The Bell System and Regional Business: The Telephone in the South, 1877–1920* (Baltimore: Johns Hopkins University Press, 1989).

11. Spratt, *The Road to Spindletop,* 13–15.

12. Diary of William Pitt Ballinger, 23 June 1860, quoted in Maxwell H. Bloomfield, "The Texas Bar in the Nineteenth Century," *Vanderbilt Law Review* 32:1 (1980): 265.

13. BBHC, *Office Review,* 12 May 1927, 168.

14. Hugh Rice Kelly, "Peter Gray," *The Houston Lawyer,* January 1976, 29–35.

15. BBHC, *Office Review,* 9 March 1922, 67–68, 79–82.

16. BBHC, Jesse Andrews historical file, Baker & Botts–Jordon, 27 June 1882.

17. BBHC, Southern Pacific files (hereafter SP) 6:1, Bryant & Dillard–DeArmond, 25 December 1889.

18. See BBHC, *Office Review,* 10 May 1923, 204; idem, "Firm Representation of 'Southern Pacific' Lines." For a discussion of Jay Gould, see Maury Klein, *The Life and Legend of Jay Gould* (Baltimore: Johns Hopkins University Press, 1986).

19. BBHC, SP 19:1, *Missouri Pacific* v. *Texas & Pacific,* 5th Circuit, Eastern District of Louisiana, 15 December 1885.

20. Before taking the SP work, the firm had received an offer to act in a similar capacity for Gould's Missouri Pacific. One reason Baker & Botts sided with Huntington and not Gould was that working for the Missouri Pacific would have entailed locating a significant portion of the office in Dallas, near the railroad's Texas hub. In choosing Huntington, Baker & Botts also allied itself with the more efficient of the two lines and the more typically modern enterprise of the two. The SP, especially after E. H. Harriman took charge in 1901, evolved into a true managerial corporation. Gould's system, by contrast, revolved almost exclusively around the personal brilliance of the financier himself and quickly declined following his death.

21. Indeed, Lovett's son—Robert Abercrombie Lovett (1895–1986)—was "widely regarded as a symbol of the so-called Eastern establishment" after spending a lifetime as a partner at the investment firm of Brown Brothers and serving as undersecretary of state (1947–1949) and secretary of defense (1951–1953) (Walter Isaacson and Evan Thomas, *The Wise Men: Six*

Friends and the World They Made [New York: Simon and Schuster, 1986]).

22. BBHC, SP 1:2, Retainer, Lovett–Kruttschnitt, 15 July 1894; Baker & Botts–Hubbard, 10 March 1897.

23. BBHC, SP 9:1, Firm Organization, Garwood memo to Tallichet, 16 October 1918.

24. BBHC, SP 1:2, Retainer, Lovett–Kruttschnitt, 15 July 1894.

25. BBHC, client files, SP, "Firm Representation of the 'Southern Pacific' Lines."

26. BBHC, SP 1:2, Retainer, Lovett–Kruttschnitt, 15 July 1894.

27. Ibid.; also BBHC, SP 1:2, Baker & Botts–Hubbard, 10 March 1897.

28. The histories of several of the New York firms are available, although the quality and coverage of those histories vary greatly. See, for example, the following published accounts of well-established corporate law firms: Eaton, *Shearman and Sterling, 1873–1973;* Swaine, *The Cravath Firm;* Lunny, *Kelley Drye & Warren;* Charles Goetsch and Margaret Shivers (eds.), *The Autobiography of Thomas L. Chadbourne* (New York: Oceana, 1985); Henry L. King, "Davis Polk Warwell Sunderland & Kiendl: A Background with Figures" (N.p.: Davis, Polk, 1966); Simpson Thacher & Bartlett, *The First One Hundred Years, 1884–1984* (New York: Simpson Thacher & Bartlett, 1984); J. Tyson Stokes, *Morgan, Lewis & Bockius: Memoir of a Law Firm, 1873–1973* (N.p.: Morgan, Lewis & Bockius, 1973); Sullivan & Cromwell, *1879–1979: A Century at Law* (New York: Sullivan & Cromwell, 1979); Herman Kogan, *Traditions and Challenges: The Story of Sidley & Austin* (Chicago: Sidley & Austin, 1983); *Ropes & Gray, 1865–1940* (Boston: Ropes & Gray, 1942); Francis Ellis and Edward Clark, *A Brief History of Carter, Ledyard & Milburn* (N.p.: Peter E. Randall, 1988); Cornelius Wickersham, *Towards Two Centuries at the New York Bar* (New York: privately printed, 1965).

29. Harold van B. Cleveland and Thomas Huertas, *Citibank, 1812–1970* (Cambridge, Mass.: Harvard University Press, 1985), 321; Walter Buenger and Joseph Pratt, *But Also Good Business: Texas Commerce Banks and the Financing of Houston and Texas* (College Station: Texas A&M University Press, 1986), 47.

30. Robert W. Gordon, "The Independence of Lawyers," *Boston University Law Review,* 68:1 (1988), has an extended discussion of this issue.

31. BBHC, SP 6:3. The sources for this episode are the two folders of the SP files from various division and local attorneys. Proctors, General Attorneys—Van Vleck (President of N.Y.T.&M. and G.W.T.&P. Rys. Cos.), 30 January 1904.

32. BBHC, SP 6:3, Baker & Botts–Messrs. Proctor, 4 February 1904.
33. BBHC, *Office Review,* 10 May 1923, 209.
34. BBHC, SP 5:1, Turney & Burgess–Baker & Botts, 27 April 1910; Kemp–Baker & Botts, 25 April 1910.
35. BBHC, SP 6:5, Parker–Kelly, 9 March 1909.
36. BBHC, SP 7:1, Baker & Botts–Garrett, 14 July 1903. SP 6:5, B&B–Kelly, 19 December 1902.
37. BBHC, SP 7:1, Baker & Botts–Garrett, 14 July 1903.
38. BBHC, SP 7:3, Baker & Botts–Bowers, 18 July 1912.
39. BBHC, SP 5:1, Baker & Botts–Beall & Kemp, 21 May 1906; SP 7:1, Garrett–Parker, 23 June 1906.
40. BBHC, SP 5:4, Garrett–Baker & Botts, 24 March 1904; Baker & Botts–de Montel, 26 March 1904.
41. BBHC, SP 7:1, Parker–Garrett, 6 December 1913, emphasis in original.
42. BBHC, Kelly & Hawes (Wharton, Texas)—Baker & Botts, 4 December 1915, Wharton local attorneys folder.
43. Since law partnerships remained quite small in this era, the death of the partner primarily responsible for the SP's work posed a serious threat to the smooth functioning of the railroad's legal system. In one particularly telling episode, Edwin Parker of Baker & Botts responded to such a death in the firm of the SP's division attorney in the important city of El Paso by forcing two remaining partners in one of that city's leading firms to admit into their partnership an outsider selected by Parker.

2. ADVOCATE FOR THE OCTOPUS

1. BBHC, "A Report on the Physical Financial Condition of the Southern Pacific Company," 1 August 1902.
2. Arden Farms, Harriman, N.Y., Schiff–E. H. Harriman, 10 November 1901 (courtesy of Maury Klein).
3. BBHC, SP 22:5, minutes of the GH&SA, 7 October 1911; 10 July 1911.
4. BBHC, SP 23:1, minutes of the GH&SA, 5 March 1910.
5. BBHC, SP 21:1, Lovett–Baker & Botts, 17 June 1910; Lovett–Baker & Botts, 23 June 1910.
6. BBHC, SP 2:7, 1905 Consolidation Act, 6.
7. BBHC, SP 2:8, San Antonio & Gulf Receivership, 5 July 1905, 26–32.
8. For a useful discussion of lawyers' functions in corporate reorganization, see Robert Gordon, "Legal Thought and Legal Practice in the Age of American Enterprise, 1870–1920," in *Professionals and Professional Ideologies in America* (Chapel Hill: University of North Carolina Press, 1983), 101–110.

9. BBHC, SP 2:2, 23 June 1904; SP 23:1, Baker & Botts–Lovett, 5 July 1905. This lengthy letter has an extended discussion of the consolidation.

10. S. G. Reed, *A History of the Texas Railroads* (Houston: St. Clair, 1941), 264–265.

11. BBHC, SP 24:2, Baker & Botts–Lovett, 10 August 1905.

12. BBHC, SP 2:7, 1905 Consolidation Act.

13. *Hubbard et al.* v. *Galveston, Harrisburgh & San Antonio Railroad et al., Federal Reporter,* vol. 200 (1st series), 504–511 (hereafter 200 Fed. 504).

14. BBHC, SP 21:1, Lovett–Baker & Botts, 23 June 1910.

15. Ibid.

16. BBHC, SP 20:2, Parker–Garwood, 19 June 1910; 200 Fed. 504.

17. BBHC, SP 21:1, Baker & Botts–Lovett, 1 September 1910.

18. 200 Fed. 510–511.

19. BBHC, SP 2:2, Lovett–Baker & Botts, 21 March 1911.

20. Ibid.; 200 Fed. 504.

21. BBHC, SP 2:2, Mahl–Lovett, 13 May 1912; SP 4:8, Mahl–Parker, 13 May 1912.

22. BBHC, SP 20:2, Lovett–Baker & Botts, 25 June 1910; Baker & Botts–Lovett, 27 June 1910.

23. BBHC, SP 25:3, Mahl–Baker & Botts, 29 March 1911; SP 23:1 Unknown–Cottingham, 17 July 1909; Cottingham–Parker, 13 August 1909.

24. BBHC, SP 4:8, Mahl–Parker, 13 May 1912.

25. Texas Railroad Commission, 2d Annual Report (Austin, 1883), 3–5 (hereafter 2TXRRC).

26. *Reagan* v. *Farmers' Loan and Trust Company, United States Reports,* vol. 154, p. 362 (hereafter 154 U.S. 362); Reed, *Texas Railroads,* 598; also Robert Cotner, *James Stephen Hogg: A Biography* (Austin: University of Texas Press, 1959), 330–331.

27. *Metropolitan Trust* v. *Houston & Texas Central Railroad et al.,* 90 Fed. 683.

28. Reed, *Texas Railroads,* 604–605.

29. *Metropolitan Trust* v. *H&TC,* 90 Fed. 683.

30. Reed, *Texas Railroads,* 605.

31. BBHC, SP 21:1, Lovett–Baker & Botts, 16 June 1910.

32. Ibid., "In the Matter of Application of the GH&SA," 7 January 1911.

33. BBHC, SP 25:3, Parker–Bryson, 14 October 1911.

34. BBHC, SP 21:1, Buck–Parker, 10 February 1911; Cottingham–Fay, 17 February 1911.

35. BBHC, personnel files, Edwin Parker. Parker left the bulk of his

estate to found a school of international relations, which became Columbia University's Parker School of International and Comparative Law.

36. BBHC, SP 21:1, "In the Matter of Application of the GH&SA," 7 January 1911; Parker–Buck, 17 March 1911.
37. BBHC, SP 25:3, Baker & Botts–Bryson, 14 October 1911.
38. An excellent example of this is the Galveston causeway case: BBHC, SP 10, *Galveston Causeway Company* v. *GH&SA;* 284 Fed. 137; BBHC, *Office Review,* 10 May 1923, 207–208.
39. BBHC, SP 1:4, memos of 17 January and 19 January 1914. Baker & Botts received $5,000 per biennium for lobbying, plus additional compensation for work on major legislation, such as the 1905 Consolidation Act.
40. BBHC, SP 1:4, memo of 19 January 1914.
41. BBHC, SP 7:1, Baker & Botts–Gregory & Batts, 5 January 1909.
42. BBHC, SP 1:4, Baker & Botts–Scott, 26 October 1914; Scott–Baker & Botts, 29 March 1917.
43. BBHC, SP 5:1, Beall–Baker & Botts, 17 April 1906.
44. *Southern Mercury,* 27 February 1890, quoted in Cotner, *Hogg,* 232.
45. BBHC, SP 7:3, circular letter, 1 June 1916.
46. Reed, *Texas Railroads,* 622–640; *Houston East and West Railway Company* v. *United States; Texas and Pacific Railway Company* v. *United States,* 234 U.S. 342. See also Kenneth Lipartito, "Getting Down to Cases: Baker & Botts and the Texas Railroad Commission," *Essays in Economic and Business History* 6 (1988): 27–37, for background on the commission and its regulatory philosophy.
47. Herbert Hovenkamp. "Regulatory Conflict in the Gilded Age: Federalism and the Railroad Problem," *Yale Law Journal* 97 (1988): 1068–1070.
48. Reed, *Texas Railroads,* 622–628.
49. Ibid., 630.
50. The result was frequently strained relations with the firm's friends at the Texas Railroad Commission. See TXRRC, *1916 Annual Report;* Reed, *Texas Railroads,* 632–634.
51. Union Pacific Railroad Company Collection, Nebraska State Museum and Archives, Lincoln (hereafter UPN), Lovett–Moroney, 19 February 1916.
52. UPN, Lovett–Moroney, 22 December 1915.
53. Ari Hoogenboom and Olive Hoogenboom, *A History of the ICC: From Panacea to Palliative* (New York: Norton, 1976), 112–118.
54. BBHC, *Office Review,* 24 March 1927, 113–116.

3. CIVIC LEADERSHIP IN A GROWING CITY

1. BBHC, *Office Review,* 13 January 1927, 1–4.
2. Ibid., 7 December 1922, 376–378.
3. Ibid, 376.
4. Ibid., 26 March 1920, item 11, emphasis in original.
5. Bruce Olson, "The Houston Light Guards: A Study of Houston's Post Reconstruction Militia and Its Membership, 1873–1903," *Houston Review* 7:3 (1985): 111–142.
6. BBHC, personnel files, Captain James A. Baker.
7. Buenger and Pratt, *But Also Good Business,* 27–35. Judge Garwood was vice-president of Lumberman's National Bank. Baker and his firm also worked closely with South Texas National, the Lumberman's National, and Union National Bank, the last two of which had strong ties to the lumber business in Houston, as well as the cotton trade.
8. BBHC, *Office Review,* 11 March 1936, 67–69.
9. Ibid., 28 February 1929, 26; 10 February 1927, 63; 8 March 1923, 92; 11 March 1936, 67. The Guardian Trust Company merged with the Second National Bank in 1945. The new bank later became Bank of the Southwest, and in 1983 it became part of MCorp, a statewide bank holding company.
10. BBHC, *Office Review,* 15 August 1925, 236–237.
11. Ibid., 17 August 1922, 256–259.
12. Olson, "Houston Light Guards," 137–141.
13. Rice University, Woodson Center (hereafter RUW), Early Rice Institute, William Marsh Rice papers, personal and business, folder 5, Rice–Baker, 9 August 1892.
14. RUW, Early Rice Institute, Rice litigation, box 2, folder 1, statement of James A. Baker.
15. RUW, Early Rice Institute, Baker & Botts–Rice Institute, box 2, folder 8, Kellogue–Baker, 18 April 1912.
16. RUW, Early Rice Institute, Baker & Botts–Rice Institute, box 4, folder 3, Baker–Downs, 23 June 1913.
17. Over the course of nearly twenty years, the Rice estate contributed more than $7 million to investments in Houston property.
18. RUW, Early Rice Institute, E. Raphael correspondence, box 1, folder 18, Houston–Raphael, 11 January 1907.
19. Fredericka Meiners, *A History of Rice University: The Institute Years, 1907–1963* (Houston: Rice University Studies, 1982), 11–50.
20. RUW, Early Rice Institute, institute materials, box 1, correspondence and questionnaires, March–July 1901.
21. RUW, Early Rice Institute, E. Raphael correspondence, box 1, folder 17, Harrington–Raphael, 23 July 1906.

22. Much material on the selection process is available in ibid., box 1, folders 10 and 17.
23. RUW, E. O. Lovett papers, president's office records, 1914–49, box 7, folder 7.
24. RUW, E. O. Lovett papers, president's office records, box 7, folder "E," Edwards–Davis, 17 November 1931.
25. RUW, Early Rice Institute, Baker & Botts–Rice Institute, box 4, folder 6, Parker–Baker, 2 February 1918.
26. BBHC, *Office Review,* 16 September 1941, 128.
27. Ibid., 26 July 1947, 137–138.

4. POWER AND POLITICS

1. See Christopher Armstrong and H. V. Nelles, *Monopoly's Moment: The Organization and Regulation of Canadian Utilities* (Philadelphia: Temple University Press, 1986), 141–169, for a definition of the term "civic populism."
2. Platt, *City Building in the New South,* 157–162.
3. Ibid., 192–194.
4. Houston City Council Minute Books (hereafter CCMB), 21 January 1906.
5. Marilyn Sibly, *The Port of Houston: A History* (Austin: University of Texas Press, 1968), 121–145.
6. BBHC, *Office Review,* 13 February 1920, 15–24.
7. BBHC, Clarence Wharton, Houston Electric Company cases, Wharton–Gray, 31 October 1932; Platt, *City Building in the New South,* 196.
8. CCMB, 21 July 1902.
9. Ibid., 22 July 1902.
10. Ibid., 28 July 1902.
11. Ibid., 20 October 1902.
12. Ibid., 15 December 1902.
13. BBHC, *Office Review,* 26 November 1946, 240–241; Houston Lighting & Power Company, "Origin and History of Houston Lighting and Power Company" (Houston, 1940), 22–23, copy in BBHC.
14. BBHC, *Office Review,* 26 November 1946, 240–241.
15. Ibid., 12 March 1920, 57–58.
16. Ibid., 18 August 1926, 266; also 31 March 1949, appendix.
17. Ibid., 12 March 1920, 57–58.
18. CCMB, 10 May 1897.
19. Ibid., 19 May 1897.
20. BBHC, Clarence Wharton, Houston Electric Company cases, Wharton–Gray, 31 October 1932. For more on this episode,

see Fran Dressman, "Yes, We Have No Jitneys: Transportation Issues in Houston Black Community, 1914–24," *Houston Review* 9:2 (1987): 69–82.

21. The best study of this problem is Thomas Hughes, *Networks of Power: Electrification in Western Society, 1880–1930* (Baltimore: Johns Hopkins University Press, 1983).

22. BBHC, *Office Review,* client index, "A. E. Fitkin & Company."

23. Ibid., 8 December 1921, appendix A.

24. Ibid., client index, "Stone & Webster Service Corporation."

25. Ibid., 8 December 1921, appendix A.

26. Ibid.

27. Ibid., 16 August 1928, 154–157, 184–185; 31 October 1929, 153–154; 10 February 1927, 56–58.

28. General Electric had created EBASCO to market the securities of local utilities that it received in lieu of payment for its equipment. EBASCO held these securities through a number of smaller regional or subholding companies it controlled. EBASCO also instructed its numerous small subsidiaries in the best technical, managerial, and financial practices of the day. After folding HL&P into this growing organization, EBASCO set the company on a new course that stressed expansion and consolidation of the numerous small power companies that served towns north, east, and south of Houston.

29. See BBHC, *Office Review,* 22 May 1926, 215–216.

30. The problem was so bad that the Humble Oil refinery was forced to build its own generating plant (HL&P, "Origin and History," 34).

31. BBHC, *Office Review,* 23 February 1922, 52–53; Millie Budd, "The Light Company," 95–96, copy in BBHC.

32. BBHC, Houston Lighting & Power files, Baker & Botts–Bertron, 14 January 1922.

33. Ibid.

34. Ibid., Bruce memorandum; Feagin–Garwood and Wharton, 24 February 1922.

35. BBHC, HL&P Files, Feagin–Garwood and Wharton, 24 February 1922; Wharton–Feagin, 20 November 1921.

36. A perpetuity is an instrument of trust and estate law that binds heirs perpetually to a certain set of dictates. Like primogeniture and entail, this legal form was banned in the Texas constitution, as well as those of many other states, as contrary to the "genius of a free people."

37. BBHC, HL&P file, Wharton–Parker, 14 April 1920; Wharton–Feagin, 20 November 1921. The franchise could be sold—alienated—thus making it nonperpetual. Because it was not exclusive, it did not constitute a monopoly.

38. BBHC, HL&P files, Wharton–Parker, 14 April 1920. The loose notion of perpetuity had been used earlier by populists to launch constitutional attacks on corporate privilege and to restrict the granting of public powers to private bodies.

39. Ibid., Feagin–Garwood and Wharton, 24 February 1922.

40. BBHC, *Office Review*, 13 January 1937, 2–3. This instrument allowed firms to issue new bonds as needed, without having to specify precisely the property to be covered by the additional financing. As more lines or stations were added, more bonds could be issued. The subsequent issues could also be of different interest rates, depending on economic conditions.

41. Ibid., 24 January 1934, 32–33; 16 December 1936, 238–259.

42. Ibid., 26 March 1925, 119–125.

43. Ibid., 13 December 1928, 209–211; 23 February 1928, 50–51.

44. EBASCO, "The Origin of Electric Bond & Share Company," March 1935, copy in BBHC.

45. BBHC, *Office Review*, 16 June 1926, 212–213.

46. Ibid., 25 November 1926, 354–355; 16 June 1927, 205–206; also HL&P, "Origin & History," 33–39.

47. Ibid., 9 September 1931, 114–117.

48. Ibid., 28 February 1930, 15–16.

49. Budd, "The Light Company," 103–104.

50. BBHC, *Office Review*, 13 November 1930, 77–79.

51. Ibid., 10 January 1940, 1–3.

52. Howard Fussell, "A History of Gulf States Utilities Company," (M.A. thesis, Lamar State College, 1966), 12–13.

53. BBHC, *Office Review*, 7 October 1926, 296–297.

54. Gulf States Utilities Company, Beaumont, Texas, Minutes (hereafter GSUM), 21 August 1925; 26 August 1925.

55. Ibid., 18 November 1926.

56. Ibid., 15 September 1926.

57. BBHC, *Office Review*, 10 November 1927, 323–324.

58. BBHC, HL&P files, Garwood–Wharton, 27 June 1929.

59. Ibid.

60. Charles Zelden, "Regional Growth and the Federal District Courts: The Impact of Judge Joseph C. Hutcheson, Jr., on Southeast Texas, 1918–1931," *Houston Review* 11:2 (1989): 73–76.

61. BBHC, *Office Review*, 16 August 1928, 152–153; 27 March 1941, 33–34.

62. Ibid., 8 March 1923, 85–87. E. F. Smith, *A Saga of Texas Law* (San Antonio, Tex.: Naylor, 1940), 271–276. A number of steel concerns had been forced out of Texas for alleged violations of the antitrust laws, a punishment that probably hurt the state's economy more than the corporations. Baker & Botts was instrumental in writing and sponsoring a 1923 amendment to the

law that permitted corporations to plead *nolo contendere* to charges of antitrust violation. With this compromise, the steel companies, including United States Steel, National Tube, and American Steel and Wire, applied for permits to do business again in Texas.

5. OIL-LED DEVELOPMENTS

1. C. A. Warner, *Texas Oil and Gas since 1543* (Houston: Gulf, 1939); Carl Coke Rister, *Oil! Titan of the Southwest* (Norman: University of Oklahoma Press, 1949); Henrietta Larson and Kenneth Porter, *History of Humble Oil & Refining Company: A Study in Industrial Growth* (New York: Harper & Brothers, 1959).
2. Joseph Pratt, *The Growth of a Refining Region* (Greenwich, Conn.: JAI, 1980), 52–56.
3. Joseph A. Pratt, "The Ascent of Oil: The Transition from Coal to Oil in Early Twentieth Century America," in *Energy Transitions: Long-Term Perspectives,* ed. Lewis Perelman (Boulder, Colo.: Westview, 1981), 9–35.
4. BBHC, SP 26:1, Parker—McEachin, 26 October 1903.
5. BBHC, SP 26:5, minutes of Rio Bravo Oil Company, 14 January 1907; SP 26:5, contract, Rio Bravo Oil Company and Hardy Oil Company, September 1908; also contract of 10 June 1908.
6. BBHC, SP 26:5, minutes of the Rio Bravo Oil Company.
7. Memorandum, 2 March 1903, Drawer A-1, papers of Joseph S. Cullinan, Houston Metropolitan Research Center, Houston, Texas (hereafter HMRC).
8. John O. King, *Joseph Stephen Cullinan: A Study of Leadership in the Texas Petroleum Industry, 1897–1937* (Nashville: Vanderbilt University Press, 1970); Marquis James, *The Texaco Story: The First Fifty Years, 1902–1952* (New York: The Texas Company, 1953).
9. Copies of these newspaper clippings and personal correspondence regarding the showdown are found in RUW, papers of James Lockhart Autry, The Texas Co.–Cullinan & Autry, resignation (1912–1913), #619.
10. BBHC, firm conferences—minutes, 27 October 1923, 2.
11. BBHC, client files, Texaco retainer, Beatty–Baker, Botts, 5 February 1914.
12. Clarence Wharton, *Texas under Many Flags,* Vol. II (Chicago: American Historical Society, 1930), 418.
13. Memorandum, 2 March 1903, Drawer A-1, papers of Joseph S. Cullinan, HMRC.
14. *Austin American,* 25 January, 27 January 1915.
15. Ibid., 11 January 1917.

16. Ibid., 18 January, 29 January, 2 February, 16 February 1915.
17. *Oil & Gas Journal,* 15 February 1917, 35.
18. For Parker's general background, see BBHC, personnel files, Edwin B. Parker.
19. BBHC, *Office Review,* "Mr. Parker's Association with the Texas Company," 9 April 1920, 76–77. The importance of this distinction was blurred somewhat by the fact that Parker was not licensed to practice in New York. His duties were more that of an adviser than a lawyer, and his legal work for Texaco involved primarily Texas cases involving Texas laws (BBHC, client files, Texaco, Edwin Parker, "First Subject—The Scope of the Firm's Activities").
20. BBHC, client files, Texaco retainer, Gannon–Feagin, memorandum, 21 September 1933.
21. Ibid., John–Baker & Botts, 26 October 1923.
22. For information on Wharton and Cole, see BBHC, personnel files, Clarence Wharton, Brady Cole.
23. "Hughes Tool Company," BBHC, *Office Review,* 13 November 1924, 354–355.
24. *Austin American,* 11 January 1915.
25. "Brady Nixon Cole," BBHC, *Office Review,* 29 October 1953, 96–104.
26. These cases are discussed in Harold F. Williamson et al., *The American Petroleum Industry: The Age of Energy, 1899–1959* (Evanston: Northwestern University Press, 1963), 150–151, 373 379. See also John Enos, *Petroleum Progress and Profits: A History of Process Innovation* (Cambridge: MIT Press, 1962).
27. Brady Cole left an extensive diary (personal log) covering the years 1934–1953. The majority of the entries record the details of his daily working life: at which hotel he stayed, whom he interviewed, what time his train departed. A copy is in BBHC.
28. This was a complicated method of distillation that used enough heat at the bottom of a tower to evaporate and separate the light hydrocarbons in natural gas that were not suitable for gasoline and then used enough cooling at the top of the tower to condense and precipitate all of the heavier hydrocarbons that were suitable for gasoline.
29. "A Very Novel and Interesting Suit," BBHC, *Office Review,* 26 May 1927, 190–197; "A Notable Victory—The Carbide Case," *Office Review,* 16 August 1927, 240–241.
30. BBHC, Brady Cole personal log, 31 December 1936.
31. Ibid., 31 January, 17 March, 21 April 1938.
32. "Schlumberger Well Surveying Corporation," BBHC, *Office Review,* 21 April 1937, 94–96; also, Brady Cole personal log, 22 March 1937.

33. Sinclair Oil Company no longer exists as a separate corporation. Many of its operations were acquired by the company now named ARCO.
34. Atlantic is now a part of ARCO.
35. Conoco has since been acquired by Du Pont.
36. For background on these clients, including major cases, see the individual folders on each company in client files, BBHC.
37. For an overview of the oil and gas clients represented by Baker & Botts before the 1960s, see "Notes on Firm Speech by James L. Shepherd," copy in BBHC, personnel files, James L. Shepherd.
38. *Rio Bravo* v. *Weed et al., Southwestern Reporter* (1st Series) 300, p. 174 (hereafter 300 SW 174).
39. A. W. Walker, Jr., "Development of Oil and Gas Law since 1925—With Some Personal Reminiscences," 1 July 1975, Hans Baade Collection, University of Texas Law School (hereafter Baade Collection).
40. "Firm History—Important Litigation—Nelson Davis Case," BBHC, *Office Review,* 17 August 1923, 282–290. In this entry, Clarence Wharton provides an excellent summary of the case.
41. Alfred M. Leeston, John A. Crichton, and John C. Jacobs, *The Dynamic Natural Gas Industry* (Norman: University of Oklahoma Press, 1963), 19–54.
42. "History of United Energy Resources, 1930–1977," copy in BBHC.
43. BBHC, *Office Review,* 31 March 1949, appendix. Baker & Botts's experience in connecting northern capital with the nascent gas industry went back even further, when Captain Baker arranged with Halsey, Stuart in New York to help finance the Houston Gulf Gas Company in 1927. Houston Gulf Gas became part of United Gas. See BBHC, *Office Review,* 24 January 1934, 32–33.
44. Ibid., 31 March 1949, appendix.
45. EBASCO, "The Origin of Electric Bond and Share Company," 11–13.
46. BBHC, *Office Review,* 30 April 1930, 29–35.
47. "Law of Oil and Gas," ibid., 3 June 1920, 130–131.
48. For background information on Shepherd, see BBHC, personnel files, James L. Shepherd.
49. James L. Shepherd, Jr., *Legal History of Conservation of Oil and Gas—A Symposium* (N.p.: American Bar Association, 1939).

6. A PERMANENT INSTITUTION

1. Buenger and Pratt, *But Also Good Business,* 78–79; David McComb, *Houston: The Bayou City* (Austin: University of Texas

Press, 1969), 142–144; Sibley, *Port of Houston,* 168–170.

2. BBHC, Ralph B. Feagin notebook, 1937–1940.
3. BBHC, personnel files, Edwin B. Parker, "Edwin Parker to All Lawyers in the Office," 31 July 1916.
4. BBHC, *Office Review,* 11 May 1922, 136–143.
5. Ibid., 27 January 1920, 2–3.
6. Ibid., 3.
7. "Edwin Parker to All Partners," 21 July 1917, BBHC, personnel files, Edwin B. Parker.
8. Parker–Baker et al., 21 July 1917, minutes of meetings of participating members, BBHC, Organization—Official Plan file.
9. "Edwin B. Parker to All in the Office," 2 January 1912, 16, in ibid.
10. Hiram Garwood, "The Firm," speech originally given in December 1913, as reported in BBHC, *Office Review,* 16 June 1921, appendix.
11. Partnership agreement between the members of the firm of Baker, Botts, Parker & Garwood, 1 January 1921, BBHC, Organization—Official Plan file.
12. Feagin entered the firm in 1916 and became a partner in 1921. During the years from 1919 to 1926, Edwin Parker was the managing partner, but he resided in New York for much of this period and Feagin served as his assistant in Houston. He left the firm from 1926 to 1933 to work for Electric Bond & Share and United Gas, but returned to Baker & Botts in 1933. He served as managing partner until his death in 1946.
13. Edwin Parker, "First Subject—The Scope of the Firm's Activities." BBHC, firm conferences, minutes, December 1922.
14. Jesse Andrews, "Our Firm in Kansas City and Longview," ibid., 21 December 1923, 36–38.
15. "Long-Bell Work in State of Washington," ibid., 12 October 1922, 1–5.
16. T. Victor Jeffries, *Before the Dam Water: Story and Pictures of Old Linn Creek, Ha Ha Tonka and Camden County* (Springfield, Mo.: Midwest Litho & Publishing, 1974), copy in BBHC, Kansas City Office file.
17. BBHC, Ralph Feagin notebook, 1937–1940.
18. BBHC, Firm conferences, minutes, 7 February 1925, 1–3.
19. Ibid., 3.
20. Ibid., 24 December 1923.
21. Such comments were voiced often in firm meetings. See, for example, ibid., 29 October 1925.
22. Parker, "First Subject—The Scope of the Firm's Activities."
23. BBHC, *Office Review,* 7 January 1925, 17–25.
24. BBHC, *Office Review,* 12 February 1936, 47–48.

25. BBHC, *Office Review,* 30 September 1946, 175–188.
26. "Women Graduates of the School of Law of the University of Texas," Baade Collection.
27. Tom Martin Davis, 2d interview, 1 September 1987, BBHC.
28. Ira Hildebrand, *The Law of Texas Corporations,* 2 vols. (Kansas City: Vernon Law Book Co., 1942).
29. Stockholders' meeting, *Texas Law Review,* 4 July 1923; Feagin–Hildebrand, 2 November 1921, Baade Collection.
30. Leon Green–Judge Garwood, 22 September 1925, Baade Collection.
31. Walne–Hildebrand, 21 May 1932, "Prizes," box 119, Hildebrand (Ira P.) papers, rare books, University of Texas law library.

7. THE TRANSFORMATION OF THE LEGAL FRAMEWORK

1. On the case method, see Robert Stevens, *Law School: Legal Education in America from the 1850s to the 1980s* (Chapel Hill: University of North Carolina Press, 1983), 50–72.
2. In the mass of historical literature on the New Deal, two "standard" works remain essential. William Leuchtenburg, *Franklin D. Roosevelt and the New Deal, 1932–40* (New York: Harper & Row, 1963), gives an excellent overview. Ellis Hawley, *The New Deal and the Problem of Monopoly* (Princeton: Princeton University Press, 1966), captures the diverse impulses of New Deal reform while suggesting the political passions and charged debate on specific issues.
3. "Memorandum Prepared by John T. McCullough as Basis for Remarks Which May be Made by Him at Firm Dinner to be Held on November 27, 1979," BBHC, personnel files, John T. McCullough. As will be discussed in subsequent chapters, McCullough served as the firm's managing partner from 1952 to 1972.
4. Reed, *Texas Railroads,* 622–640.
5. Ibid., 628, 631–634.
6. Hoogenboom, *A History of the ICC,* 112–180; Reed, *Texas Railroads,* 637; BBHC, *Office Review,* 24 March 1927, 113–116; 15 August 1924, 273–276.
7. BBHC, *Office Review,* 7 March 1934, 77–79.
8. Ibid., 11 October 1933, 230–233.
9. Ibid., 25 January 1933, 33–34; 15 June 1938, 156–158.
10. *Texas & New Orleans Railroad et al.* v. *Brotherhood of Railway and Steamship Clerks, etc. et al.,* 33 Fed. (2d) 13. Firm legend has it that Hutcheson threatened to throw Captain Baker in jail for contempt during one particularly heated moment of the trial.
11. 281 U.S. 548.

12. Tom Martin Davis, 1st interview, 21 May 1985, BBHC.
13. BBHC, SP 1:3, Carter–Tallichet & Davis, 25 September 1935; Tallichet–Dey, 15 May 1935. Davis also became labor counsel for Texaco. Davis, 1st interview, 21 May 1985; Davis, 2nd interview, 1 September 1987.
14. BBHC, *Office Review*, 22 August 1939, 182–184.
15. Christopher Tomlins, *The State and the Unions: Labor Relations Law, and the Organized Labor Movement in America, 1880– 1960* (Cambridge: At the University Press, 1985).
16. D. B. Hardeman and Donald C. Bacon, *Rayburn, a Biography* (Austin: Texas Monthly Press, 1987), 171.
17. BBHC, *Office Review*, 10 May 1934, 149–153.
18. Ibid., 23 October 1935, 179–188.
19. Ibid.
20. Ibid.
21. Ibid.
22. Ibid., 187.
23. Ibid., 188.
24. Hardeman and Bacon, *Rayburn*, 174.
25. EBASCO argued to the contrary that future growth would increase rather than decrease the need for the holding company structure, which could provide operating companies needed services more cheaply than any other source. See EBASCO, "Origin," 52–59.
26. BBHC, *Office Review*, 8 January 1936, 11.
27. Ibid., 29 June 1943, appendix. The distrust of financiers, typical of the later New Deal, was responsible for the ban on investment bankers.
28. Ibid.
29. United Gas Public Service was a subsidiary of United Gas, which was a subsidiary of Electric Power and Light, which was a subsidiary of EBASCO (ibid., 13 October 1937, 189–192).
30. Ibid., 31 January 1945, 1–5; "History of United Energy Resources," 15.
31. Ibid., 31 March 1949, appendix; 31 January 1945, 1–5.
32. "History of United Energy Resources," 15–20.
33. BBHC, *Office Review*, 30 April 1945, 46–48.
34. Ibid., 25 November 1941, 160–162.
35. Under the terms of the act, a holding company could consist of only a single, regionally integrated enterprise. Given the choice under the terms of the law to retain only one of its regional operations, Stone & Webster chose Virginia Electric and spun off Gulf States and other Texas companies such as El Paso Electric (see Fussell, "Gulf States," 168–169).
36. BBHC, *Office Review*, 8 December 1937, 241–262.

37. The best narrative account of this fascinating era in oil history remains James A. Clark and Michael T. Halbouty, *The Last Boom* (New York: Random House, 1972).

38. David F. Prindle, *Petroleum Politics and the Texas Railroad Commission* (Austin: University of Texas Press, 1981), 19–40.

39. John G. Clark, *Energy and the Federal Government: Fossil Fuel Policies, 1900–1946* (Urbana: University of Illinois Press, 1987), 220–250.

40. *Tyler Morning Telegraph* as quoted in Clark and Halbouty, *The Last Boom*, 157.

41. "Plan of Organization," BBHC, *Office Review*, 12 April 1939, 94–95.

42. Prindle, *Petroleum Politics,* chap. 5.

43. John C. Jacobs, "Public Control of the Natural Gas Industry" in *The Dynamic Natural Gas Industry*, ed. Leeston, Crichton, and Jacobs, 260–309.

44. The FPC was created in 1920, and its powers were greatly expanded by the 1938 Natural Gas Policy Act. The Supreme Court's decision in the *Phillips* case in 1954 gave the FPC the power to regulate the price of natural gas at the wellhead, at least for gas produced for interstate markets. In 1977 much of the FPC was renamed the Federal Energy Regulatory Commission (FERC) and made an independent regulatory commission within the newly created Department of Energy.

45. Dallas Morning News, *1988–1989 Texas Almanac* (Dallas, 1987), 446.

46. *Texoma Natural Gas Company* v. *Railroad Commission of Texas et al.,* 59 Fed. (2d Series) 750.

47. At the time of suit, the firms' entire names were Vinson, Elkins, Sweeton & Weems and Andrews, Streetman, Logue & Mobley.

48. "Texoma Natural Gas Company v. C. V. Terrell, et. al.," BBHC, *Office Review*, 10 December 1931, 178–179. The C. V. Terrell named in the suit was a commissioner of the Texas Railroad Commission. Coincidentally, he was also a former law partner of Clarence Wharton in Decatur, Texas, before Wharton came to Baker & Botts.

49. M. Elizabeth Sanders, *The Regulation of Natural Gas: Policy and Politics, 1938–1978* (Philadelphia: Temple University Press, 1981), 125–192.

50. Scheiber, "Federalism," 93–97. Scheiber discusses the impact of the New Deal on the southern regional economy.

51. BBHC, *Office Review*, 22 January 1936, 28–31; 27 November 1935, 228–231.

52. Ibid., 7 March 1934, 79–81; 10 February 1937, 32–33; 26 October 1938, 240–242. Antitrust was not dead; a later attorney

general initiated proceedings against the Consolidated Meat-Packing Company in another matter in 1944. See ibid., 28 January 1944, 2–4.

53. See Thomas McCraw, *The TVA and the Power Fight, 1933–39* (Philadelphia: Lippincott, 1971).
54. BBHC, *Office Review,* 25 January 1938, 29–32; 23 October 1935, 189–192.
55. Ibid., 14 December 1938, 267–269; 25 January 1938, 29–32. The deciding cases were *Alabama Power Company* v. *Ickes,* and *Duke Power Company* v. *Greenwood Company,* U.S. Supreme Court, 3 January 1938.

8. THE COMING OF AGE OF THE FIRM AND ITS CITY

1. Pratt, *The Growth of a Refining Region,* 89–119; Buenger and Pratt, *But Also Good Business,* 146–176.
2. On this period and the role of Houston's elite, see Don Carleton, *Red Scare: Right Wing Hysteria, Fifties Fanaticism and Their Legacy in Texas* (Austin: Texas Monthly Press, 1985), 64–100.
3. Buenger and Pratt, *But Also Good Business,* 177–209.
4. Thomas Eubank interview, 23 May 1985; Tom Martin Davis, 1st interview, 21 May 1985, BBHC. *Houston Chronicle,* 9 March 1964, 1; *New York Times,* 10 March 1964; *Houston Chronicle,* 20 June 1963, 1.
5. Joe R. Feagin, *Free Enterprise City: Houston in Political and Economic Perspective* (New Burnswick, N.J.: Rutgers University Press, 1988), 120–127.
6. We use the current name, Tenneco, to avoid confusion. The company's original name was Tennessee Gas Transmission Company.
7. Marvin Hurley, *Decisive Years for Houston* (Houston: Houston Magazine, 1966), 202, 207, 214–217.
8. H. Malcolm Lovett interview, 20 May 1985, BBHC.
9. BBHC, Tenneco files.
10. BBHC, *Office Review,* 30 December 1942, 138–139.
11. BBHC, Tenneco files.
12. Ibid.; Chris Castañeda and Joseph Pratt, "New Markets, Outmoded Technology," *Business and Economic History* 18, 2d Series (1989): 238–247.
13. John Mackin interview, 19 November 1986, BBHC.
14. BBHC, *Office Review,* 24 June 1948, 99–100; 26 September 1957, 135–136.
15. As will be discussed in the Epilogue, in 1972 Baker & Botts opened its own Washington office.

16. The percentage was reduced to 22 percent in 1969 before being phased out for categories of producers in 1975.
17. BBHC, *Office Review,* 27 February 1951, 20–22.
18. Ibid., 22.
19. Ibid., 28 April 1955, 41–48.
20. Ibid., 45.
21. The primary sources for this section are interviews with James Lee, Summer 1989, Gerald Hines, 22 February 1985, and Ben White, 5 June 1985, BBHC.
22. BBHC, *Office Review,* 30 May 1957, 72–77.
23. BBHC, Plan of Organization (revised 1 June 1968), 93, 129. The plan recognized the advantages of specialization, but also the need to bring together lawyers from several departments.
24. For background on Pennzoil, we have relied on Thomas Petzinger, Jr., *Oil and Honor: The Texaco-Pennzoil Wars* (New York: Putnam, 1987).
25. This early history is summarized in the *Office Review,* 31 March 1966, 41–43. Much background for Baker & Botts's involvement with Pennzoil is from interviews. Of particular importance is Baine Kerr interview, 3 May 1988, BBHC.
26. BBHC, *Office Review,* 25 July 1963, 88–92.
27. Ibid., 28 March 1968, 37–40.
28. Ibid., 27 May 1971, 65.
29. Ibid., 25 February 1971, 19–20.

9. ORGANIZING FOR A NATIONAL PRACTICE

1. BBHC, personnel files, William Harvin.
2. BBHC, Jesse Andrews historical file, Raymond–Andrews, 6 April 1931.
3. Interview with Baine Kerr, 3 May 1988, BBHC.
4. Griffin Smith, Jr., "Empires of Paper," *Texas Monthly,* November 1973.
5. Feagin, *Free Enterprise City,* 124.
6. BBHC, personnel files, Dillon Anderson.
7. For an overview of the American era, see Louis Galambos and Joseph Pratt, *The Rise of the Corporate Commonwealth* (New York: Basic Books, 1988), 127–183.
8. See BBHC, personnel files, John T. McCullough, for background.
9. Interview with John McCullough, 20 May 1985; interview with William Harvin, 16 May 1988, BBHC.
10. Statistics on "chargeable hours" for lawyers holding a top interest in the firm are difficult to compare through time, since the definition of what constitutes a "senior interest" has changed. But existing statistics show a distinct rise since 1972 in the aver-

age chargeable hours for all those with a top interest in the firm—from 1,340 hours per lawyer in 1972, to 1,462 in 1977, to 1,504 in 1982, to 1,997 in 1987. These statistics suggest that changes introduced in the early 1970s had their desired effect (BBHC, J. H. Freeman correspondence, personnel matters).

11. At least twenty of forty-four lawyers hired by Baker & Botts from 1930 to 1950 were in the top 10 percent or above of the graduating class from the University of Texas (BBHC, personnel files).

12. In one particularly stunning turnaround, Vinson & Elkins in 1963 corralled practically all the top University of Texas law graduates. This was in sharp contrast to a decade earlier, when Baker & Botts could routinely collect one-third of the top of the class (Smith, "Empires of Paper," 57).

13. Richard Abel, *American Lawyers* (New York: Oxford University Press, 1989), 192–194.

14. BBHC, Price Waterhouse & Co. survey.

15. BBHC, J. H. Freeman correspondence, personnel matters, 1967, 5.

16. Interview with William Harvin, 16 May 1988, 2–3.

17. Leon Jaworski, with Mickey Herskowitz, *Confessions and Avoidance: A Memoir* (Garden City, N.Y.: Anchor Press, 1979), 146.

18. Smith, "Empires of Paper," 58–59. For a brief time in the 1920s, Baker & Botts employed one Jewish lawyer.

19. *Texas Lawyer,* 6 June 1988, 8; Abel, *American Lawyers,* 106.

20. BBHC, Plan of Organization (revised 1 June 1968), Part III, "Departments: Objectives and General Procedures."

21. Fausto R. Miranda, "Baker, Botts & Miranda," unpublished document in BBHC.

22. BBHC, J. H. Freeman correspondence, personnel matters, 1968.

23. Ben White interview, 5 June 1985, 7; John Maginnis interview, 21 May 1985, 10–12.

24. William Harvin interview, 16 May 1988, 17–18.

25. BBHC, J. H. Freeman correspondence, personnel matters, 1969, 2.

26. Those partners who left Baker & Botts did so for exceptional reasons, as when Palmer Hutcheson resigned to practice law with his sons. The only other significant sudden changes in the partnership, besides the unexpected deaths in the 1940s and 1950s, came when partners left to join clients. Robert Lovett's move to Southern Pacific, Edwin Parker's appointment as general counsel of Texaco, Ralph Feagin's vice-presidency of EBASCO, all were part of a long and important tradition at the firm, one considered a sign of strength rather than weakness. In the postwar years, this tradition continued as Alvis Parish took over the presidency of HL&P in 1953, and corporate partners

Baine Kerr and John Mackin moved on to key clients, Pennzoil and Zapata, in 1977 and 1979, respectively.

EPILOGUE

1. Baker & Botts managing partner, Edwin B. Parker (quoting from a speech by Hiram Garwood) BBHC, *Office Review,* 27 January 1920, 1.
2. Growing indirectly out of its work for Mesa, Baker & Botts had by the late 1980s begun doing substantial work for two wealthy Midland oil producers—Cyrus Wagner and Jack Brown—who became active in mergers and acquisition areas. After several unsuccessful takeover attempts, Wagner and Brown in 1987 completed the billion-dollar-plus acquisition of Insilco. Under the direction of Joseph Cialone, this involved dozens of Baker & Botts lawyers.
3. "Pennzoil-Texaco Settlement," *Baker & Botts Office Review* 2d ser., 58, no. 1 (Spring 1988) : 1–2. This case resulted in the publication of several books. See Petzinger, *Oil and Honor;* James Shannon, *Texaco and the $10 Billion Jury* (Englewood Cliffs, N.J.: Prentice-Hall, 1988).
4. Exxon—Standard Oil of New Jersey in the years before 1975— had held a majority interest in Humble Oil & Refining, a Houston-based company, since 1919. In 1972 Exxon purchased the remainder of the stock in this company and reorganized it as Exxon, U.S.A., the international oil company's domestic subsidiary, with headquarters in Houston.
5. *American Lawyer,* July–August 1990, 14–16.
6. Abel, *American Lawyers,* 191. In 1979 the associates/partner ratio was 1.6:1 nationally; Baker & Botts was slightly below that figure, at 1:52:1. Recently, some of the nation's largest firms have raised that figure aggressively to 3.7:1 or 3.8:1. In 1988 Baker & Botts stood at 1.72 associates for each partner.
7. In 1988, Barber left to become executive vice-president and general counsel of Cabot Corporation, another client with substantial oil and gas holdings.

Index

242

*Baker & Botts
in the
Development
of Modern
Houston*

244

*Baker & Botts
in the
Development
of Modern
Houston*

246

*Baker & Botts
in the
Development
of Modern
Houston*

250

Baker & Botts
in the
Development
of Modern
Houston

252

*Baker & Botts
in the
Development
of Modern
Houston*